GENDER AND AGEING

GENDER AND AGEING

Changing Roles and Relationships

Edited by

Sara Arber, Kate Davidson and Jay Ginn

Open University Press
Maidenhead · Philadelphia

Open University Press
McGraw-Hill Education
McGraw-Hill House
Shoppenhangers Road
Maidenhead
Berkshire
England
SL6 2QL

email: enquiries@openup.co.uk
world wide web: www.openup.co.uk

and

325 Chestnut Street
Philadelphia, PA 19106, USA

First published 2003

A catalogue record of this book is available from the British Library

ISBN 0 335 21319 7 (pb)   0 335 21320 0 (hb)

Library of Congress Cataloging-in-Publication Data
CIP data has been applied for

Typeset by RefineCatch Limited, Bungay, Suffolk
Printed in the UK by Bell & Bain Ltd, Glasgow

CONTENTS

LIST OF FIGURES AND TABLES

Figures

Tables

NOTES ON CONTRIBUTORS

Sara Arber is Professor of Sociology, and Head, School of Human Sciences, University of Surrey. She is Co-Director, Centre for Research on Ageing and Gender (CRAG) at Surrey. Her books include *The Myth of Generational Conflict: Family and State in Ageing Societies* (with Claudine Attias-Donfut, 2000), and *Connecting Gender and Ageing* (with Jay Ginn, 1995).

Janet Askham is Professor of Gerontology and Director of the Age Concern Institute of Gerontology (ACIOG) at King's College London. She has a long-standing interest in marital and family relationships and has carried out research on the impact of social change on the home and family lives of older people, care giving and receiving, independent living in very old age and age gaps between marital partners.

Klas Borell is Associate Professor of Sociology at Mid-Sweden University in Östersund, Sweden. He has contributed to a number of books and articles in different fields of sociology, gerontology and family research. He is presently engaged in a research project on ageing and the meaning of home.

Toni Calasanti is Professor of Sociology, and faculty affiliate of the Center for Gerontology and the faculty of Women's Studies at Virginia Tech in the USA. Recent publications include her book *Gender, Social Inequalities, and Aging* (with Kathleen Slevin, 2001), and she is editing a special issue of *Journal of Aging Studies* on feminist gerontology (2004).

Ingrid Arnet Connidis is Professor, Department of Sociology, University of

Western Ontario, London, Canada. Her current research includes qualitative studies of multigenerational families and a multi-methods study of older workers in the new economy. Recent publications have examined conceptual frameworks for exploring family ties and social trends and their policy implications. Her book *Family Ties and Aging* was published in 2001.

Tom Daly, after retiring from the National Audit Office, has undertaken a number of projects within the Psychology and Sociology Departments, University of Surrey. He joined the Centre for Research on Ageing and Gender (CRAG) in April 2000 to undertake research on the ESRC Growing Older project 'Older men: their social worlds and healthy lifestyles', and is currently working on a project on autonomy and decision-making in later life.

Kate Davidson is a Lecturer in the Department of Sociology, and Co-Director of the Centre for Research on Ageing and Gender (CRAG) at University of Surrey. She has published on gender and ageing in national and international journals and in edited books. With Graham Fennell, she co-edited a special issue of *Ageing International* on 'New Intimate Relationships in Later Life' (2002, 27(4)).

Jenny de Jong Gierveld is Professor in the Department of Sociology and Social Gerontology, Free University, Amsterdam, and former Director of the Netherlands Interdisciplinary Demographic Institute (NIDI). She is Permanent Fellow, Netherlands Institute for Advanced Study in the Humanities and Social Sciences. Her publications concentrate on the relationships between living arrangements, social networks, well-being and loneliness of older people.

Eileen Fairhurst is Senior Lecturer, Department of Health Care Studies, Manchester Metropolitan University. She has published a number of papers on the sociology of ageing and the life course.

Sofie Ghazanfareeon Karlsson is a PhD student in Social Work at the Department of Social Work, Mid-Sweden University in Östersund. Her dissertation focuses on Living Apart Together (LAT) relationships of older people in Sweden.

Jay Ginn is Senior Research Fellow and Co-Director, Centre for Research on Ageing and Gender (CRAG), University of Surrey. Her books include *Gender and Later Life* (with Sara Arber, 1991), *Women, Work and Pensions: International Issues and Prospects* (with Debra Street and Sara Arber, 2001) and *Gender, Pensions and the Lifecourse* (2003). She was International Research Fellow, Netherlands Institute for Advanced Study in 2002–3, researching midlife attitudes to retirement cross-nationally.

Karen Glaser is a Lecturer in Gerontology at the Age Concern Institute of Gerontology (ACIOG), King's College London. She has conducted comparative research on intergenerational co-residence and proximity, and investigated the multiple work and family roles of mid-life individuals in

Britain. Together with Cecilia Tomassini, she is a member of an international network funded by the European Science Foundation (ESF), whose aim is to compare family support for older people across several European countries.

Merryn Gott is a Lecturer in Social Gerontology at the Sheffield Institute for Studies on Ageing (SISA), University of Sheffield. Her principle research interests include sexuality and ageing and 'end-of-life' care for older people.

Sharron Hinchliff is a Research Fellow at the Sheffield Institute for Studies on Ageing (SISA), University of Sheffield. She has conducted research into sexuality within the context of ageing and improving communication about sexual health matters in primary care. Her current work investigates women's experience of sexual problems.

Jenny Hislop is the Research Fellow on a European Union project on 'Sleep in Ageing Women' at the Centre for Research on Ageing and Gender (CRAG), University of Surrey. Her journal articles and presentations at national and international conferences are contributing to the development of a sociology of sleep in the UK. She is affiliated with the multidisciplinary Surrey Sleep Research Centre (SSRC).

Kim Perren is a Research Fellow at the Centre for Research in Social Policy (CRISP), Loughborough University, and was previously a researcher in the Centre for Research on Ageing and Gender (CRAG), University of Surrey. She has expertise in the secondary analysis of large-scale data sets, including the British Household Panel Survey. Her research interests include ageing and women's health across the life course.

Debora Price is a PhD student in the Centre for Research on Ageing and Gender (CRAG) at the University of Surrey, and a barrister specializing in the resolution of financial issues following separation and divorce. Her research focus is on modelling gender differences in the impact of marital status on pension provision.

Cecilia Tomassini is a Senior Research Officer in the population and demography division at the Office for National Statistics. She has carried out research on the family and social networks of older people, intergenerational transfers, survival among twins at older ages, household projections and the determinants of mortality. She is involved in several European projects on the living conditions of older people.

1

CHANGING APPROACHES TO GENDER AND LATER LIFE

Sara Arber, Kate Davidson and Jay Ginn

Changing gender roles and relationships in later life and the challenges to masculinity with advancing age are newly emerging areas in the study of gender and ageing.[1] Over recent years there have been substantial advances in our understanding of the lives of older women, but older men have been largely neglected. This book builds on Arber and Ginn's edited collection *Connecting Gender and Ageing* published in 1995, but breaks with much feminist scholarship by redressing the earlier focus on women and emphasizing changing gender identities and relationships. Turning points, such as transitions to retirement, widowhood and the onset of health problems or caring, throw into sharp relief the meanings of masculinity and identities in later life.

Cohorts entering midlife and later life in the early years of the twenty-first century grew up following the Second World War and had a very different life course experience compared with earlier generations. This is particularly so for women, who have experienced longer attachment to the labour market. Other changes relate to increases in divorce and non-heterosexual relationships. A theme running through the book is the need to reconceptualize partnership status and to improve understanding of the implications of both widowhood and divorce for older women *and* men. New forms of relationships are considered, such as Living Apart Together and the changing family relationships of gays and lesbians as they age. The meanings of ageing for men and women, and how these vary with partnership status, are key concerns of the book, as are the influence of socio-economic circumstances on the experience of ageing and on the ways in which individuals negotiate changes in roles and relationships. A life course perspective provides an orienting thread throughout the book.

Gender and diversity in later life

It is a truism to talk about diversity in later life. A key issue is whether writers consider that diversity is also a marker of inequalities in life chances. The dimensions of inequality are usually identified as gender, socio-economic status and race or ethnicity, although some authors add sexual orientation (Calasanti and Sleven 2001). It is much less usual for marital status or partnership status to be considered as a dimension of inequality. Marital status is often used purely as a socio-demographic variable that differentiates older people and, like age, is used in research as a control variable, rather than a characteristic of analytic interest.

Much research on gender in later life has taken a political economy perspective, emphasizing the disadvantaged position of older women in relation to their pensions, health status and access to care (Arber and Ginn 1991; Estes 1991). Less attention has been paid to the advantages faced by older women compared to some groups of older men. For example, older women have better social relationships with both friends (Allan 1985; Jerrome 1996) and family members, with women often characterized as the 'kin-keepers' (Finch and Mason 1993). Recent work has shown that for older women, widowhood may lead to a new found sense of freedom and autonomy, whereas widowers can see no advantages at all of being widowed compared to being married (Davidson 2001). Older women may be part of the 'society of widows' (Lopata 1973), which provides for the positive development of rewarding and emotionally supportive relationships and other activities, but for widowed men there is no equivalent 'society of widowers' as a support network and buffer. There is therefore a need to rebalance existing dominant frameworks, which focus on the disadvantages faced by older women, by also considering the disadvantages that some groups of older men may experience in later life.

Recent years have seen major research developments from a very different theoretical tradition, in particular the expansion of research on masculinities, identity and cultural studies. A recent development in the study of ageing has been an emphasis on 'new' identities in middle and old age. Such matters have been explored primarily through the concept of consumer culture, characterized by social differentiation and fragmentation (Gilleard and Higgs 2000). Retirement, within this framework, offers new 'lifestyles', centring on leisure. These new images of, and identities in, retirement are drawn, almost exclusively, from examining representations of middle age found in the media or extrapolating from statistical data sets, rather than starting from the perspectives of older individuals themselves. Hitherto there has been little attempt to integrate these developments in relation to gender and ageing.

Age represents a marker for several distinctive processes within older people's lives. First, age reflects the physiological ageing process. On average ill-health increases with advancing age, and we may expect many activities to decline with age simply because of increased frailty or restrictions on mobility. Second, ageing is associated with various social and economic changes. Some may accompany widowhood, especially for women, in terms of loss of a car or its usual driver. Others reflect declines in the value of pensions with advancing age. Therefore, changes in social roles and relationships with advancing age may be mainly due to other social and economic changes, rather than declines in health or ageing *per se*. Finally, chronological age defines membership of a particular birth cohort or generation. The group of people aged 60 and over today represents a span of over 30 years, and encompasses enormous diversity and inequality.

Cross-cutting these various meanings of ageing are gender and other dimensions of difference, especially class. In terms of physiological ageing, older women have greater reported levels of disability than older men (Arber and Cooper 1999), and therefore may experience more constraints on their social activities and everyday lives because of mobility difficulties. Older women are also more likely than older men to face later life from a position of economic disadvantage (Arber and Ginn 1991). Advanced age, ill-health and poverty are well documented predisposing factors for entry into institutional care (Oldman and Quilgars 1999). As these factors are more commonly associated with the experience of older women, they are more likely than men to spend their final years being cared for by agencies outside the family.

Inequalities in health associated with occupational class persist into later life. Those who previously had working-class occupations are more likely to suffer ill health and disability in their sixties and seventies than professionals or managers (Arber and Cooper 1999). Social and economic changes associated with advancing chronological age are more pronounced for older women than men. In terms of cohort changes, the lives of women have changed enormously over the past century with the growth of women's employment, the availability of contraception and the liberalization of abortion. These profound changes have had less effect on the oldest generation of older women, but a greater effect on those in their sixties and midlife women. The current generation of older women have had a very different life course from older men. Many of the oldest generation of women left the labour market when they married or had children, and either did not return to paid employment, or returned to part-time rather than full-time work as their children became less dependent (Dex 1984). Thus, when we study older people from age 60 to 85, we are comparing distinct age cohorts in which gendered family and labour market roles reflect the changing norms prevailing during their life course.

The present circumstances of older people can only be understood by reference to their prior life course. For example, older women's and men's current financial circumstances are intimately tied to their previous role in the labour market and thus their pension acquisition. There is likely to be substantial continuity of social activities and interests from adult years through to later life. Similarly, the pattern of friendships formed by older people during their working life and while caring for children continues to influence the nature and meanings of friendship in later life.

Gender and masculinities in later life

Despite increasing attention to gendered dimensions of ageing, insufficient attention has been paid to issues involving men and masculinities. While there has been a growth of sociological research on masculinity in recent years (for example, Seidler 1989, 1998; Segal 1990; Kimmel and Messner 2001), the focus has been on younger men, especially relating to education, crime, unemployment, sexuality and the body (Mac an Ghaill 1996; Watson 2000; Adams and Savran 2002). The literature on masculinity has largely omitted older men. A typical example is Whitehead (2002), whose book *Men and Masculinities* devotes barely two pages to ageing and masculinity, stating: 'men's ageing bodies have had little attention from gender theorists, the focus tending to be on young men, physically active men who appear to embody a dominant masculinity' (Whitehead 2002: 200). Thus, the masculinity of older men has hitherto been invisible in studies on gender, and theories of masculinity have primarily conceptualized the meaning of manhood as it applies to younger men (Seidler 1989). Indeed, some writers have proposed (Gutmann 1987; Henry 1988) that ageing can facilitate a change in masculinity: a reduction of male hormones in men could result in the development of a less aggressive, more caring lifestyle usually associated with female behaviour.

It is therefore important to examine the nature of gender identities in later life, particularly among men. Self-identities are fundamentally gendered. When the term *gendered* is used, it means ideas about gender: assumptions and beliefs on an individual level as well as societal level, and how they affect thoughts, feelings, behaviours and treatment of women and men. There is an abundance of literature on the social construction of gender and we provide only a brief review here.

Feminist discourse has argued that masculine and feminine behaviours are governed by mediating processes, such as socialization and social construction (Thompson 1993). To the extent that men and women have distinct name divisions, and dress or act differently because of societal expectations within and between cultures, their behaviour is gendered and not biologically driven. Reid and Whitehead (1992: 2) define the social construction of gender as: 'a cognitive and symbolic construct that helps individuals develop a sense of self, a sense of identity that is constructed in the process of interacting with others within a given human community'. West and Zimmerman (1987) contend that roles are learned and acted out in specific contexts, and that men and women 'do gender' all the time, in all contexts. Gender, therefore, is evoked, created and sustained daily through interaction. Gender is not the property of individuals, they argue, but a feature of social situations that both instigate and confirm gender inequality.

Susan Sontag (1978: 73) contends that 'Getting older is less profoundly wounding for a man . . . Men are "allowed" to age, without penalty, in several ways that women are not.' There is no doubt that there are heavy pressures on women to 'stay' young and 'look' young, which are less pronounced for men as they age (Featherstone and Hepworth 2000).

However, it is important to examine the maintenance of masculinity and autonomy among men in later life. Men have been described as 'in their prime' between the ages of 45 and 60, dominant in every sphere of society: academia, business, politics and religion, for example (Thompson 1994), and for a small minority, this power is little diminished even in very old age. Nevertheless, for the majority of men, advancing years herald removal from 'centre stage' in order to make room for the upcoming 'Young Turks'. Retirement from paid employment has been described as the transitional period between paid work and death following withdrawal from familiar occupational and social worlds inhabited as a 'full' member of society (Cumming and Henry 1961; Phillipson 1982; Laczko and Phillipson 1991). Leaving the occupational 'breadwinner' role, and the concomitant loss of a community of co-workers, can serve to weaken a man's sense of his male identity (Courtenay 2000). In addition, possible loss of sexual potency, diminishing physical strength and the onset of ill health can further reduce his esteem in both his own eyes and those of society. For older men, the traditional discourse of masculinity has perforce to be realigned to accommodate the changing roles and relationships created by altered life circumstances, particularly retirement.

An often overlooked aspect of gender roles and relationships in later life is that of care for a spouse with chronic physical or mental disabilities. Although women carry out the major share of informal, intergenerational kith and kin care (Finch and Groves 1983), similar proportions of men and women carry out care for their spouse in late life (Arber and Gilbert 1989). However, Davidson *et al.* (2000) found that older men retain power within the caring relationship, whether or not they are the carer or the cared for. The older men remained in control while providing care, emphasizing the organization of their daily tasks, or, as Rose and Bruce (1995) describe, carving a 'new career' of caring. In this way, men maintained a sense of order and routine corresponding to their previous employment role. When cared for, unless debilitated by dementia, ailing men maintained control over the finances and major decisions, much as they had done throughout their married years. Davidson *et al.* (2000) found that although men tend to equate illness with weakness, even physically frail men maintained their sense of self as 'head of the household' and retained control within the household and over their spouse carer.

Changing forms of partnership in later life

A reassessment of the meaning of marital status in later life is central to understanding the gendered nature of changing roles and relationships with advancing age. Older men's masculinity is reinforced and maintained by marriage or partnership. The ways in which older men who are widowed, divorced or never married seek to maintain their masculinity are a central concern of the book. Partnership status is also pivotal for material well-being and social relationships, but in divergent ways for older women and men. However, the forms of partnership status in later life are rapidly changing, with profound implications for future generations of older people.

A significant transition for many older people begins when they are widowed. Widowhood often represents the loss of a partner of 40–50 years, who may have been the main source of companionship and support, especially for men, who frequently see their wife as their primary confidante (Askham 1994; Davidson 1999). Most older men are married and therefore have a partner to rely on should they become physically disabled, whereas this is not the case for the majority of older women. Widowhood is normative for older women, since half of women over age 65 in Britain are widowed and on average women can expect to live as a widow for nine years. The common experience of widowhood for women contrasts with the norm for men, that they remain married until their death. However, this may blind us to issues that face the minority of older widowed men, and the small but growing proportions who are divorced. These groups of older men are often neglected in research studies on later life.

The proportion of older people in each marital status is not static, but shows some rapid changes between 1981 and 2021 (see Table 1.1). There is a declining proportion of men aged over 65 who are married, but even in 2021, two-thirds are married. This contrasts with older women, where the proportions married are projected to increase from 37 per cent in 1981 to 45 per cent by 2021. This change is due to improvements in mortality at older ages, especially among men. There is a corresponding projected sharp decline in widowhood, from almost half of older women in 2001 to 35 per cent in 2021. Widowhood is projected to reduce among older men from 17 per cent in 2001 to only 13 per cent by 2021 (Government Actuary's Department 2001).

The largest proportionate change between 1981 and 2021 is the massive increase in older people who are divorced. This rises from only 2 per cent divorced in 1981 to 5–6 per cent in 2001 and then more than doubles to 13 per cent of men and 14 per cent of women by 2021. This profound change means that by 2021, among women aged between 65 and 74, there will be almost as many divorcees (541,000 or 18 per cent) as widows (610,000 or 20 per cent) (Shaw 1999). Among women aged over 65, it is estimated there will be 250 widows to every 100 divorcees. This represents an

Table 1.1   Changes in marital status over time in England and Wales: 1981, 2001 and 2021, age 65 and over

	1981 %	2001 %	2021 %	Change 1981–2021
Men				
Married	73	71	66	−7
Widowed	18	17	13	−5
Divorced	2	5	13	+11
Never married	7	7	8	+1
Total number (millions)	3.0	3.5	4.8	+60%
Women				
Married	37	40	45	+8
Widowed	49	48	35	−14
Divorced	2	6	14	+12
Never married	12	6	5	−7
Total number (millions)	4.6	4.8	5.9	+28%

Source: www.gad.gov.uk/news/marital_projections.htm

enormous change from 1998, when there were 25 times more widows than divorced women. Over the same period there has been a substantial fall in the proportions of never married older women, from 12 to 5 per cent, but no change in the proportions of never married older men, at 7 per cent. Given these marked changes in the marital status of the older population, it is timely to advance our understanding of the ways in which marital status may differentiate the experiences of older men and women. However, it is important to recognize that these official figures are based on legal marital status and increasingly diverge from the *de facto* partnership status of older people, who may be cohabiting or in a Living Apart Together (LAT) relationship.

Earlier work has emphasized the feminization of later life (Arber and Ginn 1991). However, later life is becoming less numerically dominated by women. Table 1.1 shows that the expected increase in older women between 1981 and 2021 is only 28 per cent, but over the same period the expected increase for men is 60 per cent. Parallel to this, the sex ratio among the older population has steadily fallen from 1.53 women for every man over 65 in 1981 to 1.37 in 2001, and is projected to fall to only 1.23 women for every older man in 2021 (calculated from the final rows in Table 1.1). Thus, older men merit greater research attention from scholars interested in ageing.

Overview of the chapters

The chapters in this book advance understanding of gender and ageing by addressing issues relating to gender identity, masculinities, partnership status and changing roles and relationships in later life. In Chapter 2, Toni Calasanti examines the interaction between age relations and gender relations, particularly with reference to men and masculinities. Though some scholars have raised complaints about the marginal status of men as subjects of social gerontology, she argues that men *per se* have not been neglected; however, we have yet to problematize their roles in the social construction of old age. There is a need for explicit attention to men and masculine identity in a way that makes men the subjects of investigation, rather than taking them as the unacknowledged norm. It is important to highlight ways in which gender and age relations interact to exclude some men while enhancing the power base of others. For instance, the actions of some men serve to make other men as dependent upon the state in old age as are many older women. Calasanti uses care work as an exemplar to illustrate the impact of age relations on masculinities and femininities: the questions revolve not around whether men can care, but instead under what circumstances and with what gender identity negotiations.

In Chapter 3, Eileen Fairhurst examines changing perspectives on age, gender and life after work, exploring individuals' own ideas about becoming and being older and how they change as they age. She examines late life course transitions and the relationships between work, family and leisure. Three themes are examined: (a) aspirations for, and experiences of, the timing of exit from the world of work; (b) activities after exit from paid work; and (c) contrasts noted by individuals between their current experiences and those of preceding generations. These themes are examined to suggest how and, in what ways, age, gender and life after work are being redefined in contemporary Britain.

Klas Borell and Sofie Ghazanfareeon Karlsson (Chapter 4) examine the ways in which older people are creating new family forms. This is especially evident in Sweden, one of the countries in the Western world where the differentiation of family forms has progressed furthest. Older people in Sweden are active in restructuring the contemporary Swedish family and the meaning of intimacy through the establishment of lasting intimate relationships where each partner continues to live in their own home. This alternative to marriage and unmarried cohabitation is usually covered by the concept of Living Apart Together (LAT) relationships.

Their chapter demonstrates that autonomy is of particular importance to women, echoing widows' concern to keep their new-found freedom (Davidson 2001). It shows that older women play a vital role in establishing and upholding LAT relationships. For women in LAT relationships, a household of their own is a place in which personal control is ensured, a resource women can draw on to balance their need for intimacy with their need for privacy. Even if the division of labour between men and women in LAT relationships is relatively traditional when they are together, maintaining their own household enables older women to avoid some of the asymmetrical distribution of household labour and unequal demands of caring for a partner. Borell and Ghazanfareeon Karlsson examine how older Swedish LAT partners organize their lives together and the motives behind their choice of a two-household relationship. LAT relationships can offer older divorcees, widows and widowers a fulfilling intimate relationship while maintaining a significant degree of autonomy.

Despite the growing diversity of partnership forms and the 'sexualization' of contemporary society, firmly held beliefs exist about 'normal' and 'appropriate' sexual behaviours. The tendency to desexualize ageing is apparent at societal, academic and practice/policy levels. In particular, little research in this area has captured the perspectives of older people themselves. Merryn Gott and Sharon Hinchcliff in Chapter 5 draw on a qualitative study to explore whether gendered perspectives exist regarding the nature and role of sex in later life. Their research shows that sex in later life was seen by both male and female participants as an important means of expressing love and facilitating a close emotional relationship. However, older men were more likely to feel that sex had become less important to them with ageing – something they discussed within the context of their own reduced capacity to 'perform'. Some women discussed the changing meaning of sex following the menopause, with a shift in focus from procreation to their own pleasure. There were marked differences by gender regarding attitudes towards forming new sexual relationships after the death of a spouse, with women, but not men, feeling their sex life 'died' with their spouse. The chapter indicates that older people value sex, although men are more likely than women to see ageing as having a negative impact upon their sexual satisfaction but are also more likely to seek a new partner following the death of their spouse.

The issue of same-sex relationships in relation to ageing is under-researched, but Ingrid Connidis addresses this yawning gap in Chapter 6. Howard Becker's concept of 'outsiders' applies to those who are gay or lesbian in Western societies. Despite some promising signs of greater inclusion, exclusion continues to be evident in research on family ties and on ageing. Gay and lesbian adults are rarely included in discussions of family ties over the life course. However, when they are, the usual focus is on same-sex relationships in relation to parenting or to the initial response to 'coming out', particularly by parents. Research has been lacking on gay and lesbian adults' relationships with their ageing parents and their siblings.

This chapter addresses conceptual and research challenges in the study of sibling and parent–adult child relationships that involve gay or lesbian family members. The concept of ambivalence is useful because it emphasizes: (a) socially created contradictions; and (b) negotiation as an ongoing feature of family relationships. Negotiations among family members become more evident when relationships are atypical. The chapter focuses on how relationships of gay and lesbian adults with their parents and siblings change with ageing and with parents' increasing frailty and need for care. Issues of changing gender identities in relation to family relationships are addressed.

Several chapters examine the influence of partnership status on various dimensions of the lives of older women and men. Solo living is closely associated with lack of a partner, since the majority of older people who are widowed, divorced or never married live alone. Because of gender differences in life expectancy and marital status, the number of older men living alone is lower than the number of older women. However, this proportion is expected to increase in the near future. With this scenario in mind, Jenny de Jong Gierveld examines the social networks of older men living alone compared to their female counterparts (Chapter 7). Older men who live alone are often more socially isolated and lonely than women who live alone.

The chapter highlights, first, the kinds of network relationships that are associated with solo living among older people, and their frequency of social contact. Second, the determinants of the size and composition of their social networks are investigated, focusing on the life histories of the individuals involved. Among older men who live alone, key transitions and stages in their life course are shown to have a strong influence on their social relationships. Differences between never married, ever widowed and ever divorced men (and women) are examined in relation to frequency of contacts with their children (if they have any), siblings, other kin, friends and colleagues. Older people in LAT relationships are also shown to be a significant new group, who experience lower levels of social isolation and loneliness.

There is little comparative research on family support for non-married (widowed, divorced/separated and never married) older people who live in divergent cultures. In Chapter 8, Cecilia Tomassini from Italy and Karen Glaser and Janet Askham from the UK address this issue. Italy represents a familistic culture with a low level of public welfare support, while Britain has a more individualistic culture and a growing private care sector. Frail older people who are not married have to rely on help from others outside the household, state care or privately purchased care. The extent of co-residence versus solo living among unmarried men and women is analysed in these two contrasting societies, showing the impact of socio-economic circumstances but not gender on the propensity to live alone. National survey data are then analysed to examine how gender, partnership status and socio-economic circumstances influence receipt of support from relatives living outside the household, friends and neighbours, paid private care and public support, comparing Britain and Italy. The findings demonstrate the importance of differences in family structures in the two societies, as well as welfare state policies, both of which are more significant than gender *per se* in influencing living arrangements and receipt of help by older unmarried people.

A major factor that contributes to the welfare and quality of life of older people is economic independence. The financial well-being of older people cannot be considered independently of their life course and partnership history.

There has been extensive academic and political concern over the lower levels of private pension coverage among women, and the erosion of the value of the state pension in recent decades. However, simultaneously, as discussed earlier in the chapter, there have been major demographic shifts, with many men and women experiencing divorce and separation. Very little is known in the UK about the financial effects of divorce, especially for older men.

Debora Price and Jay Ginn, in Chapter 9, compare the pension prospects of men and women according to their partnership status and class, by examining those who contribute to additional private pension schemes designed to supplement the low level of state pensions in the UK. Married women have low participation rates in such pension schemes – lower than cohabiting women – reflecting their individual poverty. For divorced women and separated women who are not cohabiting, the rates are even lower. The only class of women who have higher rates of additional pension scheme participation after divorce are professionals and managers. The participation rates for men are much higher than for women, but the pension position of separated and divorced men is relatively very poor. The implications of these findings for gender inequalities in later life are discussed, especially given the projected growth in the older divorced population.

Sara Arber and colleagues, in Chapter 10, re-examine the relationship between gender and marital status with advancing age. They follow the previous chapter in showing how marital status is fundamental to the financial and material well-being of older women and men, and extend this to consider the social involvement of older people with family, friends and neighbours. They use recent British data to illustrate how marital status is linked to material disadvantage and to social roles, but in complex and gender-differentiated ways. Older men who are never married or divorced are disadvantaged both socio-economically and in their social contacts, while married men are advantaged. The pattern is somewhat different for older women, with divorced older women materially disadvantaged, but this is less for single women. In contrast to men, marital status does not differentiate older women's social contacts with family, friends and neighbours.

Kate Davidson and colleagues take the preceding chapter forward by exploring the social worlds of older men using qualitative data. Chapter 11 explores the influence of the partnership status of older men on their social networks and relationships with friends and family. They explore the gendered development of family and friendship relationships and offer possible explanations for the differential experiences of men and women in later life social interaction. Research has identified that marriage can exert a protective effect on men's well-being, with women taking primary responsibility for maintaining social networks. Lone older men face distinct challenges in successfully performing these roles.

For older men, a key issue is the maintenance of masculinity and autonomy in later life, despite changes in social circumstances. It has been argued that there is a blurring of gender roles and identities with advancing age. This is particularly relevant for older men who live without partners and who take on domestic tasks traditionally carried out by women. However, Davidson and colleagues point out that we tend to measure the social worlds of older people with a 'feminine ruler', assuming that lone older men's smaller social networks provide inadequate social support. They argue that marital history and issues of continuity and discontinuity are particularly important factors in men's social world view. They caution against seeing older men as victims of neglect by researchers who take women's experiences as their models.

The final chapter, and a fitting conclusion to the volume, by Jenny Hislop and Sara Arber, examines sleep as a social act. Until now, sleep has been theorized and researched in the domain of biomedical science. The sociology of sleep is a new and hitherto under-explored area of everyday lives. Hislop and Arber explore older women's sleep against a vivid backdrop of their social world, reflecting the multiplicity of roles and relationships that characterize their lives. As such, for many women, a central theme is the relationship with their partner and the key role this plays in shaping and influencing their sleep patterns throughout the life course. This chapter examines how older women's sleep may be affected by changes in their sleeping relationship with their partner in response to factors such as ill-health, caring responsibilities, divorce and widowhood.

The chapter uses qualitative research to show the link between women's sleep in later life and their sleeping relationship with their partner. Women's sleep may be affected physically and psychologically by their partner's activities, including increased snoring and restlessness with ageing, and caring needs associated with ill-health and dementia. Moreover, the importance of the sleeping relationship in structuring women's sleep is highlighted by the sleep changes that accompany divorce and widowhood as women seek to establish a viable sleeping pattern in the absence of a partner.

Reconceptualizing gender and ageing

The principal aim of the book has been to generate new ideas about gender and later life, in order to refresh scholarship on ageing. The contributors illustrate how an integration of issues relating to diversity, identities and partnership status provides new theoretical and policy insights into the lives of both older men and older women. A recurrent thread running through the book concerns divorced older men and women, since they will be numerically significant in years to come.

The changing nature of masculinities in later life is highlighted. An underlying theme is how the socio-economic circumstances and life course of older people continue to connect with and impact on identities, social relationships and social well-being in later life, but in differentiated ways according to gender.

Note

1 The chapters in this book are revised versions of a selection of papers presented to the International Symposium on Reconceptualising Gender and Ageing held at the University of Surrey, 25–27 June 2002. The symposium was organized as part of a grant to the editors in the Economic and Social Research Council Growing Older Programme, grant no. L480254033.

References

Adams, R. and Savran, D. (2002) *The Masculinity Studies Reader*. Oxford: Blackwell.

Allan, G. (1985) *Family Life*. Oxford: Blackwell.

Arber, S. and Cooper, H. (1999) Gender differences in health in later life: the new paradox?, *Social Sciences and Medicine*, 48(1): 61–76.

Arber, S. and Gilbert, N. (1989) Men: the forgotten carers, *Sociology*, 23(1): 111–18.

Arber, S. and Ginn, J. (1991) *Gender and Later Life: A Sociological Analysis of Resources and Constraints*. London: Sage.

Arber, S. and Ginn, J. (eds) (1995) *Connecting Gender and Ageing: A Sociological Approach*. Buckingham: Open University Press.

Askham, F. (1994) Marriage relationships of older people, *Reviews in Clinical Gerontology*, 4: 261–8.

Calasanti, T. M. and Sleven, K. F. (2001) *Gender, Social Inequalities and Aging*. Walnut Creek, CA: AltaMira Press.

Courtenay, W. H. (2000) Constructions of masculinity and their influence on men's well-being: a theory of gender and health, *Social Science and Medicine*, 50: 1385–401.

Cumming, E. and Henry, W. (1961) *Growing Old: The Process of Disengagement*. New York: Basic Books.

Davidson, K. (1999) Marriage in retrospect: a study of older widows and widowers. In R. Miller and S. Browning (eds) *With this Ring: Divorce, Intimacy and Cohabitation from a Multicultural Perspective*. Stamford, CT: JAI Press.

Davidson, K. (2001) Late life widowhood, selfishness and new partnership choices: a gendered perspective, *Ageing and Society*, 21(3): 279–317.

Davidson, K., Arber, S. and Ginn, J. (2000) Gendered meanings of care work within late life marital relationships, *Canadian Journal on Aging*, 19(4): 536–53.

Dex, S. (1984) *Women's Work Histories: An Analysis of the Women and Employment Survey*. Department of Employment Research Paper Number 46. London: Department of Employment.

Estes, C. (1991) The new political economy of aging: introduction and critique. In M. Minkler and C. Estes (eds) *Critical Perspectives on Aging: The Political and Moral Economy of Growing Older*. New York: Baywood.

Featherstone, M. and Hepworth, M. (2000) Images of ageing. In J. Bond, P. Coleman and S. Peace (eds) *Ageing in Society: An Introduction to Social Gerontology*. London: Sage.

Finch, J. and Groves, D. (1983) *A Labour of Love: Women, Work and Caring*. London: Routledge and Kegan Paul.

Finch, J. and Mason, J. (1993) *Negotiating Family Responsibilities*. London: Routledge.

Government Actuary's Department (2001) *Marital Projections: England and Wales* (http://www.gad.gov.uk/news/marital_projections.htm). Accessed 12 November 2002.

Gilleard, C. and Higgs, P. (2000) *Cultures of Ageing: Self, Citizen and the Body*. Harlow: Pearson Education.

Gutmann, D. (1987) *Reclaimed Powers: Towards a New Psychology of Men and Women in Later Life*. New York: Basic Books.

Henry, J. (1988) The archetypes of power and intimacy. In J. Birren and V. Bengtson (eds) *Emergent Theories of Aging*. New York: Springer.

Jerrome, D. (1996) Continuity and change in the study of family relationships, *Ageing and Society*, 16(1): 91–104.

Kimmel, M. and Messner, M. (2001) *Men's Lives*. Boston: Allyn and Bacon.

Laczko, F. and Phillipson, C. (1991) *Changing Work and Retirement*. Buckingham: Open University Press.

Lopata, H. Z. (1973) *Widowhood in an American City*. Cambridge, MA: Schenkman.

Mac an Ghaill, M. (ed.) (1996) *Understanding Masculinities*. Buckingham: Open University Press.

Oldman, C. and Quilgars, D. (1999) The last resort? Revisiting ideas about older people's living arrangements, *Ageing and Society*, 19(3): 363–84.

Phillipson, C. (1982) *Capitalism and the Construction of Old Age*. London: Macmillan.

Reid, B. and Whitehead, T. (1992) Introduction. In T. Whitehead and B. Reid (eds) *Gender Constructs and Social Issues*. Urbana: University of Illinois Press.

Rose, H. and Bruce, E. (1995) Mutual care but differential esteem: caring between older couples. In S. Arber and J. Ginn (eds) *Connecting Gender and Ageing: A Sociological Approach*. Buckingham: Open University Press.

Segal, L. (1990) *Slow Motion: Changing Masculinities, Changing Men*. London: Virago.

Seidler, V. (1989) *Rediscovering Masculinity*. London: Routledge.

Seidler, V. (1998) *Man Enough*. London: Sage.

Shaw, C. (1999) 1996-based population projections by legal marital status for England and Wales, *Population Trends*, 95: 23–32.

Sontag, S. (1978) The double standard of ageing. In V. Carver and P. Liddiard (eds) *An Ageing Population*. Milton Keynes: Open University Press.

Thompson, E. (1994) Older men as invisible men, in E. Thompson (ed.) *Older Men's Lives*. Thousand Oaks, CA: Sage.

Thompson, L. (1993) Conceptualizing gender in marriage: a case of marital care, *Journal of Marriage and the Family*, 55: 557–69.

Watson, J. (2000) *Male Bodies: Health, Culture and Identity*. Buckingham: Open University Press.

West, C. and Zimmerman, D. (1987) Doing gender, *Gender and Society*, 1(2): 125–51.

Whitehead, S. (2002) *Men and Masculinities: Key Themes and New Directions*. Cambridge: Polity Press.

2

MASCULINITIES AND CARE WORK IN OLD AGE

Toni Calasanti

At least two different groups decry the neglect of men and masculinities in social science scholarship. In much the same way that whites in the USA have complained of 'reverse discrimination', some argue that feminism concentrates too exclusively on women and fails to attend to men and their needs. Others agree that men and masculinities have been neglected but not because men have been ignored. Instead, this latter group acknowledges that previous theory and research have used men as an unexamined standard, noting that 'Research on men is as old as scholarship itself, but a focus on masculinity, or men as explicitly gendered individuals, is relatively recent' (Coltrane 1994: 41).

These contrasting perspectives result in two broad types of scholarship on manhood. The first, non-feminist, approach examines the ways in which masculinity has confined men; but it does not explore men's privilege. Essentially, this work 'celebrates male bonding and tells men they are OK' (Coltrane 1994: 42). For instance, the US mythopoetic men's movement uses weekends full of therapeutic and story-telling techniques to help men to 'claim their "inner" power, their "deep manhood," or their "warrior within" ' (Kimmel 1994: 136). The popularity of this perspective is based on the fact that many men do *not* feel powerful, and may be frustrated and angry at their lack of power. The statistical realities that demonstrate men have power are contradicted by men's feelings of powerlessness (Kimmel 1994).

A second, pro-feminist, approach considers men's power over women. It explores the socially constructed aspects of this dominance and of 'hegemonic masculinity' (Connell 1995): the dominant masculinity that encompasses the 'normative constellation of attitudes, traits, and behaviours that become the standard against which individual men measure the success of their gender accomplishments' (Kimmel 1994: 139). Present hegemonic masculinity would include physical strength, professional success, wealth, heterosexual prowess and self-control over certain emotions, such as grief or shame. Alongside this cultural ideal, to which many men aspire and against which they measure themselves but generally do not achieve, are many coexisting and competing masculinities. Recognizing these diverse masculinities as well as the 'contradictory meanings and experiences of manhood' (Coltrane 1994: 42), this perspective acknowledges that many men *are* relatively powerless – because of their relationships with *other men*.

> In this sense, men's experience of powerlessness is *real* – the men actually feel it and certainly act on it – but it is not *true* – that is, it does not accurately describe their condition. In contrast to women's lives, men's lives are structured around relationships of power and men's differential access to power, as well as the differential access to that power of men as a group.
>
> (Kimmel 1994: 135)

The pervasiveness of men's feelings of powerlessness is due to the fact that manhood has been constructed in such a way that only a tiny percentage can really 'achieve' and feel it. The vast majority are disempowered, often due to discrimination on the basis of other social hierarchies. What is important across masculinities is that they all take pride in, and in many ways reward themselves for, being different from women and femininity. Thus, this second approach 'link[s] the ways that men create and sustain gendered selves with the ways that gender influences power relations and perpetuates inequality' (Coltrane 1994: 44).

This chapter builds upon this latter approach to address how we should treat men and masculinities in the study of ageing. I consider how the intersections between gender and age relations shape manhood over the life course, particularly in old age. The chapter begins by exploring why men and masculinities have been neglected in ageing studies, and outlines the theoretical bases for their inclusion. Next, I apply this lens to informal, unpaid care work, to illustrate ways in which we might examine manhood more fruitfully. While I am aware of the importance of examining the intersections of social locations, given space constraints I do not do so in depth. Finally, in this chapter I use the term 'old' rather than 'older' for political reasons (for a more in-depth discussion, see Calasanti and Slevin 2001). While 'old' is socially constructed, reified and stigmatized, as are many other terms for oppressed groups, using the term 'older' conveys that the old are more acceptable if we think of them as more like the middle-aged. In much the same way that many would find it ludicrous to refer to Blacks as 'darker' and instead recognize the efforts to reclaim the word 'Black' and imbue it with dignity, so too I use 'old' to recover and instil the term with positive valuation.

The omission of men and masculinities in ageing: ignoring gender and age relations

Backlash against feminists in the USA has taken, among others, the form of claims in the popular press (including those of social scientists) that feminists have gained too much power in many realms, including power over the production and dissemination of knowledge (Faludi 1991; Kimmel 1996). In gerontology, this would translate into the view that feminists had deemed the study of masculinities inappropriate and, as a result, left men out.

From a different vantage, Thompson (1994) maintains that, in addition to the fact that there are far more old women, old men have been ignored in part because ageing and ageism do not influence men and women equally. Old men are relatively better off than women financially; they are more likely to be married and hence living with others and not experiencing the grief of widowhood; and they also experience less disability than do women. Consequently, Thompson argues that researchers tend to see old women as 'problems' (see also Gibson 1996); thus, old women receive more research attention than do old men.

While Thompson's claim has some validity, the deeper issue is theoretical. Despite an increased interest in old *women*, few scholars use a feminist approach. For the most part, gender has not been a concern among sociologists of ageing (Hooyman 1999). For example, when researchers do focus on old men and their higher mortality, their lives become medicalized to the extent that other, non-medical aspects of their lives, such as support networks, become trivialized or ignored altogether (Thompson 1994), as are the gender relations that shape these. And, in those rare instances when scholars do bring in gender, it is often in relation to women only. We are far less prone to research those with privilege from the standpoint *of* that privilege. As a result, whether or not they have been included *in* studies, old men have not been critically examined. However, despite contentions of the anti-feminist backlash, feminist perspectives would advocate that 'The sociology of ageing . . . be fully, not partially, gendered' (Hearn 1995: 98).

Feminist approaches are grounded in an appreciation of gender *relations* – understanding both women and men, and femininities and masculinities as inextricably linked. Thus, these perspectives require a focus on manhood. However, rather than assuming men's experiences as unexamined standards, or that research on men is synonymous with the study of 'everyone', this gender-relations approach views men and masculinity critically, as integral parts of a system of inequality. Doing such research implies more than including women or men as respondents. The lens one uses makes the difference. A feminist, gender-sensitive lens takes male privilege *itself* as problematic and incorporates it into the research questions (Calasanti and Slevin 2001).

When we use this feminist approach to review the contention that old men have been ignored because of their relative comfort, for instance, it is clear that we need to go further: we must contextualize the relative comfort of old men in terms of underlying gender relations. Further, positing men's relative advantage does not help us to understand why other, more negative aspects of old men's lives are not seen to be problematic. For instance, if men do not live as long as women, why do we not pose them and their shorter life expectancies as problems? Why do we not ask: what is it about old women that makes them stronger (Gibson 1996)? Why have we not examined how *masculinity diminishes* health (Courtenay 2000)? Such questions go beyond simply noting demographics, such as the fact that men tend to engage in more unhealthy behaviours than women. They ask, how does masculinity help us to account for this?

Bringing old men into research involves more than treating them as victims of neglect; it requires making manhood visible, a subject of inquiry, and not merely listing gender differences. Again, using health as an example, we do not simply enumerate the realities that men drink more than women, or engage in other adverse health-related behaviours. Instead, we explore how 'doing masculinity' leads men to hurt their health by engaging in behaviours that will reproduce their privilege over women and at the same time neglect their social networks and physical safety. Similarly, we would look at how 'doing femininity' reproduces women's subordination.

To understand more fully the neglect of manhood within studies of ageing, we need also to examine the ways in which age relations intersect with gender to influence knowledge production. Within social gerontology, a middle-aged bias often pervades research, such that earlier theories depicted being old as a 'problem'. In addition to seeing old women's lives as problems (Gibson 1996), applying a middle-aged lens to old men rendered retired men as:

> ... outside the 'normal' work spaces ... Older men were portrayed as obsolete currency in a culture that cherishes power; in disengagement terms, the spotlight was on younger men's welfare. Later discourses of activity theory similarly emphasized the core values of a masculinity that best fits younger employed men's lives.
>
> (Thompson 1994: 15)

More recent perspectives continue to incorporate this middle-aged bias. The continued emphasis on productivity and activity, often through the lens and promotion of 'successful ageing', is ultimately geared towards showing that the old are not different from younger people and are therefore worthy of esteem (Calasanti 2003).

The influence of age relations and ageism can also be seen in scholarship on gender. Those in gender studies – whether focusing on women or men – also tend to ignore the old (Arber and Ginn 1991; Hearn 1995; Calasanti and Slevin 2001). Among those who study masculinity, even in those few instances where scholars adopt a life course view, 'the theoretical discourse on masculinities has concentrated on social practices of young to middle-aged men and, by default, marginalized the masculinities of elderly men' (Thompson 1994: 9).

Taking both gender and age relations into account in the study of men requires that we simultaneously explore relations among men of different ages, as well as relations between old men and old women. Given that masculinity is both dynamic and multiple, our goal in ageing studies would include examining 'the ways in which "men" are constructed as meanings through and by reference to "age". This is both a matter of the social construction of the category "men" and of particular men and a question of the construction of men's experiences through the lens of age' (Hearn 1995: 97). What does manhood mean to different old men? We should explore how age relations shape old masculinities such that old men are often depicted as 'other' even as some may be able to approach hegemonic masculinity. We need to explore the ways in which age relationships shape masculinities, leading to lower status (and even invisibility) for old men; and how masculinities shape old men in relation to old women, maintaining gender inequality.

To illustrate this approach to manhood and old age, this chapter briefly examines unpaid care work, a primary area in which scholars have been critiqued for omitting men. Some (for example, Thompson 2000) have accused analysts of both ignoring male care workers and discussing men's care work as deviant – different from, or not as good as, women's – by taking women's experiences as the norm. By doing so, the complaint goes, researchers miss the possibility that men's care work may actually be better than women's, at least in so far as men appear to suffer less stress. In briefly examining these allegations, this chapter does not address all of the data or nuances involved in these contentions, but focuses instead on the extent to which researchers have actually examined men and masculinities from the standpoint of gender relations. I then suggest a feminist approach to research on male care workers.

Unpaid care work

Although feminists generally do not concern themselves with ageing issues, women's preponderance among care workers throughout the life course has prompted attention to this activity. Centring on women's experiences, feminists have revealed many aspects of care, including the fact that it is *work*. To understand the invisibility of care work, one needs to consider the distinctions between physical tasks and emotional labour as well as managerial/ organizational aspects of care (Davidson *et al.* 2000). Of special importance to a discussion of gender relations and old age is what Mason (1996) has termed 'sentient activity', a type of care that may not be totally conscious, but that considers such things as the preferences of another person, which is a form of knowledge developed over time (Davidson *et al.* 2000: 537). This type of care is generally invisible, often only revealed by its absence. Like much of the work that goes into feeding a family (DeVault 1991), if done well, remembering preferences, dislikes, time sequences and the like, and arranging all of these to occur seamlessly, is not apparent to those who receive this care, but becomes notable when it is withdrawn or when one is no longer called upon to perform it (Davidson *et al.* 2000).

Feminists have long noted that, whether paid or unpaid, some dimensions of care work are not only invisible but also undervalued, particularly in care of the old (Diamond 1992; Hooyman and Gonyea 1999; Milne and Hatzidimitriadou 2002). In part, this is apparent in the greater value accorded to care performed by men, a topic to which I return below. But in addition, care for younger 'dependants' (children) seems to be far more highly valued. For instance, 'skewed' dependency ratios, when reflecting a large young population, do not create the sort of uproar that those relating to an older population do, despite the reality that young children are more likely to *need* care than those, say, aged 65–70 (Calasanti and Slevin 2001). The greater value placed on care for the not-old is also apparent in the fact that feminists have paid relatively little attention to the care of old people, except in relation to how this influences the lives of younger (middle-aged) carers.

Because women engage in far more care work than men, their experiences and definitions of such work have guided much gerontological scholarship, and have provided the standards against which men's experiences are compared (Walker 1992). As a result, some of what men do, which might in fact be care work, can be overlooked. For instance, men undertake instrumental tasks that do not match conventional notions of care; therefore this work is discounted by both men and women (Matthews 1995). At the same time, of course, ignoring this work does not change the reality that, if men primarily engage in instrumental care only but women perform both personal and instrumental tasks, women are performing more care work.

In addition, we are only beginning to examine what care work means to men, including their motivations and experiences (Kirsi *et al.* 2000). For instance, what do men mean when they say they are 'involved' in personal care? Do they assume primary responsibility, or do they help their spouses, children or others in this task? How do they view their activities? Some may see themselves as having primary responsibility for care work, even if they do not perform certain tasks: 'My wife does most of it. It is a joint effort' (Vonhof 1991, cited in Martin Matthews and Campbell 1995: 143). Indeed, recent research on men's care work suggests that their participation is conditioned by their relationships with women: the care activities of their wives and daughters draw them into engaging in care work, whereas sisters' involvement serves to decrease and effectively substitute for men's contributions (Gerstel and Gallagher 2001).

These preliminary questions and findings suggest that researchers have much to learn about male carers. However, some of the claims concerning men's care work being treated as deviant, or being ignored by researchers, appear overblown. For instance, consider the complaint that 'The categorical variable in multivariate analysis is frequently coded "female", which is a label for a demographic characteristic . . . "male" remains the background, contrast effect, and distinctiveness of men's caregiving remains invisible' (Thompson 1997, cited in Russell 2001: 356). If the argument here is that gender is being treated, incorrectly, as a categorical variable, then why would it matter which gender was coded as one versus zero? Such coding hardly erases men, and the author's odd misunderstanding of quantitative analysis suggests a desire to find discrimination against men in all sorts of places. It hardly lends credence to a complaint that seems overstated from the beginning. The use of a dummy variable neither omits men nor treats them as deviant.

As another example, consider the (probably unintentional) conflation of diverse studies by some of those who complain of discrimination against men carers. Among other important factors, we need to distinguish among types of relationships between care worker and care receiver in terms of spouse, child, in-law, aunt, sibling, friend and so on. Such differences have significant effects on care work in terms of motivation and frequency. For instance, although men and women do nearly equal amounts of care-giving as spouses, non-spousal care-givers are far more likely to be women. In addition, the fact of providing care does not tell us how much time is devoted to it, and again, outside of spousal care, women expend far more hours and are more likely to have the primary responsibility for care work (Arber and Ginn 1995; National Alliance for Caregiving and AARP 1997). Scholars keen to claim that men do as much care work as women sometimes mingle research on spouses with studies conducted on other types of caring relationships, or look at studies that include all care workers alongside those that only include primary care workers (for example, Kaye and Applegate 1994; Russell 2001). Comparing across such different care relationships cannot identify gender similarities or differences, or render much insight into how men versus women have been examined. Men and women in similar care work relationships may be more similar than not; but women are more frequently care workers overall, more likely to spend more time providing care and to have primary responsibility. We must not lose sight of the fact that being a man means having far less chance of taking on care work. This is not to say that sons do not provide care, for instance, but they do not do so nearly as often as daughters (Harris 1998; Connidis 2001). Care work *is* devalued labour, reserved primarily for women except when it is undertaken by husbands for their wives. To note women's disproportionate care work is not to ignore men.

My larger concern with this gender and care work debate, however, is theoretical. To what extent are claims of ignoring men coming from a pro-feminist perspective that concerns the need to understand gender relations, versus an uneasiness that men are somehow being ignored or discriminated against, despite the fact that we know that for the most part this is not the case? Further, if we accept that men *have* been ignored from the standpoint of being *subjects* of inquiry, how shall we go about filling the gap in our research?

Beginning with a comparison of similar types of care work relationships, one could explore the ways in which gender relations within the family influence the meaning of care. For instance, because women assume primary responsibility for domestic labour, they view much of the care work they perform for their spouses as a part of that everyday duty (Davidson *et al.* 2000). As a result, they may not see spousal care work as requiring as many *extra* hours, and are likely to under-report their work. By contrast, husbands, who do comparatively little domestic labour, are likely to report *all* of their care tasks. Therefore, in spousal care, researchers may find husbands report spending as many or more hours of care than do wives (Dwyer and Seccombe 1991; Milne and Hatzidimitriadou 2002). When we take a close look at similarly situated men and women, and their different approaches to care work, we learn how gender relations shape the reporting and indeed meaning of care work in later life.

One subject in which there has been a push to include considerations of old men is in relation to 'care-giver stress', an area in which men are characterized as having an often unrecognized advantage over women. Female care workers tend to report more anxiety, depression, physical strain and health problems and lower life satisfaction than do equivalent men; and wives who provide care report higher levels of depression than do husbands who provide care (Shirey and Summer 2000; Yee and Schulz 2000). To explain this gender difference, some scholars have pointed to men's more 'managerial style' of caring, a mode that Thompson (2000) argues is devalued by an implicit bias towards women's modes of caring. He and others suggest that men approach care as 'work' in which they seek 'control', attempting to provide care 'in the most efficacious manner with the least engulfment' of the self (Thompson 2000: 337). Similarly, Russell (2001: 355) asserts that this 'managerial strategy provides the caregiver greater perceived control, the sense of being in charge, feelings of self-efficacy, as well as the ability to choose to act or not'. Thus men can often separate *caring for* from *caring about*, and this assumed ability to detach and separate emotional from functional aspects of care is thought to provide a buffer to stress (Thompson 2000: 338). Whether this control and detachment is devalued is, of course, debatable. On the one hand, research that notes men's lower stress levels often suggests that men respond 'better' to care work than women do. Indeed, some speculate that greater attention to men's care work might teach us lessons that could be helpful to women (Thompson 2000; Russell 2001). At the same time, others might find the notion of emotional separation problematic, as it would seem to run counter to a notion of 'caring'. Of course this leads to a host of other questions, about, for instance, the extent to which our ideas about care itself are gendered. Do we view 'detachment' by men and women in the same way? Further, how do we assess 'better' or 'worse' styles of care, versus 'different'?

To address these issues more carefully, we need to place the insightful arguments concerning men's care work within a larger theoretical framework. From this vantage, it appears that the assertions about men's care work *begin* to explore masculinities and gender relations, but do not go far enough theoretically. Using the example above, why would feelings of greater control or a sense of being in charge matter for self-efficacy? Would this ease stress for everyone, regardless of social location? What sorts of masculinities are we really talking about? *Which* men are able to choose to engage in care work, and under what conditions? How does the ability to *choose* whether to act relate to masculinities and gender relations? While exceptions certainly exist (for example, Harris 1998), typically, men who engage in primary care are spouses, or sons with no available female siblings. The issue of 'choice' is itself gendered.

Further, when we assert that men's style may be more 'efficacious' and 'professional/managerial' because of their work experience, we imply that women's labour, which often involves at least two 'jobs', including paid employment, is less 'efficient'. Yet research on women and work shows that women in fact have to juggle far more tasks in many realms than do men. They certainly must be efficient.

Finally, the ability to take time for oneself or detach is shaped by gender differences in the ideology surrounding how care ought to be performed. Such gendered beliefs concerning care are apparent in the ways in which people judge male and female care workers. Do people use the same standards? Further, how is care work shaped by distributions of economic resources and informal networks, which tend to favour men? For example, sons caring for parents tend to receive more support from wives than daughters do from husbands (Yee and Schulz 2000). In addition, husbands are more likely to use outside assistance in care work than are wives (Russell 2001), perhaps because providing care is not seen to be central to their identities as men. Thus, men's privileged positions influence their experiences of caring as a lighter burden than for equivalent women and they experience lower levels of depression. Pointing to this privilege does not devalue men's care work, dedication or commitment, as is sometimes charged. Instead, it reveals the ways in which such dedication may be differently expressed by, or present divergent problems for, men and women, based on gender relations.

Many of these points are evident in Rose and Bruce's (1995) research on spousal care. They argue that husbands and wives experience different sources of stress and rewards in care work, distinctions that can be tied ultimately to gender relations. They suggest that husbands are less distressed by caring for their demented wives in part because they feel useful and able; their care evokes a sense of accomplishment. Rose and Bruce do not doubt either the men's suffering or dedication to their care work, but instead note the gendered nature of their care work:

> . . . we began to think of men's caring as a pet rabbit relationship. A pet rabbit's survival requires conscientious care; indeed its condition is a source of pride for its carer, and the well cared for pet, or rather its owner, receives much admiration. For women, the husband with Alzheimer's

fails to become an equivalent pet, so they grieved. Their equally conscientious care . . . produced little of the real, if subdued, sense of pride that the men displayed.

(Rose and Bruce 1995: 127)

Women did not find comfort or pride in providing care, perhaps because such care had always been expected of them; instead, they grieved for the lost relationship. For the men, such care was 'extraordinary' and brought them attention and respect; the task of caring also gains value when men perform it. Indeed, recent research on men's care work in Japan and the USA confirms that husbands receive more praise and recognition for their activity than do equivalent women, due to the perception in both cultures that the work is more 'natural' for women (Harris and Long 1999). Rose and Bruce (1995) found that the caring tasks themselves continued to be seen as feminine, or at best gender-neutral; they were never seen as masculine. Even when men performed them, caring tasks remained women's work. Perhaps, rather than challenging their masculinity, these men garnered admiration for doing 'women's work'.

Documentation of the lower stress levels of husbands compared to wives who are carers is generally based upon quantitative research, which draws upon typical, close-ended indicators of levels and sources of stress. However, qualitative research has shown that husbands' care work experiences are far more complex than can often be assessed by such quantitative measures. For instance, men may indeed report feelings of accomplishment, while they may also express frustration that much of the care they provide is invisible to others, or feel socially isolated (Russell 2001). Indeed, the fact that men are often used to having their work in the paid realm acknowledged may cause them to feel greater frustration over the invisibility of their care work than women feel; women face a lifetime of invisible domestic labour. Men may respond to such stress with stoicism (Harris 1998).

Furthermore, embedded within this depiction of men's style of care work as managerial and more like their paid work is often the image of a White, professional, heterosexual man. But the causes and *expressions* of stress may vary across gender and racial/ethnic groups (Aranda and Knight 1997). Preliminary qualitative work among Puerto Rican, Black and White men and women carers finds that, though all groups report strain, they speak about it differently, and in response to divergent questions. For example, Whites note feelings of burden and, among women, anger; Puerto Rican women feel isolated; and Black and Puerto Rican men express frustration (Calderon and Tennstedt 1998). Researchers have tended to overlook aspects of the stress men do in fact experience because they do not attend to the intersections of age and gender with race and ethnic relations.

Along these lines, MacRea's (1998) research on emotion work – the processes by which care workers 'manage feelings' in themselves and in the care recipient – suggests ways we might think about how social hierarchies interact in producing stress. She shows that care workers are aware of the 'feeling rules' that govern interaction: they are conscious of expectations concerning the range of emotions one 'ought' to feel in a particular context, and they experience stress when they deviate from these norms. Along these lines, carers who fail to manage their emotions appropriately experience negative self-evaluations. However, those who succeed also do so at a cost. By controlling or suppressing their emotions in order to cope, 'they are at risk of becoming estranged from them and of perhaps even losing the capacity to feel' (MacRea 1998: 157).

Drawing on this research and a gender-sensitive lens, we might ask: do male carers experience less stress because they have greater latitude in the emotions they are allowed to express? Or, because care work is not supposed to be a part of their identity, can they circumvent the guilt and consequent stress for *not* managing their feelings appropriately? How might such feeling rules vary among *different* masculinities? Combined with research that demonstrates how some masculinities encourage men to deny stress or to express it in unhealthy ways (such as alcohol consumption, smoking and risk-taking behaviours; Courtenay 2000), we might also ask whether men deny stress. What price do they pay for its suppression, such as loss of the capacity to feel? Rather than positing men or women as more or less able to handle stress, we might ask what 'care' means to diverse men and women, and how they integrate this into their sense of selves as masculine and feminine and thus shape experiences of stress.

We could hypothesize that stress relates to the ways in which women and men as care workers see themselves, and the resources at their disposal to alleviate difficulties. It might be that both men and women find care work less stressful to the extent that they can enact particular femininities (such as their ability to evoke calm in the care recipient, thereby reinforcing their perception of their own ability to 'nurture') and masculinities (such as their ability to be 'in control' of themselves or the situation). We might examine how men negotiate their identities in relation to care work, and the impact this has on a variety of outcomes. For instance, Kirsi *et al.* (2000) find evidence of a gendered notion of care among the 15 men in their study: these men recognized the existence of 'sensitive' styles of care work that are seen as being more 'female'. Some men who ascribed to this style experienced an implicit tension between being a care worker and being a man. For instance, one man felt a need to explain how he could be both a sensitive carer and still a man; another sought to explain how he was able to express emotions that are not typically masculine. Research on men as care workers in both the USA and Japan finds a similar tension between caring and masculinity (Harris and Long 1999).

Greater attention to negotiating masculinities within a context of care work suggests additional questions. For instance, is men's provision of personal care rendered more difficult to the extent that it deviates too far from hegemonic masculinity? Or, since sexuality is an important part of some masculinities, does such cross-sex care for a spouse interfere with the sexual relationship? While preliminary evidence shows that in fact husbands do provide such care to spouses (Arber and Ginn 1995), the process by which masculinity continues to be negotiated is not clear. Interestingly, Bowers (1999) finds that men carers score higher on masculinity scales than men not providing care. She speculates that these men focus on the managerial aspects: the need to organize, take charge and invest time and energy, traits all reflected on masculinity measures. Such scores could also represent a type of over-compensation, as a way to justify what might appear to be 'non-masculine' behaviour.

The commonly used term 'care-giving' is a misnomer for many reasons, including the implied passivity of the 'receiver', who actually plays a critical role in shaping the care relationship, including the care worker's experiences of stress and rewards (Rose and Bruce 1995; Arber and Ginn 1995; Harris and Long 1999; Kirsi et al. 2000). Davidson et al. (2000) trace the differences in older wives' and husbands' experiences of both care work for a spouse and its receipt to gender relations throughout their long marriages. While the wives saw such work as an extension of their domestic duties, men viewed it as a break with their previous roles – but not with their masculinity in terms of autonomy. That is, the power relations that characterized their marriages and gave the husbands greater control did not cease when the husband became dependent upon his wife for care. As a result, wives who provided care still experienced constraints upon their time and decision-making abilities.

Husbands who received care, except for those who experienced dementia, continued to exert control over decisions and were demanding, perhaps because, for them, disability meant weakness and thus threatened their masculinity. Not having been relegated to domestic labour previously in their marriages, husbands did not have an appreciation for what this work entailed. In many respects, they tried to retain as much independence as they could as care receivers, reproducing what they could of their dominance. By contrast, dependent wives were well aware of what caring entails, as they had long been providing it. As a result, they were described as 'good patients', expressed gratitude for their husbands' care work and were not demanding. Thus, the men who cared for wives continued to exercise control and thus found their independence less constrained by care work than did the women. When combined with the positive feedback husbands received from professionals and their dependent wives for stepping outside their usual roles, male carers found sources of self-esteem and independence, while women carers found constraints without the positive feedback (Davidson et al. 2000). Thus, not only was the experience of giving care gendered, but so too was the experience of care receipt itself.

Research finds that the greater a care receiver's personal control and autonomy, the higher is their well-being (Connidis 2001). This suggests that wives who receive care would experience lower well-being than similarly situated husbands. However, it is unclear if men and women define control in the same ways. Given the differences in control experienced throughout their lives, it is unlikely. Similarly, we need to examine multiple masculinities and femininities; that is, how gender intersects with race, ethnicity, class and sexual orientation in influencing care work and care receipt in the context of intimate relationships.

Conclusions

This chapter has emphasized the importance of examining old men and masculinities through a feminist theoretical lens. To date, however, few studies, including those that decry the neglect of men, have looked at manhood critically. I have provided an exemplar by exploring research on unpaid care work, particularly by spouses.

It is clear that men are *capable* of care work (see, for example, Risman 1987). Given this, the questions involve not whether men can care, but under what circumstances and with what gender identity negotiations. How do different masculinities and femininities shape rewards and stresses associated with care work?

This chapter has focused on spousal care in order to address the debate over men's contribution to care work, and in part because it is the only care relationship in which men and women perform similar amounts and types of care work. But what of other types of care relationships? Gender differences among adult children providing care for parents are suggested not only by the greater prevalence of daughters over sons among care workers, but also by the ways in which they handle the work (Matthews 1995; Yee and Shultz 2000). Of interest is how gender relations influence these variations. For instance, given women's predominance in care work over the life course, including emotion work and care management, it is not surprising to find that daughters tend to be more proactive in their care, and sons more reactive (Connidis 2001). That is, daughters anticipate needs whereas sons often wait and respond to requests from parents, illustrating 'sentient activity' (Mason 1996).

Feminist approaches to care work, or to ageing more generally, do not imply a correct way to do care work, or that men or women are deviant when they do it. The feminist perspectives acknowledge similarities and differences, based in an understanding of social locations. Evaluative comparisons of 'better' and 'worse' are far less important than understanding that the methods used by men, for instance, may not work for women, and why. Some types of emotional detachment, for example, would not fit with some femininities and could instead create more stress for the care worker. Rather than evaluating forms of care, we would study how others make those judgements. Age relations intersect with masculinity, class, race, ethnicity and sexual preference to shape people's perceptions of the quality of care. Researchers can ask whether younger men draw more praise than old men when they do care work, and how intersecting relations of inequality influence that valuation.

In closing, let me make two final points. First, we should not leave it only to men to study masculinity; women's views are also important (Coltrane 1994). Second, the idea of masculinity as socially constructed and historically shifting reminds us of our ability to alter what we do not like. As Kimmel (1994) notes, we do not just have to say 'boys will be boys' – we can change what 'boys' are. From this standpoint, we should understand masculinity and femininity in old age so that we can intervene: to make retirement a time of equality; to fashion policies that will help all unpaid care workers and ensure that women do not bear the brunt of such care work; to make old men and their masculinities just as valued as younger men's. Our theories and research are not merely academic or abstract pursuits, but should play a role in social change.

References

Aranda, M. P. and Knight, B. G. (1997) The influence of ethnicity and culture on the caregiver stress and coping process: a sociocultural review and analysis, *The Gerontologist*, 37(3): 342–54.

Arber, S. and Ginn, J. (1991) *Gender and Later Life*. Newbury Park, CA: Sage.

Arber, S. and Ginn, J. (1995) Gender differences in informal caring, *Health and Social Care in the Community*, 3: 19–31.

Bowers, S. P. (1999) Gender role identity and the caregiving experience of widowed men, *Sex Roles*, 41(9/10): 645–55.

Calasanti, T. M. (2003) Theorizing age relations. In S. Biggs, A. Lowenstein and J. Hendricks (eds) *A Need for Theory*. New York: Baywood Press.

Calasanti, T. M. and Slevin, K. F. (2001) *Gender, Social Inequalities, and Aging*. Walnut Creek, CA: Alta Mira Press.

Calderon, V. and Tennstedt, S. L. (1998) Ethnic differences in the expression of caregiver burden: results of a qualitative study, *Journal of Gerontological Social Work*, 30(1/2): 162–75.

Coltrane, S. (1994) Theorizing masculinities in contemporary social science. In H. Brod and M. Kaufman (eds) *Theorizing Masculinities*. Thousand Oaks, CA: Sage.

Connell, R. W. (1995) *Masculinities*. Berkeley, CA: University of California Press.

Connidis, I. A. (2001) *Family Ties and Aging*. Thousand Oaks, CA: Sage.

Courtenay, W. H. (2000) Behavioural factors associated with disease, injury, and death among men: evidence and implications for prevention, *Journal of Men's Studies*, 9(1): 81–142.

Davidson, K., Arber, S. and Ginn, J. (2000) Gendered meanings of care work within late life marital relationships, *Canadian Journal of Aging*, 19(4): 536–53.

Diamond, T. (1992) *Making Gray Gold: Narratives of Nursing Home Care*. Chicago: University of Chicago Press.

DeVault, M. (1991) *Feeding the Family: The Social Organization of Caring and Gendered Work*. Chicago: University of Chicago Press.

Dwyer J. W. and Seccombe, K. (1991) Elder care as family labour: the influences of gender and family position, *Journal of Family Issues*, 12(2): 229–47.

Faludi, S. (1991) *Backlash: The Undeclared War against American Women*. New York: Crown Publishers.

Gerstel, N. and Gallagher, S. K. (2001) Gender and the contingent character of care, *Gender and Society*, 15(2): 197–217.

Gibson, D. (1996). Broken down by age and gender: 'the problem of old women' redefined, *Gender and Society*, 10(4): 433–48.

Harris, P. B. (1998) Listening to caregiving sons: misunderstood realities, *The Gerontologist*, 38(3): 342–52.

Harris, P. B. and Long, S. O. (1999) Husbands and sons in the United States and Japan: cultural expectations and caregiving experiences, *Journal of Aging Studies*, 13(3): 241–67.

Hearn, J. (1995) Imaging the aging of men. In M. Featherstone and A. Wernick (eds) *Images of Aging: Cultural Representations of Later Life*. London: Routledge.

Hooyman, N. R. (1999) Research on older women: where is feminism?, *The Gerontologist*, 39(1): 115–18.

Hooyman, N. R. and Gonyea, J. G. (1999) A feminist model of family care: practice and policy directions, *Journal of Women and Aging*, 11(2/3): 149–69.

Kaye, L. W. and Applegate, J. S. (1994) Older men and the family caregiving orientation. In E. H. Thompson Jr (ed.) *Older Men's Lives*. Thousand Oaks, CA: Sage.

Kimmel, M. (1996) *Manhood in America*. New York: The Free Press.

Kimmel, M. (1994) Masculinity as homophobia. In H. Brod and M. Kaufman (eds) *Theorizing Masculinities*. Thousand Oaks, CA: Sage.

Kirsi, T., Hervonen, A. and Jylha, M. (2000) A man's gotta do what a man's gotta do: husbands as caregivers to the demented wives. A discourse analytic approach, *Journal of Aging Studies*, 14(2): 153–70.

MacRea, H. (1998) Managing feelings: caregiving as emotion work, *Research on Aging*, 20(1): 137–60.

Martin Matthews, A. and Campbell, L. D. (1995) Gender roles, employment and informal care. In S. Arber and J. Ginn (eds) *Connecting Gender and Ageing: A Sociological Approach*. Buckingham: Open University Press.

Mason, J. (1996) Gender, care and sensibility in family and kin relationships. In J. Holland and L. Adkins (eds) *Sex, Sensibility and the Gendered Body*. London: Macmillan.

Matthews, S. H. (1995) Gender and the division of filial responsibility between lone sisters and their brothers, *Journal of Gerontology: Social Sciences*, 50B(5): S312–20.

Milne, A. and Hatzidimitriadou, E. (2002) Isn't he wonderful? Exploring the contribution and conceptualisation of older husbands as carers. Paper presented at the Reconceptualizing Gender and Ageing Conference, University of Surrey, UK, 25–27 June.

National Alliance for Caregiving and AARP (1997) *Family Caregiving in the US: Findings from a National Survey*. Washington, DC: National Alliance for Caregiving.

Risman, B. J. (1987) Intimate relationships from a microstructural perspective: men who mother, *Gender and Society*, 1(1): 6–32.

Rose, H. and Bruce, E. (1995) Mutual care but differential esteem: caring between older couples. In S. Arber and J. Ginn (eds) *Connecting Gender and Ageing: A Sociological Approach*. Buckingham: Open University Press.

Russell, R. (2001) In sickness and in health: a qualitative study of elderly men who care for wives with dementia, *Journal of Aging Studies*, 15(4): 352–67.

Shirey, L. and Summer, L. (2000) Caregiving: helping the elderly with activity limitations. *Challenges for the Twenty-first Century: Chronic and Disabling Conditions*, no. 7. Washington, DC: National Academy on an Aging Society.

Thompson, E. H. Jr (1994) Older men as invisible in contemporary society. In E. H. Thompson Jr (ed.) *Older Men's Lives*. Thousand Oaks, CA: Sage.

Thompson, E. H. Jr (2000) Gendered caregiving of husbands and sons. In E. W. Markson and L. A. Hollis-Sawyer (eds), *Intersections of Aging: Readings in Social Gerontology*. Los Angeles: Roxbury Publishing Company.

Walker, A. (1992) Conceptual perspectives on gender and family caregiving. In J. W. Dwyer and R. T. Coward (eds) *Gender, Families, and Elder Care*. Newbury Park, CA: Sage.

Yee, J. L. and Schulz, R. (2000) Gender differences in psychiatric morbidity among family caregivers: a review and analysis, *The Gerontologist*, 40(2): 147–64.

3

NEW IDENTITIES IN AGEING: PERSPECTIVES ON AGE, GENDER AND LIFE AFTER WORK

Eileen Fairhurst

This chapter addresses themes of retirement and new 'identities' in middle and old age, focusing on how individuals view becoming and being older. Such concerns link with conceptual categories such as the life course and transitions. There has been a recent revival of interest in transitions into adulthood, with particular emphasis on the relationship between work, family and leisure (for instance, Hollands 1990; Bynner *et al.* 1997; Bradley *et al.* 2002; Dunne and Prendergast 2002). This chapter shares an interest in transitions and those substantive topics but at later stages of life.

The examination of retirement as a life stage transition is a well trodden path (Phillipson 1987; Donovan and Street 2000; Hirsch 2000). While the explication of transitions *per se* is not the major focus here, it should be noted that retirement may not be just one discrete transition from work to non-work but also one that entails movement from full-time to part-time paid work and/or to unpaid work. In this sense, retirement may set up a number of work-related transitions that result in 'multiple retirements' (Fairhurst 2002a). Given the predominant focus on retirement as primarily a male phenomenon in which work is a central life interest, we know little about women's experiences (Bernard and Mead 1993; Bernard *et al.* 1995). Moreover, the depiction of retirement as 'the return of the dominant breadwinner to the home' has neglected the study of couples in retirement (Phillipson 1997: 509). The sparse literature on the experience of both partners suggests that, for women, their husband's retirement may be anticipated either as entailing a loss in their personal space (Hilbourne 1999) or as an encroachment into their domestic space (Mason 1987). For men, early retirement may enable the renegotiation of the division of domestic labour and the development of new notions of masculinity (Cliff 1993). Cliff's study is important, as it is one of the first to outline how structural economic changes may have implications for the traditional linkage between masculine identity and the division of domestic labour.

In general terms, the studies by both Cliff (1993) and Hilbourne (1999) accept the premise noted by Phillipson (1997) of connecting the economic sphere and marital relationships. Their emphases, though, are rather different. Whereas Cliff's study was of male early retirees, Hilbourne's was on the anticipated effects of men's forthcoming retirement on husband and wife relationships. Cliff's concern with traditional gender roles both within and outside the home points to the continuation in early retirement of the gendered domestic division of labour and the 'domestic division of leisure' (Cliff 1993: 46), and notes the kind of adjustments made by couples to avoid men 'getting under the wife's feet'. By contrast, for the participants in Hilbourne's (1999: 172) study the 'impact of the division of labour in the home . . . was a minor detail' and 'apprehension was focused on emotional and interpersonal aspects almost to the exclusion of instrumental ones'. More women than men anticipated retirement having an impact on their marriage. Although the research reported here was not intended to address aspects of marriage in retirement, nevertheless it will be seen to constitute a background 'relevance' (Schutz 1970) in which people situated their prospective and current orientations to retirement.

A different understanding of what might be considered 'conventional' retirement is offered by the emergence of 'new' identities in middle and old age. The development of these ideas stem from recognition of the consequences of higher educational levels of attainment, an increase in access to occupational pension schemes, a rise in the general standards of health and the approaching retirement of the post-Second World War 'baby boomer' generation. Such matters have led to an emphasis on consumer culture characterized by social differentiation and fragmentation. Retirement, within this framework, offers new 'lifestyles', centring on leisure (Hepworth and Featherstone 1982; Featherstone and Hepworth 1993; Hepworth 1995, 2000; Benson 1997; Evandrou 1997). Others, however, have predicted that increasing polarization among the over-fifties may mean that, while some may be able to pursue hedonistic lifestyles, others may lead lonely and financially stricken lives (Scase and Scales 2000; Scase 2001).

Irrespective of controversies about the extent to which these new lifestyles are experienced, an important methodological issue is raised. These new images of, and identities in, retirement are drawn, almost exclusively, from examining representations of middle age found in the media or by extrapolating from statistical data, rather than starting from the perspectives of individuals themselves. This chapter is grounded in how those below, as well as those above, the age of retirement think about their own ageing. In addressing how matters of age, gender and life after work are being redefined in contemporary Britain, it casts a wider net across generations than hitherto; the research included individuals between the ages of 30 and 79 although data relating to the under-forties and over-seventies are not included here. While Anderson *et al.*'s (2000) study was directed at the under-fifties, their concern, unlike here, was confined to financial preparations for and expectations in retirement.

The chapter has four major sections. Following an outline of the study upon which this chapter is based, attention is focused on how mid-life and older people talk about how the intended and actual timing of exit from work is contextualized in terms of life stages. That, together with a focus on activities after work, provides an entrée into the relatively neglected area of marital relations in retirement. Examination of such emotional matters embraces not only 'his' but also 'her' retirement (Szinovacz 1996). Indeed, talk about how time is or will be spent in retirement calls upon ideas about marital relationships and demonstrates how distinctions in language usage are made between the categories of married and 'coupleness/togetherness'. Finally, the changing nature and expectations of retirement are addressed. Individuals' acknowledgement and assessment of social change are situated through contrasts made between their current experiences and those of preceding or ascending generations. This is particularly evident in talk about lifestyles in retirement and intergenerational relationships.

Genesis of the study and research methods

The data upon which this analysis is based come from a focus group study undertaken in Greater Manchester as a contribution to Age Concern England's Millennium Debate of the Age, a national policy debate on the implications of an ageing society. Participants in focus groups were identified by Age Concern chief officers. Discussions from the focus groups were tape-recorded, transcribed and analysed for emergent themes (see Fairhurst 1999, 2002b for further details of how the study was undertaken). Data reported in this chapter are from five focus groups with individuals between the ages of 40 and 69 and relate to just two of the study's wider concerns: age/timing of retirement and activities in retirement.

No claims are being made about the generalizability or representativeness of these research findings. The participants in the study were contacted through the local networks of Age Concern groups, since Age Concern chief officers saw their involvement in this process as part of their active contribution to the research. While this course of action meets current expectations of including 'end-users' in the research process, it also had theoretical ramifications. Since the purpose of focus groups is to gather together individuals to discuss a shared experience and/or ascertain their meanings of it, the use of these local networks resulted in both male and female participants being familiar with, rather than being strangers to, each other (Bloor *et al.* 2001). A consequence of this familiarity was that participants addressed each other with first names and engaged with each other's views in either agreement or advancing another view, and humour was a feature of the focus groups. An important point follows from all of this. The findings of this study tell us *how* 'ordinary' individuals 'theorize' age and ageing (Gubrium and Wallace 1990).

Timing the exit from work

Leaving the world of work is more than a matter of reaching a particular age: people make connections between chronological age and consequences of work for the realization of personal needs or 'the self' and between chronological age and life stages (Fairhurst 2002a). In relation to the latter, it was shown how discussions about turning from full- to part-time employment linked the category of age to other life stage events. The initial analysis of how the timing of the exit from work links with life events/stages will be furthered through a more explicit focus on how cultural knowledge about marital relationships is employed. As Bloor *et al.* (2001: 17) note, 'focus groups provide a valuable resource for documenting the complex and varying processes through which group norms and meanings are shaped, elaborated and applied'.

Sacks's (1992) ideas about the use of membership categorization devices demonstrate how cultural knowledge about marriage is used in talk. Membership categorization devices refer to taken-for-granted, common-sense knowledge for members of society and they enable the selection, from a number of possible descriptions, of an appropriate category to describe an individual. Hence, mentioning the category 'family' carries expectations of including the categories mother, father, son and daughter. Furthermore, these membership categorization devices provide a link with interaction through the idea of category-bound activities, which are activities tied by common sense to certain membership categories. For example, if someone has a broken limb set, it is assumed that this was done by a doctor. The way in which everyday knowledge about marital relations is called upon in matters of timing the exit from work is indicated here.

Extract 1

Male: My wife and I, when we sat down and devised our life plan, it was that we would both try and retire at 55. My retirement came five years early through hearing problems. My wife looks like, because they've changed the rules for teachers, she's going to have to go on till she's 60, so I've lost five years and she's gained five years. So I have, I did retire. I was retired for six months before, I had a six-month break and then came back. I'm doing what Mary [another focus group member] says she wants to do.

I've got a job for three days a week and there's no stress. If the stress builds up, I can wave two fingers at it and walk away because I've got a good pension coming in and thoroughly enjoying it you know . . . I've been involved with the voluntary sector for a long time, although my job wasn't with the voluntary sector. It was the public sector. I take on other things in my spare time with other voluntary organizations. That's I mean, if Martha [his wife] was to retire at 55, I'd say it's unlikely that she would, I would certainly go back to just doing three days a week. But unless we move away from the area completely, you know, I'm quite happy to go on till I'm fed up basically.

Facilitator: You said that you and your wife sat down and made a life plan. How long ago was that? At what age?

Male: I can't remember to be honest. I think I remember when we were in our early forties, we sort of started taking out, thinking about insurance policies and all the rest of it, working out pensions and that, when we would retire. So it was in our early forties when we hit the 'big four-O'. We suddenly realized that things were coming on a-pace . . . At that age, you know, people, I mean we had our children quite young. So they were at that stage then, when we were 40, they were doing A levels and going on to university. And life takes on a different meaning when you're suddenly faced with the fact that soon there will be only two of you as opposed to having a house full of kids and their friends. (Male in his fifties)

In the unfolding of this account of his exit from the world of work, matters of age, life stage and marital relationships are clearly connected. He and his wife, when in their early forties, were 'at the stage' when their children were about to leave home to go to university and this led to the realization 'that life takes on a different meaning'. Moreover, this account points to a subtle distinction between marital relationships and 'coupleness'. In devising a 'life plan' the couple had aimed to retire together at the age of 55 but circumstances had altered their plans; disability for him, and a change in occupational retirement policy for her. Thus, at the intended age of retirement, he had already left, and she would remain in, full-time work. He has a part-time job for three days a week and 'takes on other things with voluntary organizations' in his 'spare time'. That the marital relationship takes primacy over 'spare time' activities is suggested by his declaration that, if his wife was to retire at 55, he 'would certainly go back to just doing three days [work] a week'. The continuation of his 'spare time' activities is contingent upon his wife not being retired and remaining in full-time work. That, together with the use of the plural pronoun 'we' in the account, points to 'coupleness'. The account describes joint activities. Hence, 'when we sat down and devised our life plan it was that we would both try and retire at 55' and 'unless we move away from the area completely, I'm quite happy to go on'. 'When' and 'unless' signal contingent activities. Moreover, 'coupleness' is an activity linked to the category of married.

Unlike other members of this focus group, one woman was thinking about returning to, rather than leaving, the world of work. She described herself as 'nearly 50' and as not having 'gone out to work' since she was 24. She had recently started voluntary work and saw unpaid as opposed to paid work as not involving stress. Voluntary work enabled her to 'learn things without being pressurized' and would give her 'more confidence' if she 'wanted to do something else or get a paid job'.

Extract 2

Female: I've four children and I've done various things, but I've never actually gone out to work. I've always pleased myself and I've got fed up of always pleasing myself actually. You know, because I've had so much time to do things you tend not to stick to any routine. You can sort of amble along. Whereas now I find, if I'm going to do a certain thing, I'm more organized ... I was getting very depressed, which I think is another syndrome because your role has changed, because the children have grown up. I've no grandchildren and I just realized, I thought, well I've spent my life running after everybody and I'm very available, which I've enjoyed. I can't say I've not enjoyed it, but then you realize they go and leave and then there's nothing. There's nothing else really and my husband tends to, we tend to, do our own things in a lot of aspects, I would say. You know we don't do things together, so I thought, what am I going to do?

Just as in extract 1, linkages were made between chronological age and children leaving home as a life stage, but in this extract how 'work' is implicative of marital relationships is quite different. For this woman, 'work' typified women's domestic work: children had remained at home, she had no grandchildren and she had spent her 'life running after everybody'. Her invocation of cultural knowledge about changing roles, and consequences, for middle-aged women's emotional life is evident in her linkage of depression with 'children growing up' (see Fairhurst 1998). Since she and her husband 'tend to do our own things in a lot of aspects', voluntary work promised to replace the 'nothing' left by the eventual departure of children from home. The marital relationship is assessed as not involving 'coupleness'. 'Things' are undertaken as an individual, as indicated by the use of 'I' rather than 'we'. Attending to that life stage, characterized by children leaving home, is an individual matter too, for 'we don't do things together so I thought what am I going to do?' The use of 'together' emphasizes the way 'coupleness' is an activity conventionally bound to the category of married and its absence warrants justification. Since wife and husband 'tend to do their own things', what was to be 'done' upon the children's departure from home became problematic for her.

Activities after exit from work

This section continues to examine 'coupleness' in retirement, with a particular focus on activities. Those thinking about or experiencing retirement derive emotional satisfaction from giving time to their families, grandchildren or voluntary activities or make time to take up new activities (Fairhurst 2002a). The implications of leaving work for being a couple are outlined. The extensive sociological literature on marital relationships tends to focus on the consequences of economic activity for the gendered division of labour inside and outside the household. Often these concerns are pursued in relation to the topics of decision-making and power, undertaking of household tasks and leisure activities (for recent examples of such literature on later stages of life see Cliff 1993; Hilbourne 1999; Kulik 2001). The research reported here was undertaken not to address those particular matters but to cover a number of other features of later life. In order to identify current and prospective orientations to 'life after work', discussion focused on 'spending time' rather than specifically on 'men's and women's' perspectives on who does what in the house. Nevertheless, discussions about life after work were organized in the mundane realities of marriage and 'coupleness'. Here a man and a woman in their sixties are talking about what is involved.

Extract 3

Male: I think you need to know what's going to happen and I think you need some training, just as you would need training for the job you were doing, and I just don't think you can change your job and take up retirement and, particularly, where people are married because it's not just a question of one person's life changing. When they retire it's a couple's life changing and usually it's an enforced retirement or the spouse isn't actually involved in it. I know people said that 'I can't stand him around under my feet all the time.'

Female: No. It's the woman who says it. This is what drove me back to work. It was loss of space.

Male: I think, if I can recollect, somebody actually said, 'I couldn't resist being in the kitchen and organizing things' but by 'things' he meant his wife. I think there's a lot to be worked at when thinking of retirement. I think there needs to be flexibility but I'm not quite sure if it is for some of the reasons that you raise. I think it's dangerous to say you should make it [retirement] flexible so that younger people should be stepping in [to work].

At least two points arise from this extract. First is the explicit acknowledgement by both men and women of the ramifications of retirement for marital relationships and also for men and women as a 'couple'. 'It's not just a question of one person's life changing'; instead, 'it's a couple's life changing'.

References to 'flexibility' and needing 'to work at' retirement suggest that this a matter for both rather than just one party in the marriage. Second, the woman notes that she was 'driven back' to work because of 'loss of space'. These data point to the reversal of the typification of men 'being driven out' of the house because of the gendered categorization of the domestic domain as belonging to women. At the same time, this offers an interesting variation on Hilbourne's (1999) finding that middle-class wives anticipated loss of their domestic space upon their husband's retirement. Here not only has this woman experienced her husband's retirement but also, unlike the majority in Hilbourne's study, she, as well as her husband, had been in employment. Therefore, she had available the alternative space of work to return to upon the loss of 'domestic space'. Another woman's retirement had lasted six months before her return to work. During that time she had:

Extract 4
Female: Tidied every cupboard, asked neighbours for coffee.
Facilitator: And when you came to the end of that?
Female: Went for walks, tidied more cupboards, started hobbies that I'd no intention of continuing with, that I'd waited fifty years for. I got fed up. I needed something to do with the adrenaline flow and, you know, I wanted a bit of anger. (Woman in her sixties)

This, like the previous extract, casts the view of retirement as the return of men to the domestic sphere, with their subsequent 'encroachment' upon their wife's 'personal space', in a different light. Both women who had themselves retired from work subsequently returned to paid work; one had 'lost control of' and the other had got 'too much control over' her domestic space. Neither tidying cupboards or inviting neighbours for coffee, activities of domesticity and sociability respectively, which are conventionally linked with the category of femininity, nor walking or starting new hobbies, lifestyle activities linked to 'new identities' in retirement, satisfied her. Indeed, she 'got fed up' with them. Wanting 'a bit of anger' and needing 'the adrenaline flow' are feelings that she attributed to the category of work. Moreover, such descriptions reflect the emotional response conventionally attributed more to masculinity than to femininity.

Taken together, material presented in this section suggests that marital relations in retirement are much more complex than either Cliff (1993) or Hilbourne (1999) propose. The new identities of masculinity revealed by Cliff are not as clear cut in this study, since both men and women describe their own activities in ways that typically are assigned to 'masculine' or 'feminine' identities. Indeed, 'his' and 'her' retirement has no ontological status. Arguably, constructing marital relations in later life in terms of 'sharing' leisure activities or not, or as 'togetherness versus personal space' (Hilbourne 1999: 175), serves to perpetuate the dualism of subjective–objective, structure–agency and so on found in much social science. Ordinary theorizing, in comparison, involves an emotional assessment of the activity rather than the person who does the activity. It should be noted, too, that in this study, focus groups were composed of both men and women, whereas not all couples in Cliff's study were interviewed jointly and those in Hilbourne's were researched separately.

Lifestyles, later life and redefining ageing

The focus of the chapter now turns to how orientations to lifestyles in later life are redefining ageing; by so doing it picks up themes found in literature on 'new' identities of middle and old age that were noted in the chapter's introduction. Unlike most of that literature, though, this section relies upon the perspectives of individuals. Data, arising from this study, point to the ways in which the category of age, as a determinant of lifestyle or of how to lead one's life, is questioned, while state of health, financial position and 'who you mix with' are assessed as of greater relevance. Just as in the previous section, the evaluation of activities was seen to offer a more complex picture of marital relations in retirement than hitherto; similarly, this is the case in relation to chronological age as a determinant of lifestyle. In particular, Sacks's (1992) use of category-bound activities will be seen to be of relevance. In the following extract, a man and two women in their forties are comparing the kinds of activities older people do now with what they did when these middle-aged people were younger.

Extract 5

Male: I think there's more for that age group to do now than there was 20 to 30 years ago, when my parents retired. There's more for people to do now. They're encouraged to do more now.

Female 1: I don't think age is as much of an issue as it used to be.

Male: If you're well.

Female 2: Yeah. Again it goes down to having your health, and being more agile and articulate and that, but I don't think age is an issue as much as it used to be. I mean when you think of people when we were younger, if they said somebody was 50, I thought they were ancient and that's not just because you were children. It was because of the lifestyle in a lot of ways. You know a woman of 60 was quite an old woman and had a very old lifestyle, didn't they? You didn't see anybody of 60 go out to aerobics when we were kids, or going to the [swimming] baths and that, did you? Which they do now . . .

Female 1: I know people, you know, you see them in the street and you think, 'I went to school with him. Crikey, do I look as old?' It's when they're old fashioned in their ways. Old fashioned and whether they're living in a group of the same, I'm trying to say it's who you mix with, isn't it? I have a niece who's thirtyish, but

> I would say she is 30 going on 60 because her family has always been old fashioned: old fashioned in their ways, old fashioned in their whole lifestyle.

This extract indicates an awareness of the typification of children as 'inflating' the chronological age of adults and also that children's orientations to temporal matters are different to those of adults. That acknowledgement prefaces the explication of lifestyle in terms of physical activities of aerobics and swimming. Whereas now women of 60 do such activity, in Female 2's childhood they did not. Lifestyle, though, is not just restricted to physical activities. Being 'old fashioned' refers not just to physical activities but also to wider social actions, such as 'ways' and those 'you mix with'. That chronological age is not a sufficient matter to be connected to 'old fashioned' is underscored by the description of a niece 'who's thirtyish, but I would say she is 30 going on 60'. Just as Atkinson (1973) showed how knowledge about particular activities/lifestyles is linked to specific ages, this is happening here through men and women binding cultural knowledge about lifestyles to a category, age.

The mundane reasoning about particular types of 'age-related' activity being associated with specific patterns of social 'mixing' is elaborated much more explicitly in the next extract of men and women in their sixties.

Extract 6

Male 1: If you plan on an age basis and if you move to somewhere where it is 'better for older people to be', you finish up in age ghettos, away from younger people. I think it is seeing younger people that you need.

Female 1: I would agree with you. My father-in-law and his wife moved to [retirement coastal town] where the whole of the north seem to have gone, en masse, of the same age group. Now he is on his own and all around him are old people and all he needs is lifting out into a family life.

Male 2: And there is the reverse as well. I moved into a New Town when I was 20 and another one [baby] on the way and everyone else was the same. We all worked. The fellas [men] all worked in the same place. It was one age group, segregated from the wider society.

Male 3: I look at it differently, in a way, than that because I am at the stage now where I have put our house up for sale. It isn't because of my age, but realistically I am going to be ageing and we are looking around. Up to now I have painted all the outside. I have painted the gutters and all that but realistically I am not going to be able to do all that, nor will I be able to afford to pay for someone to do it. So what I'm looking for is something that is easy to maintain, knowing full well that I don't want to be stuck in a ghetto. There is a row of bungalows near us where they are all the same age and they come out and count the blades of grass every morning. I don't want to do that. I want to be in a vibrant society and in much the same role that I have now . . . I have been abroad with them and there is no way I am going to Benidorm with a thousand grey geese . . . Individually I can take them but en masse I can't cope.

Male 1:   You do it [move home] for financial or health [reasons], but just to do it because you are getting old is crazy. I can believe it when you say you can't go to a ghetto because I'm told in [another retirement coastal town] the only traffic you see around is hearses.

Age of itself, as in Extract 5, is of less relevance than financial or health reasons for how later life is led, but in Extract 6 these matters centre on discussions of 'moving house'. For Male 3, implied awareness of declining physical ability to maintain his house, rather than age *per se*, had led to thinking of moving home. Others in the group oriented to age in a similar way and considered the adverse consequences of entry into an 'age ghetto' after moving home because of 'being old'. Clearly, the term 'ghetto' is a category conventionally associated with being 'cut off' or 'separated' and has ramifications for interaction. Not only is it more difficult to interact with younger people but also there are implications for the type of interaction. There is a predictability and routinization of activity: 'they come out and count the blades of grass every morning'. Male 3's declaration that 'there is no way I am going to Benidorm with a thousand grey geese' implies that just as geese, as a group, tend to be in 'formation', so do older people act in predictable ways together. In addition, this typification of routinized interaction is consequent upon a group of older people being together, as opposed to an assessment of an individual person being old. Hence, Male 3's assessment of 'Individually, I can take them but, en masse, I can't cope.' However, the implications of living with a homogeneous age group for social interaction are not specific to 'old age'. Male 2 refers to his own experience when, as a young man, at an earlier stage of his married life, he lived and worked in a New Town with others in a similar situation and was 'segregated from the wider society'.

This section has continued highlighting the ways in which talk about social ageing is situated in assessments of activities. Using Sacks's (1992) category-bound activities has shown how 'lifestyles' are elaborated in terms of activities rather than chronological age. In both Extracts 5 and 6, activities such as swimming or other type of social interaction are bound to the category of 'lifestyle', rather than such activities being contingent upon chronological age. In this way, evaluation of an activity links back to the category, here that of 'lifestyle'. Orientations to 'lifestyles' in middle and old age follow from assessing an activity rather than chronological age *per se*. Identifying an individual as 'old fashioned', then, is less a matter of 'advanced' chronological age and more a consequence of weighing up activity.

Situating change in contrast with 'times past'

The chapter has presented how ordinary individuals theorize prospective or current views on their own ageing by concentrating on the ways mundane knowledge informs their accounts. This path is pursued now by examining contrasts made between their own and other generations, either their children's or their parents', in order to situate orientations to social change. There is an extensive literature on inter-generational relations in terms of care-giving responsibilities and how they are negotiated in practice (for a current example see Brannen *et al.* 2002). Although that topic is not of concern here, this section shares interest in one of its intellectual antecedents, Laslett's historical studies, famously conveyed in his book title *The World We Have Lost* (Laslett 1965). Irrespective of scholarly endeavours to show the 'inaccuracy' of claims about the existence of the three-generation extended family dwelling in which older members of the family were cared for, the typification of older people as 'within the bosom of the family' in the past continues to have powerful resonance. Such a typification was the baseline against which assessments were made by focus group participants about 'being older' now or in the future, as contrasted with 'the past', usually relying on images drawn from their own childhood.

'The past' was evaluated as some kind of 'golden age' in a focus group of men and women in their sixties, from which the next extract comes. At one point, the view was expressed that 'our generation are the last to experience this'. Associated with the 'golden age' typification is the categorization of older people as a source of advice/wisdom. Again we can see how the identification of social change resides in the interactional use of the typifications.

Extract 7

Female 1:   There is a great breakdown in our society, of course, which means that there are not enough people valued when they are old, but I think a lot of people miss out on that, the 'granny syndrome'. A lot of women who have a lot of granny time aren't using it, because they are divorced, split up, move around. You are not close together. Granny has lost its importance to family life and there is a great deal they can do. There was some talk recently on whether you could actually match up 'unwanted grannies' with children who have not got grannies. I think there is a lot of advice and help they can give.

Male 1:   In all my friends' houses and in South Wales, where I was born, every house had a granny or a granddad in the corner in a rocking chair and people didn't necessarily take any notice of them . . . Mind you, having said that, I queried with an aunt of mine about the grandma or granddad who used to sit in the corner. I called him ancient, an ancient man, and he was 71 when he died. So, in fact, people were younger than what we thought, so

	they were not that old. Now they are working and doing all sorts of things.

Male 2: I was a grandfather at 48 and now I'm an old codger. I don't know what they think of me now. I see a lot of them but not continually, because I was only 48 when I was first a grand-parent. My grandmother brought us up and I can remember thinking how ancient she was, but she was only 66. I used to think she was absolutely ancient, but I don't think my kids think I am ancient.

Male 1: I don't know whether it's changed as we go on holidays a lot and things like that. We go out a lot, walking, that sort of thing, which my grandparents didn't do. They were there as a sort of base.

Female 1: And I think they did work a lot harder and they aged a lot quickly, and their health wasn't as good. I think our grand-parents at 60 were equivalent to somebody of 70, 75 [now].

The woman's references to a 'breakdown in society', the resulting decline in 'valuing older people', changing patterns of marriage and residence and the 'loss' of advice and help from 'granny', portray the 'world we have lost'. Although the 'world we have lost' typification provides the yardstick against which social change is being gauged, it is not literally accepted by all. Male 1, on the other hand, acknowledges that, in his childhood, the presence of a grandparent did not necessarily lead to their 'help' or 'advice' being 'valued'. It can be seen how the identification of social change resides in the inter-actional use of typifications. Moreover, Gubrium and Wallace's (1990) point about what counts as 'warrantable evidence' in 'ordinary' theorizing of ageing is illustrated here. Whereas the woman considered the presence of older people within a family as both a necessary and a sufficient condition for them giving 'help' or being 'valued', Male 1 saw this as neither. This extract not only outlines how social change is oriented to, but also how lifestyle changes are constituted in material matters such as holidays, physical activities, employment conditions and improvements in health status.

Conclusion

The purpose of this chapter has been to place alongside changing perspectives on later life, which have emerged from the academy, those that are rooted in 'ordinary' theorizing about ageing. The ways in which talk about the timing of retirement is contextualized in terms of categorizations of a life stage rather than chronological age have been examined. In turn, those categories imply cultural knowledge about marriage and marital relationships. Such matters are apparent in theorizing about current or expected future activities in retirement during which mundane knowledge about 'coupleness' in marriage is invoked. So much is this part of 'background relevancies' informing the social organization of later life that, even though facilitated discussion was not specified in terms of husbands and wives sharing or separately undertaking activities, that was how talk about life in retirement was interactionally achieved. The talk of retirement found in this study adds, too, to our understanding of changing aspects of gender. The implications of women's increasing participation in the world of work for their perspectives on retirement were evident. Data from this study offer a more fluid picture of masculinities and femininities in retirement than those suggested by both Cliff (1993) and Hilbourne (1999).

The nature of the study's data collection may have particular salience. Not only did almost all focus group participants know each other before the research took place, but also the groups consisted of both men and women unrelated to each other. Arguably, this has repercussions for the type of data generated here. Participant interaction could call upon relevant background knowledge about specific individuals to which people were privy by virtue of membership of particular networks that existed, irrespective of a focus group. Consequently, there did not appear to be any difficulties in, or reservations about, responding to facilitated discussion. Getting men and women to talk about their current and expected future perspectives on ageing may not be an insurmountable matter but may be a consequence of the way data are collected.

Data in this chapter supplement the 'new' lifestyles in later life literature by replacing a reliance on representations, or analysis of survey data sets, with analysis grounded in individual's own orientations. Just *how* ordinary theorizing problematizes age as a determinant of a range of activities in retirement has been outlined, showing that health, financial status and with whom one 'mixes' are of greater salience than chronological age. That patterns of interaction and 'ways' or 'kinds' of behaving are keys to the appraisal of lifestyles was evident in the discussion of 'being old fashioned' and enscapulated in the category '30 going on 60'.

A thread running through data extracts was the ways in which participants addressed each other's views in their discussions. One instance of this was the use of the typification of 'the world we have lost' as a yardstick against which assessments of change were made. 'Ordinary' theorizing about ageing, rather than being 'tacit', features disagreement and the 'sifting' and 'comparative evaluation of evidence' (Gubrium and Wallace 1990: 147). It should be noted that new identities of ageing, masculinity and femininity in retirement are not 'out there' waiting for experts to collect but, as has been shown through a close analysis of language in use, are a product of ordinary interaction. Moreover, reconceptualizing ageing and gender is an ongoing matter, demonstrably undertaken by men and women in the mundane organization of their own lives.

References

Anderson, M., Yaojun, L., Bechhofer, F., McCrone, D. and Stewart, R. (2000) Sooner rather than later? Younger and middle-aged adults preparing for retirement, *Ageing and Society*, 20: 445–66.

Atkinson, M. (1973) Formulating lifetimes: the normally ordered properties of some life cycle properties. Unpublished MA(Econ) thesis, University of Manchester.

Benson, J. (1997) *Prime Time: A History of the Middle Aged in the Twentieth Century*. London: Longman.

Bernard, M. and Mead, K. (eds) (1993) *Women Come of Age: Perspectives on the Lives of Older Women*. London: Edward Arnold.

Bernard, M., Itzin, C., Phillipson, C. and Skuda, J. (1995) Gendered work, gendered retirement. In S. Arber and J. Ginn (eds) *Connecting Gender and Ageing*. Buckingham: Open University Press.

Bloor, M., Frankland, J., Thomas, M. and Robson, K. (2001) *Focus Groups in Social Research*. London: Sage.

Bradley, H., Devadason, R., Fenton, S., Guy, W. and West, J. (2002) Home and work: priorities in the lives of young adults. Paper presented to the ESRC Seminar on Work-Family Challenges across the Generations, Aberdeen University, February.

Brannen, J., Moss, P. and Mooney, A. (2002) Care-giving and independence in four generation families. In J. Brannen and P. Moss (eds) *Rethinking Children's Care*. Buckingham: Open University Press.

Bynner, J., Ferri, E. and Shepherd, P. (1997) *Twenty Something in the 1990s. Getting on, Getting by and Getting Nowhere*. Aldershot: Ashgate Press.

Cliff, D. (1993) 'Under the wife's feet': renegotiating gender divisions in early retirement, *Sociological Review*, 41: 30–53.

Donovan, N. and Street, C. (2000) *Transitions after 50: Older People and Paid Work*. York: Joseph Rowntree Foundation.

Dunne, G. and Prendergast, S. (2002) Young LGB people making it through education: can families be relied upon? Paper presented to the ESRC Seminar on Work-Family Challenges across the Generations, Aberdeen University, February.

Evandrou, M. (ed.) (1997) *Baby Boomers: Ageing in the 21st Century*. London: Age Concern.

Fairhurst, E. (1998) Suffering, emotion and pain: towards a sociological analysis. In B. Carter (ed.) *Perspectives on Pain*. London: Arnold.

Fairhurst, E. (1999) *Thinking about Becoming and Being Older: Some Findings from Greater Manchester*. Manchester: Manchester Metropolitan University.

Fairhurst, E. (2002a), 'If you had a whole year of week-ends, it would be a very long day': situating and assessing time in the context of paid and unpaid work. In G. Allan and G. Jones (eds) *Social Relations and the Life Course*. London: Palgrave.

Fairhurst, E. (2002b) Emotions and linked transitions from work to non-work: looking towards and experiencing retirement. Paper presented to the ESRC Seminar on Work-Family Challenges across the Generations, Aberdeen University, February.

Featherstone, M. and Hepworth, M. (1993) Images of ageing. In J. Bond, P. Coleman and S. Peace (eds) *Ageing in Society: An Introduction to Social Gerontology* 2nd edn. London: Sage.

Gubrium, J. and Wallace, J. (1990) Who theorises age?, *Ageing and Society*, 10(12): 131–49.

Hepworth, M. (1995) Change and crisis in mid-life. In B. Davey (ed.) *Birth to Old Age: Health in Transition.* Buckingham: Open University Press.

Hepworth, M. (2000) *Stories of Ageing.* Buckingham: Open University Press.

Hepworth, M. and Featherstone, M. (1982) *Surviving Middle Age.* Oxford: Basil Blackwell.

Hilbourne, M. (1999) Living together full time? Middle-class couples approaching retirement, *Ageing and Society,* 19: 161–83.

Hirsch, D. (ed.) (2000) *Life after 50: Issues for Policy and Research.* York: Joseph Rowntree Foundation.

Hollands, R. (1990) *The Long Transition.* London: Macmillan.

Kulik, L. (2001) Marital relations in late adulthood, throughout the retirement process, *Ageing and Society,* 21: 447–69.

Laslett, P. (1965) *The World We Have Lost.* London: Methuen.

Mason, J. (1987) A bed of roses? Women, marriage and inequality in later life. In P. Allat, A. Bryman and B. Bytheway (eds) *Women and the Life Cycle: Transitions and Turning Points.* London: Macmillan.

Phillipson, C. (1987) The transition to retirement. In G. Cohen (ed.) *Social Change and The Life Course.* London: Tavistock.

Phillipson, C. (1997) Social relationships in later life: a review of the research literature, *International Journal of Geriatric Psychiatry,* 12: 505–12.

Sacks, H. (1992) *Lectures on Conversation.* Oxford: Blackwell.

Scase, R. (2001) *Britain towards 2010: The Changing Business Environment.* Swindon: Economic and Social Research Council.

Scase, R. and Scales, J. (2000) *Fit and Fifty.* Swindon: Economic and Social Research Council.

Schutz, A. (1970) Selective attention: relevances and typification. In *On Phenomenology and Social Relations.* Chicago: Chicago University Press.

Szinovacz, M. (1996) Couples' employment/retirement status and perceptions of marital quality, *Research on Ageing,* 18: 243–68.

4

RECONCEPTUALIZING INTIMACY AND AGEING: LIVING APART TOGETHER

*Klas Borell and
Sofie Ghazanfareeon Karlsson*

The family life cycle perspective defines the existence of a set of develop-mental stages – from marriage to widowhood – and attributes to each of these stages typical 'developmental needs' and 'developmental tasks' (Duvall 1957). For many years, and especially during the 1950s, the family life cycle model dominated the study of family change. However, during the 1970s the limitations of this model became increasingly apparent. New research into family history demonstrated that the family in traditional and early modern societies was far too complex a phenomenon to be studied through the application of an *a priori* developmental model (Hareven 1996). At the same time, it became clear that significant changes were taking place in contem-porary family life. The increasing divorce rate and constant diversification of family forms made it impossible to adopt the analytical approach that had been seen as 'natural' during the 1950s, an era of unusual marital stability (Rice 1994).

Present-day family research has almost entirely abandoned the family life cycle approach in favour of a life course approach. The unit of analysis is primarily the individual, rather than the family, and the focus of interest is on the alternative paths chosen by the individual in moving from one intimate relationship or family constellation to another (Hareven 1996). However, research on the family life of senior citizens seems to have been almost unaffected by the change of approach. Although the family life cycle is rarely referred to directly, the influence of this approach is still clearly evident in much research on older adults. Lifelong marital relationships are often assumed to be the norm, and the focus of the studies has been on 'developmental tasks' following the 'contraction' and 'decay' of the family. Examples of this are studies of 'the empty nest syndrome', i.e. the need for adjustment in marriages after the children leave home and studies of the ways in which widows and widowers cope with adjusting to a life without their lifelong partners (for a research review, see Borell 2001). When, on rare occasions, the important changes that have occurred in family life and intimate relationships are recognized, they usually deal with the *indirect* effects these may have on older people. For instance, a number of studies focus on the consequences that an adult child's divorce can have for the status and roles of the older generation as grandparents, and, more seldom, on the relationships members of the older generation may develop with their adult child's stepchildren (e.g. Cherlin and Furstenberg 1986; Creasey 1993).

For each new cohort of the ageing population the omission of older people from the study of contemporary family differentiation becomes less defensible. To an increasing extent the 'young old' (65 to 74 years of age) in particular are *actors* in the process of the differentiation of family forms and practices. This is especially evident in Sweden, one of the countries in the Western world where the differentiation of family forms has progressed furthest. The change in the proportion of divorcees to widows and widowers in the age group 65 to 69, i.e. the youngest of the 'young old', illustrates this. While the improved health of this age group has meant that the number of widows and widowers has decreased by almost half in the period 1968 to 2000, the number of divorcees has more than quadrupled in the same period. Since 1997 it has become more usual in the age group 65 to 69 to be a divorcee than to be a widow or widower (Swedish Central Bureau of Statistics 1968–2000, authors' analysis).

One of the least researched contributions of senior citizens to the restructuring of contemporary Swedish intimate relationships and family life is the establishment of lasting intimate relationships that do not include a mutual home, i.e. an alternative to different forms of cohabitation, which is sometimes referred to as Living Apart Together (henceforth LAT) relationships.

Beyond the boundaries of a single household

A house or an apartment, whether rented or owned, is often assumed to constitute the setting in which intimate family relations take place. But a common feature of several of the emerging patterns of family and intimate relationships is that they – in different ways and to different degrees – challenge the link between a single household and family life that is often taken for granted. Contemporary family life is characterized not only by an open and flexible concept of the family, but also by a significant spatial flexibility. Family and intimate ties have a tendency to extend beyond the boundaries of a physical household, which leads to the creation of *multi-household families* (Borell 2002, 2003). In 'commuter marriages', usually a temporary arrangement where career development is identified as the primary motive, partners work in different locations during the week and share a residence only at weekends (Winfield 1985). Gay and lesbian families do not share a particular family form, but members of these *families of choice* often belong to two or more households (Weston 1991). Networks of support and exchange between divorced men and women may also be included in these spatially flexible family constellations. Some authors speak about 'recombinant' or 'binuclear' families, where the children regularly move between the households of their divorced parents and maintain a double membership of two households (Ahron and Rodgers 1987; Maccoby and Mnookin 1992).

LAT relationships are probably the least studied of these new intimate multi-household constellations, and the LAT relationships among senior citizens have hardly been studied at all (but see Borell 2001; Borell and Ghazanfareeon Karlsson 2000, 2002). However, it is clear that LAT relationships constitute an increasingly popular alternative to co-residence (with or without marriage) in Sweden. Approximately 4 per cent of all adults in Sweden live in LAT relationships and despite the uncertain nature of the data, the proportion appears to be highest among the 'young old' (Levin and Trost 1999). This chapter examines LAT relationships between older couples and the motives that might lie behind their choice to live in multi-household relationships.

The ontological status of LAT relationships

Remarriage is unusual between couples over the age of 65 in most countries in the Western world, even though it has recently increased to some degree (Burch 1990; Steitz and Welker 1990). The difficulties involved in finding a new partner are only part of the explanation for this. Previous research has shown that older women are doubtful about remarriage, not only because they run the risk of becoming 'locked into' a traditional marriage role, but also, and more specifically, because they do not want to run the risk of eventually becoming a 'nurse' to an often older man (Lopata 1996; Davidson *et al.* 2000; Davidson 2001). This does not necessarily mean that they are therefore uninterested in intimate relationships. Even though the empirical data are limited at present, a number of studies indicate that there is a growing trend among older divorcees, never married and widows and widowers towards finding new forms of dyadic relationships that allow for long-term intimacy without necessarily involving marriage or cohabitation (for a research review, see Borell 2001). Even though this trend can be identified in several countries in the Western world, there are nevertheless cultural differences that should be noted.

One notable feature of American studies of intimate relationships among the older generation is the absence of an established terminology to describe long-term relationships that do not involve cohabitation. When interviewees refer to intimate relationships of this kind they often borrow terms that relate to youth culture, which they then have to qualify or delimit. For instance, they use expressions such as 'going steady' or 'dating' as approximations, since more suitable terms do not exist (e.g. Bulcroft and O'Connor 1986). In Sweden, on the other hand, a term for long-term relations between two adults who are not co-resident has existed for the last twenty years, namely *särbo* (where *sär* stands for 'apart' and *bo* for 'live'). This linguistic differentiation is probably of far greater significance than is first apparent. The acceptance of the concept *särbo* gives an ontological status to a type of relationship that involves separate domiciles, but is not a transitional form leading to cohabitation, within or outside wedlock. By being named, and thereby defined in relation to other family forms or intimate relationships, this type of relationship becomes a distinct alternative that people can consciously make a choice about (Borell 2001).

Nevertheless, it is important to stress that LAT relationships in Sweden are not institutionalized to the same degree as marriage or cohabitation. While married life tends to follow certain articulated and generally accepted patterns, partners in LAT relationships have few conventions or established patterns of relating to one another to fall back on. They have to construct their own set of rules and roles, without the help of more specified cultural patterns that apply to this type of relationship. Our study of LAT relationships among older people aims to focus on these rules and roles, i.e. to examine how older LAT partners organize their lives together, and how they define the commitment they have to one another. Furthermore, it aims to examine the motives behind their choice of this particular form of relationship.

Method

Individuals who form LAT relationships are not registered in any official statistics. They are therefore part of a 'hidden population', the exact size and contours of which are unknown. It was therefore impossible to obtain a statistically representative sample of older couples living in LAT relationships. In view of this, we choose to obtain a sample through advertising. Naturally, one of the disadvantages of this approach is that the researcher lacks control over who responds in terms of their representativenes. In order to compensate for this problem as much as possible we chose to advertise in local newspapers, which are read in Sweden by a large proportion of the older population (Hadenius and Weibull 2000). In total, nine advertisements were placed in the local newspapers of three different regions, which together represent both rural and urban areas of Sweden.

The advertisements sought individuals and couples aged 60 years or older to take part in a study of LAT relationships among older people. As a result of this advertising, 116 individuals involved in heterosexual LAT relationships took part in a self-completion questionnaire, including 18 couples. There was a considerable range of ages in the sample – from 60 to 90 years of age – but the majority (52 per cent) were young old (65 to 74 years of age), and the median age across the sample was 70. Slightly more women than men responded to the survey, with the sample containing 57 per cent women and 43 per cent men. Almost half of the respondents were divorced and approximately 40 per cent were widows or widowers. The vast majority of the respondents had children of their own (91 per cent) and grandchildren (84 per cent). Over half of the participants lived in medium-sized towns, but about 20 per cent lived in rural and 20 per cent in metropolitan areas of Sweden.

The sample is not representative of the older Swedish population in two important respects. First, the sample has a considerably higher level of education. Comparing the age group 65 to 74 in our sample with data about the same age group in the entire population, the percentage with a low education (without senior high school or higher qualifications) is much greater among the general public (76 compared with 44 per cent) and the percentage with higher education (at college or university level) is more than three times greater in our sample: 49 compared with 15 per cent among the general public (Swedish Central Bureau of Statistics 2000a). Second, the sample is characterized by relatively better health. Over 80 per cent of the respondents between 65 and 74 years of age in the sample claim that their health is good to very good, while representative data from an equivalent group of the general public shows that only 65 per cent make this claim (Swedish Central Bureau of Statistics 2000b). Differences of this sort must of course signal caution and be seen in the light of the method of sampling used. It is probable that healthy, active and well educated older individuals are more likely to respond to an advertisement asking for participation in a survey than other older people. However, the extent of the differences and the fact that the advertising was done in a way that should have reduced social bias indicate that there really is a difference between the groups, i.e. older people who choose to live in LAT relationships are those who are healthier and have a higher level of education.

In the following discussion, data from this self-completion survey are presented together with qualitative data from a previous pilot study, which involved in-depth face-to-face interviews with 14 men and women (from 62 to 75 years of age). Most of these interviews were carried out in the respondents' home and they took, on average, 70 minutes to complete. Pseudonyms are used for individuals throughout the paper.

Living apart together in old age

LAT relationships among older people are in certain respects not a uniform experience. The partners may live on the same block of housing or far apart; the distance between the domiciles of the partners in the survey sample varied from virtually nil (the couple lived in the same apartment block) to 450 kilometres (with a median distance of 6 kilometres). The partners in all the relationships studied keep in touch with each other by telephone on a more or less daily basis, but the time actually spent together varies; 36 per cent meet almost every day, 51 per cent a couple of times a week and 12 per cent twice a month or less often. All the respondents see their relationship as long term, but the length of time they say they have been LAT partners varies widely, from 1 to 28 years (with a median length of 6 years). Despite this variation, relatively clear patterns emerge, both regarding the motives for living in LAT relationships and in the rules and roles that have been adopted by the partners.

Autonomy

Many older couples are obliged to live apart against their will, because of changes brought about by illness: one spouse may be institutionalized while the other still lives in the community (Kaplan 2001). In contrast to these involuntarily separated couples, LAT partners choose of their own free will to live in separate households, i.e. to 'live apart together'. However, it would be a mistake to assume that this is a result of LAT relationships being less focused on intimacy or less emotionally close than other relationships between older men and women. Both our survey data and our in-depth interviews indicate that LAT partners see their relationships as deeply intimate in the widest sense of the word, i.e. they represent mutual trust, understanding and the sharing of confidence. A 75-year-old divorced woman, Carin, explains that when she became older she felt a strong need for a close relationship:

> that can provide intimacy. I think that we need one another now when we are old . . . My partner is my support and I think he feels the same way . . . If, for example, I feel sick sometimes, I can call him and tell him about it. It is so good to have someone who will listen to me at times like that.

A 67-year old woman, Sally, gives a similar picture of the situation, saying:

> My partner is fantastic at backing me up! He listens to me when I read poetry and when I sing in the choir . . . He cares about me, quite simply, in a wonderful way. When I was taken ill one evening a couple of years ago I called him up and he came over and stayed with me overnight. My children live so far away, so it is my partner I turn to if I have any problems. It was the same when he was taken ill. It was me he turned to, first of all.

Faithfulness is also a central part of these relationships. A 75-year-old man, Eric, says that he often goes out dancing and there he meets other women. 'Some of the women', he says, 'show a certain interest in me, but no, I never let it go beyond that point. My partner and I meet every day, so it would be disastrous for both of us. Moreover, she has warned me: if I go out with anyone else, that will be it!'

What is it that motivates these older couples to choose to live in a multi-household relationship rather than as married or cohabiting? The results of the survey do not give a consistent picture of these motives. Instead a pattern appears that indicates a considerable difference between the answers of men and women. In general the women tend to give more unambiguous and unanimous answers about their motives for choosing this particular kind of relationship. This gender difference suggests that it is the women rather than the men who are the driving force behind the choice to live as LAT partners.

The survey respondents were asked about eight potential motives for choosing a LAT relationship, using a scale of 0 (indicating of no importance) to 10 (of great importance). The median value of men and women for each item is shown in Table 4.1, as well as the mean rank resulting from a Mann–Whitney U-test. The men, and similarity the women, deny that their choice of a LAT relationship is motivated by financial considerations or based on unhappy experiences from earlier relationships (Table 4.1, items b and c). On the other hand, significantly more women than men mention the difficulty involved in adapting to a new partner's habits or ways (item h) and the

Table 4.1   The motives of older men and women for choosing a LAT relationship

Item	Median		Mean rank		N =		
	Male	*Female*	*Male*	*Female*	*Male*	*Female*	*p*
(a) Importance of having a home of one's own	7	10	47	65	50	63	< 0.01
(b) Importance of economic factors	0	0	53	61	50	64	n.s.
(c) Importance of negative experience from earlier relationships	0	1	53	60	50	63	n.s.
(d) Importance of being freed from duties that would arise if one was married	4	8	47	64	49	63	< 0.01
(e) Importance of being accessible to children and grandchildren	1.5	5	49	59	48	60	n.s.
(f) Importance of own habits	5	5	53	61	50	64	n.s.
(g) Importance of practical reasons concerning living arrangements	7	8.5	51	63	50	64	< 0.05
(h) Importance of the habits of partner	2.5	5	50	64	50	64	< 0.05

Each item is scaled from 0 (indicating of no importance) to 10 (indicating of great importance). The Mann–Whitney U-test is used to test the null hypothesis that the mean rank of men and women is identical.

practical difficulties of living together (item g), e.g. that one of the partners is a heavy smoker while the other is allergic to smoke. But the gender disparity is above all evident regarding two further motives, namely the importance of having a home of one's own and the importance of being freed from duties that would arise if one was married (items a and d). These two latter motives revolve largely around *autonomy*.

The autonomy theme was even more apparent in the face-to-face interviews that were conducted. In these interviews, women emphasized the fact that LAT relationships mean that they can combine intimacy with what they repeatedly refer to as their strong desire to 'be by themselves' or 'live their own lives'. Retaining a home of their own is an essential factor. It is a place in which personal control is ensured and optimized; a boundary-making resource that these women draw on to balance their need for privacy and time alone with their need for intimacy and closeness.

'Having a home of my own', says Patricia, aged 62, 'lets me feel I am deciding for myself and that I don't have to consider other people. It wouldn't work if we lived together. Then I couldn't say: "It's time for you to go".' Throughout the interviews, women described their own home and their self-imposed single status as a privilege, and marriage or other forms of cohabitation as a loss of this privilege. Anne, 70, thinks that it 'feels good to be able to take it easy a few days a week and to be yourself, after having been married for so long and having been responsible for the home. Then, somehow, you were tied and couldn't do as you wanted.' Glory, 75, although she meets her partner almost daily, says that she 'needs to be alone, at least during the morning. Then I do the washing or baking. These things are more easily done when I am alone. I take it easy. I can organize the morning as I wish: that's what's so wonderful.' Helen, 66, states that her friends sometimes try to encourage her to move in with her partner for financial reasons, but she says, 'I would rather be less well-off and live alone. Then I can get up when I want and eat when I want. I explain this to my friends and after listening to me for a while they say, "How wise of you, I would also like to live like that".'

Household labour and collective resources

The women involved in the LAT relationships that we studied value their own home as a means of protection against the gendered duties implicit in a marriage. Having a home of one's own acts as a demarcation for the distribution of domestic labour. 'His home is his, and my home is mine', says one of the women interviewed. This does not mean that the LAT relationships entered into by old people in all respects nullify a traditional division of labour. Certainly relationships exist in which partners visit each other's homes in turn and, to give just one example, take it in turns to prepare meals. However, as our survey data show, it is more common that the couple meet in the woman's house and that she also prepares the meals on these occasions: 18 per cent of the participants say that they generally meet in the man's home, 35 per cent that they alternate between each other's homes and 45 per cent that they most often meet in the woman's home (which is also where they usually spend the night together). It is also usual that the woman cooks the meals that they eat together, even when they take it in turns to meet in each other's home or meet in the man's home, and that the man often repairs things in the woman's home.

Despite the existence of this traditional division of household labour, LAT relationships provide a vital boundary-setting resource for women. The face-to-face interview with Patricia illustrates this. She describes how she usually prepares the food when she meets her partner, but emphasizes that this does not mean that she is prepared to take on responsibility for her partner's home: 'We each do our own cleaning in our own homes. I can moan at him a little and say that he should clean the windows or do other things, but I would never do them for him.'

A consequence of having separate households is that the couples also have separate finances. A married couple that live together usually have a joint private economy and over the years acquire a number of shared resources (house, car, holiday home, etc.). The LAT partners that we have studied all have their own private household economies and very few have many joint resources. Usually they divide current expenses (often for the meals they eat together) between them (77 per cent), although in some cases the men pay for the ingredients, perhaps as a way of 'compensating' for the woman's work in preparing the meal. Most participants (79 per cent) have no joint savings of any kind. Those who do save together with their LAT partner are all saving towards some specific goal, such as a planned holiday together. There are also very few that say that they have shared possessions: over 85 per cent of the respondents say that they do not have any shared possessions at all. In the cases where a couple does have joint ownership it is never of expensive items, such as a car. A typical example is that one of the LAT partners owns a holiday home where the couple spends time together, but they might own things such as the household utensils there jointly.

An interesting, and counter-intuitive, finding is that joint ownership and saving does not appear to increase in relation to the duration of the LAT relationship. Relationships that have stretched over a period of eight years or more do not seem to be characterized by a greater degree of joint ownership than relationships of less than eight years (and the shorter relationships actually report a significantly *higher* degree of joint saving than the longer ones). These results indicate that LAT relationships do not tend to lead to an increasing amount of common commitments or, expressed in another way, become more 'marriage-like' over time.

Future care

LAT relationships between senior citizens do not lack mutual commitments, but these commitments primarily focus on the giving and receiving of emotional support. However, we ought to bear in mind that the majority of the people we interviewed are both 'young old' and in relatively good health. An interesting question is therefore the way in which LAT partners see how the commitment between them would develop were one of them to become seriously ill.

The participants in the survey were asked to envisage a future scenario where their partner became seriously ill and try to describe how they would handle this situation. Table 4.2 shows the median responses of men and women to eight different ways of coping with the situation, ranging from 0 (completely disagree) to 10 (completely agree), as well as the mean rank compared using a Mann–Whitney U-test. The answers to this question show that only a few would refuse to take care of their partner in any way (item c), and practically no one would end the relationship because of their partner's ill health (item d). Most of them, however, envisage taking on a more or less limited degree of care for their partner. They can consider caring for an ill partner for some months (item a), a few days a week (item e) or a few hours a day (item f), but not full time (item g).

Table 4.2   Attitudes to future care of their LAT partner among older men and women

	Median		Mean rank		N =		
Item	Male	Female	Male	Female	Male	Female	p
(a) Would consider taking care of partner for some months if he/she were seriously ill	8.4	7.7	61	55	49	65	n.s.
(b) Would consider taking care of partner for any length of time	6.6	4.8	65	51	49	64	< 0.05
(c) Would not consider taking care of partner if he/she were seriously ill	1.9	2.6	53	51	47	65	n.s.
(d) Would end the relationship if partner became seriously ill	0.8	1.3	56	58	49	65	n.s.
(e) Would consider taking care of partner a few days a week	6.9	5.9	63	52	49	64	n.s.
(f) Would consider taking care of partner a few hours a day	6.9	5.5	64	51	48	64	< 0.05
(g) Would consider taking care of partner 24 hours a day	3.7	2.6	61	54	48	65	n.s.
(h) Would move to live with my partner if he/she became seriously ill	4.6	3.1	64	53	49	65	n.s.

Each item is scaled from 0 (completely disagree) to 10 (completely agree). The Mann–Whitney U-test is used to test the null hypothesis that the mean rank of men and women is identical.

It is important to emphasize that this result should not be interpreted entirely on the basis of the form of intimate relationship that the individual has chosen. It is also influenced by the fact that the Swedish welfare system still offers its citizens high quality public care and service in their old age. Despite the cut-backs that have taken place within the old age care sector during 1990s, older people in Sweden still have high expectations of good care in their old age (National Board of Health and Welfare 2000). Nevertheless, there are important differences between the views of women and men (see Table 4.2). Significantly more men than women say they are prepared to take care of their partner for a few hours every day (item f), and significantly more men than women say they would consider taking care of their partners full-time if necessary (item b).

There are various ways in which the difference between men's and women's attitudes to taking care of their LAT partner in the future can be interpreted. However, an obvious starting point is the systematic gender differences that exist in the care of older people. In Sweden, as in most countries, care for older people is, to a disproportionate degree, the province of women, especially wives, and, historically, women's unpaid and often inconspicuous care for husbands has been taken for granted as part of the marriage contract (Davidson *et al.* 2000). The women that choose to form a LAT relationship no doubt see the risk of becoming imprisoned in a traditional marital role, and ultimately of taking on new caring commitments in their old age, as a major issue, and have therefore chosen a form of intimate relationship that does not involve either marriage or unmarried cohabitation. Thus, although both men and women in the study were asked to say to what degree they would hypothetically be prepared to care for their LAT partner, we found that the women much more than the men had seriously considered this aspect of the relationship. For the women it relates to an issue that they were fully aware of, and which had undoubtedly been a major factor in their decision to 'live apart together'.

The restructuring of old age care that has taken place in Sweden in the past decade throws further light on the differences between men's and women's attitudes to care of their partner in the future. The number of older people who have access to social services has decreased as the most needy in the ageing population have been prioritized. In certain municipalities it has become increasingly difficult for older *couples* living under the same roof to get assistance (National Board of Health and Welfare 2000). 'I'll do everything I can to help and support my partner when he becomes ill and really old', says Ruth. But at the same time she adds that as long as she appears to have her 'feet under the table, then the welfare services won't do their bit'. In other words Ruth, like many of the other women interviewed, sees a separate home of her own as a protection against potential demands made by society that she, as a partner, should provide the care and attention that would otherwise be the responsibility of the local authority's welfare service.

Discussion

It is not exclusively the older generation that enter into LAT relationships (Levin and Trost 1999), but the fact that this type of relationship occurs among those over 65 (and is possibly most common in Sweden among the 'young old') raises interesting questions about what makes this particular form of intimate relationship attractive to older people.

In order to understand what makes LAT relationships of older people distinctive, a comparison can be made with marriage, which is still the most highly institutionalized form of heterosexual partnership. Although they have differing theoretical approaches and conceptual perspectives, Becker (1960, 1981) and Johnson (1991) have both noted the complex nature of the commitments that married couples have towards one another. Marriage today is usually based upon romantic love and attraction, and also tends to include a sense of moral obligation to each other. But the bond between spouses also includes ties that can be described as structural commitments, i.e. ties that imply that a relationship has to continue because of joint investments that have been made. These structural ties – which can keep a marriage together, even when the relationship has lost its mutual emotional and moral bonds – are multiple. Over the years a couple acquire a number of jointly owned resources (of which their shared home is usually the most expensive investment). If they have children they are bound together through this common relationship to a third party. Marriages with children usually develop over time an increasingly specialized division of labour, which also increases the couple's mutual interdependence. Moreover, through marriage the couple becomes interwoven with each other's network of kin and friends, which also leads to long-term and complex loyalties and commitments. Furthermore, although contemporary family life is characterized by increasing differentiation, the still strong institutional and cultural sanctioning of marriage constitutes another element of the structural bonds. Marriage is a legally sanctioned form of cohabitation and it is also a type of relationship for which there are clearly defined rules and roles.

Marriage can, of course, be structurally bonded to a greater or lesser degree, but nevertheless marriage and LAT relationships start out from different *baselines* or different *levels of organization* (Borell 2001). Just like marriage, LAT relationships are based on mutual love and attraction, and in addition the partners develop various moral commitments to one another. However, LAT relationships have few, if any, of the structural foundations that marriage rests upon. As this study of LAT relationships of older people shows, the partners have virtually no common ownership of resources. Their private economies are quite separate and they have a very limited degree of shared possessions or savings (moreover, there is no indication that joint ownership tends to increase over time, making LAT relationships more 'marriage-like'). Furthermore, older LAT partners do not usually have children in common and neither do they have a shared extended family network that binds them together.

LAT relationships are also characterized by a low degree of institutionaliza-
tion; that is, there are no legal bonds between the partners and there are
few clear cultural conventions or established patterns of behaviour that the
partners can fall back on. In many, if not in all, of these circumstances,
the multi-household organization of the relationship plays a crucial role.
Establishing a multi-household LAT relationship, as opposed to living under
the same roof, places radically different demands on the need for coordination
of time, action and resources.

In consequence of this, the bond between LAT partners is principally about
mutual emotional and moral commitment. The focus of the relationship is
on the intimacy itself and on the giving and receiving of chiefly emotional
support. Thereby, it depends fundamentally on the mutual satisfaction
generic to the relationship, rather than on structural bonds.

LAT relationships can offer older divorcees, never married, widows and
widowers a fulfilling intimate relationship, but they can also ensure the individual a significant degree of autonomy. As this study has clearly shown,
autonomy is of particular importance to the women. They want to have an
intimate relationship, but still have time for their daily choice of activities.
Above all, women are not prepared to accept a gendered division of household labour in return for intimacy. This does not mean that the new LAT
relationships lack mutual commitments, but these commitments are less to do
with traditional gender-based demands of personal service within marriage
than they are with the giving and receiving of emotional support (and
a limited instrumental support when necessary, e.g. if one of the partners
falls ill).

This balance is achieved through each partner retaining a home of
their own. For women in LAT relationships a home of their own is a place in
which personal control is ensured and optimized; a resource that they draw
on to balance their need for privacy with their need for intimacy. Thus,
even if the division of household labour between men and women in LAT
relationships is relatively traditional when they are together, their own home
represents a central boundary-setting resource: 'His home is his, and my
home is mine.'

The instrumental role older women seem to play in the formation of contemporary LAT relationships is not coincidental. The history of contemporary
older women who are active in the everyday 'experimentation' of finding
new forms of intimacy is, to a great extent, the history of a cohort who have
been pioneers in the restructuring of family life over the past 30 to 40 years.
The women in today's LAT relationships experienced, when still quite young,
a unique period of history, the 1950s, when the ideal of the nuclear family
became more generally widespread, i.e. an ideal characterized by a distinct
segregation of public and domestic spheres. Here the household, or rather, in
this context, the *home*, was identified as primarily a female sphere: the mother
and wife was the heart of the home, and caring and household chores were
female tasks. But equally they belong to the cohort of women who gradually

participated in a massive shift from unpaid work to wage labour. The altered position of women in the public sphere did not, however, bring with it an equivalent change in the domestic sphere. Instead, women had to take on a 'second shift' of housework and childcare (Hochschild and Machung 1989). During a period stretching from the 1960s onwards the number of divorces increased dramatically across the Western world, which can be seen as the first indication of women's dissatisfaction with what was, in many respects, an unaltered family model. But women not only initiated divorces to a greater extent than men, they were also instrumental in efforts to create more autonomous and equal relationships, both inside and outside the framework of marriage (Crosbie-Burnett and Giles-Sims 1991).

The everyday 'experimentation' by older Swedish women with LAT relationships can be seen as an extension of this goal, as the gender revolution continuing into old age. But if their previous marital households represented a constitutive force in the reproduction of traditional gendered relations, their own household today constitutes a resource base from which they may avoid an asymmetrical distribution of household labour and unequal demands of caring for a partner. However, it would probably be premature to interpret LAT relationships as the product of an *exclusively* female strategy or interest. It is reasonable at least to speculate about the connection between the inherent qualities of LAT relationships, suggested by this study, and the psychological processes of ageing.

Adherents to the socio-emotional selectivity theory have in recent years drawn attention to the fact that older people often tend to avoid superfluous social interaction; they seem to value the emotional side of social relationships more than younger adults (Carstensen 1992). According to this theory, individuals strategically adjust their social networks to maximize the emotional quality of their social interaction. LAT relationships are well suited to these psychological processes. In LAT relationships the emotional context of the relationship is brought to the fore and, in contrast to marriage, there is no automatic development of increasing commitments and responsibilities in the relationship.

Conclusions

The growing differentiation of family life has gradually transformed the agenda of family research and a pluralistic life course perspective has replaced the previously dominating monolithic family life cycle approach. Research into the family life and intimate relationships of older people has, however, hitherto remained surprisingly unaffected by this change of approach. In a number of studies of family life, senior citizens have been treated as an isolated segment of the population, who are affected, if at all, only *indirectly* by the process of differentiation of family life. But the diversity of family trajectories characterizes not only younger adults. To an increasing extent the 'young old' and, in particular, 'young old' *women* are innovators in the process of family change. LAT relationships are intimate in the deepest sense of the word, but combine at the same time intimacy with autonomy. Living together under the same roof, as opposed to establishing a dual-household LAT relationship, places radically different demands on the coordination of time, action and resources. By initiating multi-household relationships, 'young old' women may avoid the burden of what they consider an unfair demand for personal service and care, but at the same time enjoy intimacy.

This chapter takes a first step towards understanding one aspect of the differentiation of the family life of older people, the development of LAT relationships following divorce and widowhood in later life in Sweden. We hope that our study will inspire further research not only on LAT relationships, but also on other under-investigated aspects of the increasingly important and independent role older people play in the growing differentiation of contemporary family life.

Acknowledgements

An earlier version of this paper was published in *Ageing International* (Ghazanfareeon Karlsson, S. and Borell, K. (2002) Intimacy and autonomy, gender and ageing, *Ageing International*, 27(4): 11–26). Many thanks to Sara Arber, Kate Davidson and Graham Fennell for valuable comments.

References

Ahron, C. R. and Rodgers, R. H. (1987) *Divorced Families. A Multidisciplinary Developmental View.* New York: W. W. Norton & Company.
Becker, G. (1960) Notes on the concept of commitment, *American Journal of Sociology*, 66: 32–40.
Becker, G. (1981) *A Treatise on the Family*. Cambridge, MA: Harvard University Press.
Borell, K. (2001) I stället för äktenskap. Åldrande och nya intimitetsformer, *Gerontologia*, 15: 147–56.
Borell, K. (2002) Familj och hushåll. Familjeforskningen och de nya hushållsöverskridande familjeformerna, *Fokus pa familien*, 30: 265–79.
Borell, K. (2003) Family and household. Family research and multi-household families, *International Review of Sociology*, in the press.
Borell, K. and Ghazanfareeon Karlsson, S. (2000) Äldre kærestefolk – hvert sit hjem, *Gerontologi og Samfund*, 16: 85–7.
Borell, K. and Ghazanfareeon Karlsson, S. (2002) Intimitet och autonomi, kön och åldrande. Hushållsöverskridande relationer mellan äldre, *Aldring og Livsløp*, 19: 22–7.
Burch, T. K. (1990) Remarriage of older Canadians: description and interpretation, *Research on Aging*, 12: 546–59.

Bulcroft, K. A. and O'Connor, M. (1986) The importance of dating relationships on quality of life for older persons, *Family Relations*, 35: 397–401.

Carstensen, L. (1992) Social and emotional patterns in adulthood: support for socioemotional selectivity theory, *Psychology and Aging*, 7: 331–8.

Cherlin, A. J. and Furstenberg, F. (1986) *The New American Grandparent*. New York: Basic Books.

Creasey, G. L. (1993) The association between divorce and late adolescent grandchildren's relations with grandparents, *Journal of Youth and Adolescence*, 22: 513–29.

Crosbie-Burnett, M. and Giles-Sims, J. (1991) Marital power in stepfather families: a test of normative resource theory, *Journal of Family Psychology*, 4: 484–96.

Davidson, K. (2001) Later life widowhood, selfishness and new partnership choices: a gendered perspective, *Ageing and Society*, 21: 297–317.

Davidson, K., Arber, S. and Ginn, J. (2000) Gendered meanings of care work within late life marital relationships, *Canadian Journal on Aging*, 19: 536–53.

Duvall, E. M. (1957) *Family Development*. Philadelphia: Lippincott.

Hadenius, S. and Weibull, L. (2000) *Massmedier: en bok om press, radio och TV*. Stockholm: Bonnier.

Hareven, T. K. (1996) The impact of the historical study of the family and the life course paradigm in sociology, *Comparative Social Research*, Suppl. 2, 185–205.

Hochschild, A. and Machung, A. (1989) *The Second Shift: Working Parents and the Revolutions at Home*. New York: Viking.

Johnson, M. E. (1991) Commitment to personal relationships. In W. H. Jones and D. Perlman (eds) *Advances in Personal Relationships*. London: Jessica Kingsley.

Kaplan, L. (2001) A couplehood typology for spouses of institutionalized persons with Alzheimer's disease: perception of 'we'–'I', *Family Relations*, 50: 87–98.

Levin, I. and Trost, J. (1999) Living Apart Together, *Community, Work and Family*, 2: 279–94.

Lopata, H. Z. (1996) *Current Widowhood. Myths and Realities*. Thousand Oaks, CA: Sage.

Maccoby, E. E. and Mnookin, R. H. (1992) *Dividing the Child. Social and Legal Dilemmas of Custody*. Cambridge, MA: Harvard University Press.

National Board of Health and Welfare (2000) *Äldreuppdraget. Slutrapport*. Stockholm: Socialstyrelsen.

Rice, J. K. (1994) Reconsidering research on divorce, family life cycle, and the meaning of family, *Psychology of Women Quarterly*, 18: 559–84.

Steitz, J. A. and Welker, K. G. (1990) Remarriage in later life: a critique and review of the literature, *Journal of Women and Aging*, 2: 81–90.

Swedish Central Bureau of Statistics (1968–2000) *Befolkningsstatistik*. Stockholm: Statistic Sweden.

Swedish Central Bureau of Statistics (2000a) *Befolkning och utbildning*. Stockholm: Statistic Sweden.

Swedish Central Bureau of Statistics (2000b) *Befolkning och hälsa*. Stockholm: Statistic Sweden.

Weston, K. (1991) *Families We Choose. Lesbians, Gays, Kinship*. New York: Columbia University Press.

Winfield, F. E. (1985) *Commuter Marriage: Living Together, Apart*. New York: Columbia University Press.

5

SEX AND AGEING: A GENDERED ISSUE

Merryn Gott and Sharron Hinchliff

The idea of fundamentally different male and female sexual 'natures' is powerful, despite long-standing evidence that physiologically, male and female sexual 'responses' are very similar (Masters and Johnson 1966). These sexual natures are commonly popularized as biologically fixed and largely oppositional, with male sexuality conceptualized as active and powerful, and female sexuality by contrast as passive and nurturing. As such, 'genital and reproductive distinctions between biological men and biological women have been read not only as a necessary but also as a sufficient explanation for different sexual needs and desires' (Weeks 1986: 45). These have both reflected, and reinforced, wider cultural understandings of masculinity and femininity.

The premise of this chapter is very different. We argue that sexuality, frequently described as 'the most natural thing about us', is not natural at all but is socially constructed in complex ways. Although biology may provide the potential for gender differences in sexual understanding and expression, how and why men and women are sexually active with whom, when, where and how is largely socially determined (Foucault 1979). From this perspective, the key to understanding how gender mediates the influence of ageing upon later life sexuality lies not in biology, but in exploring the sexual attitudes and behaviours of older women and men within a wider socio-cultural and historical context.

That societal norms determine 'normal' and 'appropriate' sexual behaviours becomes apparent when the relationship between sexuality and ageing is explored. Indeed, although sex has assumed a greater importance within society than perhaps ever before, old age remains outside this 'sexualized world' (Hawkes 1996), with the stereotype of an asexual old age pervading not only popular culture, but also policy, practice and research. The belief that sex is either not important or not relevant in later life, for example, appears to underpin both the failure to address sexuality within studies of older people and the failure to include older age cohorts within studies of sexuality and sexual health (see, for example, the latest National Survey of Sexual Attitudes and Lifestyles: Johnson *et al.* 2001).

What little research evidence there is regarding the influence of ageing upon sexuality is primarily derived from quantitative surveys aiming to identify rates and correlates of sexual activity in later life. This work has shown that many older people are 'sexually active' and that sexual behaviours differ by gender. In particular, in the samples studied, sexual activity among older women was found to be largely dependent upon the availability and health of older men, with the cessation of sexual activity for older women typically attributed to a male partner dying, or being unable to have 'sex' (Pfeiffer *et al.* 1972; Bretschneider and McCoy 1988; Diokono *et al.* 1990; Matthias *et al.* 1997). However, these studies provide limited information about how gender mediates wider aspects of sexuality – gender is treated as just another 'add on' variable, rather than a fundamental basis of inequality.

Further limitations of this approach are also apparent. Perhaps most importantly, what is meant by 'sex' and 'sexual activity' is rarely defined and, where it is, penetrative sexual intercourse between a man and a woman is taken as the norm. Not only does this give primacy to a heterosexual, and some would argue (LeMoncheck 1997) male-centred, model of sexuality, but it also leaves little room for the understandings, experiences and attitudes of older people themselves. Terms such as 'sex' and 'sexual activity' are unproblematically accepted with little recognition of the fact that these are socio-culturally defined and, as such, likely to vary by gender and age.

Recent qualitative work has gone some way to address the wider social context within which sexuality and ageing are situated. Ley *et al.* (2002), for example, found that older women's understandings of sexuality were located within a male frame of reference. Men were seen as the instigators of sexual encounters and as fundamental in determining women's self-perception of their own sexual attractiveness. Having a close emotional relationship with a (male) partner was also seen as key to maximizing sexual satisfaction. Jones (2002) used a social constructionist perspective to explore older women's discourses around sexuality, an approach that recognizes the socio-political implications of how people talk about sex, including heteronormativity (the belief that only heterosexual sexual behaviour is 'normal') and ageism.

Our research has also contributed to this body of work by adding the voices of older people themselves to debates around the importance and meaning of 'sex' within the context of ageing (Gott and Hinchliff 2003). We have identified that sex remains important to quality of life until the point where people do not think they will have another sexual partner during their lifetime and can be termed 'sexually retired'. Of relevance to this chapter was our finding that men and women differed with regard to the factors precipitating a position of 'sexual retirement'. For older men, experiencing health problems and/or erectile dysfunction determined the adoption of a position of 'sexual retirement' – they viewed this as their 'luck running out'. For older women, widowhood was the key determinant of sex no longer assuming any importance to them – they 'didn't want anyone else'.

This latter finding highlights the importance of marriage as a context for expressing sexuality, particularly for older women, as indeed would be expected given dominant social attitudes in Britain during the early to mid-twentieth century, which saw heterosexual marriage as 'ordained by God' (Hawkes 1996: 72) and 'affirmed by men of science' (*ibid.*). Moreover, as Giddens (1992: 53) has identified, 'the experience of older women was almost always framed in terms of marriage, even if the person in question did not marry. Marriage was to them the core experience of a woman's life.' Yet we know little about marriage in later life (Askham 1995) and even less about the role of sexuality within this context.

The role of sex in decisions to remarry following widowhood has been explored and a gender difference in attitudes has been identified. Davidson (2000), for example, found that 'not wanting sex' was key to decisions not to remarry among some older widows, but no older widowers. Moreover, for some widows sex was seen as one of the 'marital duties' that, along with domestic chores, they had been freed from through widowhood. This finding indicates that the sexual attitudes of this cohort of older people continue to be influenced by sexual standards current when they were younger. Indeed, this notion of sex as a marital 'duty' received considerable attention at the time when this age cohort was newly married. Concerns about small family size and rising divorce rates led to attention being paid to 'sexual compatibility' between husbands and wives in the popular literature of the mid-twentieth century (Lewis 1984: 134). This promoted the idea that a wife's responsibility was 'not only [to] be the provider of food and home comforts but of sexual pleasure as well. Failure to do this meant at least tacit encouragement for extra-marital infidelity by the man' (Hawkes 1996: 98). Some older women are therefore likely to conceptualize sex in terms of duty rather than pleasure, and the research findings that widowhood can be perceived as bringing liberation from this duty are therefore not unexpected.

Moreover, even where a spouse is still alive, it would be expected that the notion of providing sex as a 'wifely duty' would assume less importance with ageing. This is partly because of known declines in sexual interest and ability (to have penetrative sex) among older men (Schiavi 1999), but also because it has been suggested that women become more confident and assertive as they age (Gutmann 1987) and may challenge and resist socialized gender roles within marriage that were barely questioned when they were younger

(McDaniel 1988). There is some research evidence to support this position (for example, Sinnott 1986), although studies of middle-class couples have found that some female 'duties' within marriage – for example, household tasks – remain clearly defined into later life (Ginn and Arber 1995). It would therefore be interesting to explore whether ageing enables older women to challenge the traditional female role as provider of sexual pleasure. However, at the same time it is important to recognize that the popular notion of sex as 'a service or favour that women render to men, and not vice versa' (Symons 1979: 27), also indicates that sex may represent a source of power for women within marriage. Again, the influence of ageing upon this aspect of gender relations within marriage is under-researched.

There is evidence that gender may play an important role in mediating the influence of ageing upon individual sexual identity, as well as gendered sexual relationships. Person (1980: 619), for example, argues that 'in men, gender appears to "lean" on sexuality . . . the need for sexual performance is so great . . . In women, gender identity and self-worth can be consolidated by other means.' This position is consistent with gendered attitudes towards remarriage and sex following widowhood, as it indicates that remarrying and resuming a sexual relationship following widowhood may be important for older men as a means of asserting their masculine identity.

These ideas point to ageing being more challenging to male sexual identity than female sexual identity, given that it has already been identified that a man's ability to 'perform' sexually is the central determinant of men's later life 'sexual activity'. This is partly due to the known increase in experiences of erectile dysfunction with ageing – it has been estimated, for example, that by the age of 70, 67 per cent of men will experience some degree of erectile dysfunction (Feldman et al. 1994). Sexuality is considered central to current conceptions of masculinity (Tiefer 2000), resulting in erectile dysfunction being seen as a challenge to inherent masculinity (Person 1980), and 'a fate worse than death' (Doyle 1983: 205). In addition, a study exploring sexual satisfaction among hospital patients concluded that experiencing erectile dysfunction represented a trigger to 'feeling old', even among younger men (Daker-White and Donovan 2002).

This finding is theoretically important, as it supports the argument that physical failings in later life can represent a 'potential catalyst for the transition between the Third Age and the Fourth Age . . . that is, from a successfully ageing person to someone who is unsuccessful in dealing with the challenges of age' (McKee and Gott 2002: 85). A transition of this type has been termed a 'body drop' (McKee 1998), a concept that links outward physical failings to a transition in self-identity: 'the individual comes to think of himself or herself no longer as someone who is in an endless "middle-youth" (Featherstone and Hepworth 1991), but as someone who is old' (McKee and Gott 2002: 85). Emerging insights about the cultural dimensions of ageing (Gilleard and Higgs 2000) indicate that the transition in self-identity need not be permanent. The increasing availability of 'age-resisting technologies' may enable people to postpone self-identifying as 'old'. The obvious example relating to sexuality is Viagra, which, it is claimed, 'has rapidly bypassed its role as a treatment for specific pathologies to become a means for older men to "reverse" their ageing and restore a synthetic youthful sexual performance that is widely seen as crucial to their self-esteem' (*ibid.*: 77). However, whether older men perceive such resistance as either possible or necessary remains unclear.

For older women, few equivalent age-resisting technologies are currently available (although interest in treatments for 'female sexual dysfunction' is growing) and it may be that ageing is more likely to compromise female sexual identity through challenging conceptions of feminine sexual attractiveness, rather than any more direct impact upon sexual 'function'. This is certainly a perspective put forward by feminist authors, most famously in Susan Sontag's recognition of the 'double standard of ageing' (Sontag 1978) where ageing is seen to compromise gender identity for women in a way that it does not for men.

The influence of ageing upon female sexual behaviour has received less attention and, where it has, this has typically been in relation to the menopause. Gannon (1999), for example, identifies that 'regardless of time and place, aging and menopause have meant an increased freedom for women (Gannon 1985; Smith-Rosenberg 1985) – if only freedom from pregnancy and child bearing' (Gannon 1999: 124). It is worth noting that such 'freedom' may have particular significance for this cohort of older women, whose experiences mostly preceded the advent of the contraceptive pill in the 1960s and the 'uncoupling of sex from marriage and reproduction' (Hawkes 1996: 105). However, aside from discussions such as these around the menopause, little has been written about the impact of ageing upon female sexuality. In particular, it is unclear whether the increased visibility and attention paid to female sexuality in recent decades has influenced older women's perceptions of their own sexuality, or whether their current beliefs and behaviours were determined when they were younger.

The research study

This chapter focuses on the views of older cohorts about the role of sex in marriage and gender relations. Drawing on qualitative interviews conducted with 14 women and 17 men aged 60 to 92 years living in Sheffield in the North of England, we explore similarities and differences by gender in under-standings and expressions of sexuality. Participants' discussions of their current sexual beliefs and behaviours are situated within the context of their earlier lives and of particular interest is how the changes in sexual mores during their lifetimes have influenced their individual attitudes and experiences. We also examine the ways in which ageing impacts upon male and female sexual identities, as well as gender relations within marriage and following widowhood.

The chapter is part of a larger study described in detail elsewhere (Gott and Hinchliff 2003). To summarize, participants comprised a sample of patients registered at one general practice surgery in Sheffield, situated in an area of 'medium deprivation' as measured by the Townsend Deprivation Index. Only 25 per cent of those originally contacted agreed to participate in the study (this varied by age group, marital status and gender, with participation rates being lower than average among women over 70 years). Semi-structured interviews were conducted at the surgery or the participant's own home by an experienced female researcher, and lasted between one and two hours. Interviews were tape recorded and transcribed verbatim, and analysis was undertaken using the National Centre for Social Research 'framework' approach. This involves a structured process of 'sifting, charting and sorting material' according to key issues (Ritchie and Spencer 1994). Recurring themes were identified to develop a thematic framework, which was systematically applied to all transcripts. Confidentiality was assured at all times and the study had the approval of the local ethics committee.

There was a marked gender difference in marital status among participants (Table 5.1), with men being more likely than women to be currently married. The majority of men were married, two were widowed and one was divorced. Five women were married, five were divorced, two were never married and two were divorced. No participant identified as other than heterosexual.

Understandings of 'sex' and ageing

The meanings participants attached to 'sex' were explored to provide a context for examining how age-related changes in sexual beliefs and behaviours were experienced and understood. These discussions identified that sex was perceived as something 'natural' and 'normal' for 'adults' of all ages, including for older people: 'sexual relationships are part of the totality of human relationships and for adult people or adult adolescent people that's a normal aspect of life and a normal aspect of the pleasurable side of life' (Married woman, aged 63).

Table 5.1   Marital status of participants by age group and gender

	60 to 69		70 to 79		80 and over		All	
	Men	*Women*	*Men*	*Women*	*Men*	*Women*	*Men*	*Women*
Married	5	1	6	3	3	1	14	5
Divorced	1	2	–	–	–	–	1	2
Widowed	–	–	–	5	2	–	2	5
Never married	–	–	–	2	–	–	–	2
All	6	3	6	10	5	1	17	14

Most participants discussed 'sex' in terms of penetrative sexual intercourse between a man and a woman, although there was some recognition that what was meant by the term 'sex' could change with ageing. This was particularly the case for people who were experiencing barriers to engaging in penetrative sex. Altering notions of what 'sex' involved seemed to represent part of the process of adapting to these barriers:

> As you get older you act differently and you adjust to your age, but I consider that a cuddle is sex . . . obviously intercourse doesn't take place as much when you're getting older, you're not able, but the desire to love someone is there, and love, it takes a different form. That's love when we are gardening together and doing things.
>
> (Married man, aged 74)

Issues regarding adaptation to barriers to remaining sexually active within the context of long-term marriage are explored in more detail elsewhere (Hinchliff and Gott, in press).

Sexuality and gender

Gender underpinned participants' discussions of their sexual beliefs and behaviours, with sex seen as 'normal' and 'natural' only within a hetero-sexual context. Within this context, sex was identified as key to facilitating a relationship, and particularly marriage, between a man and a woman. Participants saw this role as having been very important when they were younger and first involved in a relationship, because sex 'brings you together in the first place, opposites – a man and a woman' (Married man, aged 74). Sex was also seen as providing a means of bridging the 'difference' between men and women because 'you find out qualities of your partner through having sex' (Married woman, aged 71).

The notion of men and women as 'different' and 'opposite' was reinforced in discussions of the nature of sexual desire. Such discussions conceptualized male sexuality as active and female sexuality as passive. These beliefs trans-lated into sex being seen as a 'need' for men, but not for women: 'I think it's time we got modernized in this country and recognize the fact that it's man's nature to have sex with a woman to relieve himself' (Widowed man, aged 92). Among these older respondents, the male sexual 'urge' was seen as a natural force over which men could exert little control. 'Basically when you look at animals, a stallion will jump a four foot fence to get to a mare, even if he kills himself doing it, he's going to do it and we [men] are only the same' (Married man, aged 79). However, the male sexual need was seen to lessen with ageing, something that was attributed to an age-related decline in male libido. This had implications for gender and sexual relationships within marriage, as explored below.

Overall, both male and female participants used more passive language to describe female sexuality. Indeed, this was not seen as an 'uncontrollable' biological urge like male sexuality. Instead, women tended to talk about sex as something *done to* them, rather than something they did, and male participants reinforced this notion of a 'passive' female sexuality: 'My missus . . . has always gone along with it, if you know what I mean, not in a promiscuous way' (Married man, aged 65). A key influence upon the sexual attitudes and behaviours of older female participants was seen to be beliefs about female sexuality that were dominant during the first half of the twentieth century. Indeed, many participants talked about how women of their age cohort had been socialized into thinking of sex as something 'dirty' that 'had to be endured' (Widowed woman, aged 78).

I can't say that they [sexual relationships] have been very important to my life because I've been born in the wrong era . . . My mother was just frightened of being pregnant, so I am sure she didn't enjoy her sex life that she had, and my mother-in-law thought it was dirty . . . so you grow up with that, that it's dirty, and it takes some growing out of really.

(Married woman, aged 71)

As in this extract, many participants focused discussions about sexually related issues upon their earlier life experiences. These were relevant to explore because they provided a key determinant of the current sexual attitudes and behaviours of this older cohort. This was particularly true for female participants, notably in relation to discussions of marriage.

Marriage, gender and 'sex roles'

Nearly all of these older men and women saw marriage as providing the only context for appropriate expressions of sexuality for people of all ages. Indeed, within marriage sex was seen as a 'normal part of life'. This was again related to the attitudes participants had grown up with and, in particular, the stigmatization of sex outside marriage for women: 'You see when you went for sex, you were bringing her down . . . and you fully expected to be rejected. It was a girl's duty to be a virgin when she married' (Married man, aged 79).

Gendered understandings of the 'sex roles' of men and women within marriage emerged, and these were related back to beliefs about the different 'need' for sex between men and women. Indeed, a key 'duty' for women within marriage was seen to be managing the male 'urge', particularly in the early years of marriage. For women, this was seen as a task they had to undertake in order to maintain the stability of the marriage. Moreover, some women described sex as something they could 'use' to exert power and control over their husbands:

If you have a good relationship, as far as sex is concerned, then you know how to use it and ... you understand your husband and if you have similar needs, or if you don't even have similar needs, you try as a woman, that is the way I look at it, that is the way I worked it, you try and accommodate your husband's needs and this is survival of a marriage.

(Widowed woman, aged 78)

However, the power that women could potentially exert through their sexuality was acknowledged to be limited because of the risks inherent in not meeting a man's sexual needs. These centred on extra-marital relationships, which both men and women saw as a justifiable response to this situation. 'I can only speak from a man's point of view, I can imagine him looking elsewhere occasionally, either for another liaison or going to see a prostitute' (Married man, aged 77).

Being older and in a long-term marriage was seen to reduce the need for wives to provide sex for their husbands because of an identified age-related decline in male sexual desire. In addition, many female participants reported that sex within long-term marriage became more focused upon their own pleasure, rather than driven by any sense of duty, as described below. However, discussions revealed that marriage itself remained crucial as a context for sex, even for older people. This became particularly apparent during discussions of remarriage following widowhood. Indeed, for most participants, remarrying was considered to be the only appropriate means of resuming a sexual relationship following death of a spouse.

Remarriage, gender and sexuality

A gender difference in attitudes towards remarriage following widowhood emerged. The two widowers within the sample had both been widowed more than once, whereas none of the eight widows had remarried or formed a new sexual relationship following the death of their spouse. Again gendered attitudes towards sex were seen to influence attitudes to remarriage, with the male participants stating that a desire to resume a sexual relationship played a key role in their decisions to remarry. Indeed, the central reason given by a widower of 92 as to why he was not looking to remarry was his loss of libido: 'I only wish I was still [sexually] active, I would be looking for another wife.' However, none of the widowed female participants discussed wanting a sexual relationship, and implicitly marriage, with anyone else. 'I could not envisage myself, the intimacy of married life, one would have to get used to another person and I personally could not' (Widowed woman, aged 78). This respondent also linked the discussion to the potentially liberating effect of widowhood, stating that, following the death of her husband, 'I arrange my life to suit myself.'

This is not to say, however, that all older widows felt 'liberated' from their 'sexual responsibilities'. One widow in particular discussed how she had 'missed' sex when her husband had died eleven years ago:

I don't think I could have gone through life without sex, particularly with [name of husband] anyway, he was the type of person it was easy to have sex with because you loved them so much, and you knew for a fact that they loved you, and it wasn't one of those things like 'shall we have a go then' . . . At first when he died, I wasn't upset about not having sex, but I missed it, I missed the sex part of life you know, but you've got to move on haven't you?

(Widowed woman, aged 76)

She went on to state that she no longer missed sex, something she partly attributed to her current age, as well as the fact that she had never felt attracted to anyone other than her late husband.

Ageing and male sexuality

As previously described, these older participants typically equated 'sex' with sexual intercourse, and within this context the male ability to 'perform' was seen as central. Indeed, not only was this 'performance' crucial to sex taking place, but it was also seen by male participants as a means of expressing both 'maleness' and 'youthfulness'. 'Impotence' therefore became powerfully symbolic and challenged self-identity. However, the specific impact it had on self-identity differed according to men's age. For a 60-year-old male participant in the sample, experiencing erectile dysfunction was seen as a challenge to his inherent masculinity: 'I've lost confidence in it, of being able to perform like a normal man' (Married man, aged 60). This may be because erectile dysfunction was considered 'abnormal' outside of the context of old age: 'There's something wrong with you if you're young and you can't . . . [laughs] I should say you're ready for shooting if you're a young bloke and you can't manage it' (Married man, aged 76).

However, for male participants in their seventies and eighties, erectile dysfunction was seen as normal if they already identified themselves as 'old'. Moreover, within this context, it was also seen as less of a challenge to masculinity, indicating that sexual potency is not as important as a component of masculinity in old age. This may be because sex is not an expected part of old age. 'You think about liking it, and you think what you are missing, but you are getting old' (Married man, aged 81). The idea that not being sexually active equated with old age was reinforced by accounts by male participants indicating that sex in later life was seen as embarrassing and potentially laughable:

Int: Yes, you have seen him [GP about erectile dysfunction]?
P: No, I've contemplated seeing him, but I just don't know how much

importance the doctor would attach to it, you know what I mean? I mean getting to our age, he says it's about time you packed up anyway. [laughs] You know what I mean, I don't want him to think I'm a sex maniac or anything like that. (Married man, aged 65)

There was also evidence that experiencing erectile dysfunction represents a trigger to self-defining as old. This was particularly evident in the account of one male participant experiencing erectile dysfunction, who talked about resisting this transition to old age through the use of Viagra. However, he still expressed concerns about his sexual 'performance' and explicitly linked these to wider worries about ageing: 'What worries me is that it's petering out and I just wonder what happens when it starts. [laughs]. Bring out the slippers!' (Married man, aged 70). For others, the availability of medications to treat erectile dysfunction was seen as beneficial and something they wanted to explore further. However, for one male participant, Viagra was seen as 'artificial', interfering with the 'natural' progression of old age: 'We accept the fact that we are what we are and it's interfering with nature' (Married man, aged 74). This indicates that a complex process is likely to mediate between the availability of 'age-resisting' technologies such as Viagra and their actual use.

Ageing and female sexuality

Female participants did not describe a similar sexually related trigger to self-definitions of old age. Indeed, some female participants who had been sexually active into later life saw this as a time when sex could 'improve'. This was partly attributed to age freeing women from sex performed as a marital 'duty': 'You do it because you really love each other, sometimes I think when you're younger you feel it's your duty to do it' (Widowed woman, aged 76). It was also noted that older age brought changes in the meaning of sex for women, with a shift in focus from reproduction to their own pleasure. This shift began with the menopause, but continued to have a significant impact upon sexual attitudes and behaviours into later life. The liberation from a need to control sexuality tightly to manage reproduction was considered to be of particular significance by this age cohort of older female participants, because of the limited availability of effective contraception when they were younger.

However, there was also evidence that changing societal attitudes towards female sexuality, particularly within the past two decades, had influenced the sexual attitudes and behaviours of the older female participants. For two older women in particular, the increased availability of information about female sexuality, as well as sex aids, had opened up new sexual possibilities to them. 'A few months back I watched a programme . . . for women to get more sexual pleasure, I was watching this thing and I was absolutely fascinated, so

I watched the next two or three' (Married women, aged 71). This female participant went on to say that the information had challenged her attitudes towards sexuality generally, but that she did not feel able to discuss the sexual knowledge she had acquired with her husband. This was something she attributed to their earlier life experiences.

> I think the younger generation must talk a lot more about sex between them and it's a thing we never did really. I mean with him having a mother that thought that sex was dirty and didn't want to get pregnant, it does rub off on you, you're not brave enough to talk about it, which seems a bit silly, but I wouldn't want to embarrass my husband.
>
> (Married women, aged 71)

For another woman, the use of a sex aid had completely changed her attitudes towards her own sexuality. She began by explaining that she and her husband weren't 'made right', as she had never had an orgasm during (penetrative) sex with her husband: 'Oh yes, he said it was the nicest thing there was. It was no good telling me that because I didn't know' (Widowed woman, aged 77). However, following his death she had used a sex aid and found that 'it was probably there' all along:

> I never felt like it in all my married life, never felt like sex, but I've done more in these last two years than in all the time I was married, you see it was probably there. I probably just needed one of those in the shops.
>
> (Widowed woman, aged 77)

The current sexual attitudes and behaviours of these older female participants were therefore seen to be influenced both by the dominant 'sexual standards' of their youth and by recent societal changes in attitudes towards female sexuality. These findings indicate that the sexual beliefs and behaviours of this age cohort must be considered within a broad socio-historical context if they are to be fully understood.

Discussion and conclusions

This chapter has explored gender differences in understandings about sexuality among 31 people aged 60 to 92 years of age living in Sheffield, England. We have identified that, within this cohort of older people, gender underpins beliefs about appropriate 'sex roles' for men and women within marriage, channels how ageing impacts upon sexual identity and influences attitudes towards sexuality and remarriage following widowhood. Moreover, these gendered understandings and expressions of sexuality were shaped by the historical context within which participants grew up and, in particular, reflected the moral and religious standards of the early to mid-twentieth century.

Among older cohorts, sex was seen as 'normal' and 'natural' within the context of heterosexual marriage. As expected, marriage had a significant impact upon participants' attitudes towards sex and this was particularly the case for women, supporting the argument of Giddens (1992) discussed earlier. However, for both male and female participants marriage was seen as continuing to provide the only appropriate context for sexual relationships, even in later life. Within marriage, a complex relationship between ageing, gender and sexuality was identified. There was some evidence that sex was seen as a marital duty for this cohort of older women (a duty rooted in the perceived biological difference between the active male sexuality and the passive female sexuality), but that ageing enabled a degree of liberation from this duty. This was partly because married women felt more able to resist this 'duty' when older, suggesting that sex represents one of those female marital responsibilities that can be challenged in later life (McDaniel 1988).

Ageing did appear to affect differentially men's and women's sexual attitudes and behaviours. There was evidence to support Person's (1980) argument that masculinity is more dependent on 'sexual performance' than femininity. In this study a high proportion of male participants experienced erectile dysfunction. We found that the challenge represented to male self-identity varied by age. For younger men, erectile dysfunction was seen as abnormal and as such challenged masculinity, as Tiefer (2000) has argued. However, for men who defined themselves as old, erectile dysfunction was seen as expected and there was little evidence that it challenged their masculinity. The finding that erectile dysfunction could represent a trigger to self-definition of being in old age supports earlier work (Daker-White and Donovan 2002) and lends weight to the theory of 'body drop' outlined earlier (McKee 1998). There was also evidence of the use of Viagra as an age-resisting technology within this context, as argued by Gilleard and Higgs (2000). However, some male participants saw these new technologies as inherently 'unnatural', indicating that complex factors at an individual level are likely to structure whether and how forms of age resistance are manifest.

For older women, gender identity did not seem to be dependent upon sexual performance, supporting Person (1980). Ideas of ageing as 'liberating' in relation to sexuality for older women did emerge. As Gannon (1985) and Smith-Rosenberg (1985) suggest, being post-menopausal was seen as freeing women from managing their sexuality around their fertility. This was seen to be particularly significant in relation to older women's accounts of the tight control they had had to exert over their sexual behaviours during early adulthood in order to manage family size and, in particular, to avoid the stigma of pregnancy outside of marriage. Being post-menopausal facilitated a relaxation of this control. In addition, their responsibility to 'provide' sex for their husband was increasingly resisted, but where older women were sexually active this was often seen as more centred on their own sexual pleasure than previously. This was facilitated for some female participants by the increased information available about female sexuality within contemporary society.

Gendered attitudes to remarriage following widowhood were identified, and these were highly complex. They partly support Davidson's (2000) findings that for some women, sex was seen as one of the marital duties that, along with domestic chores, they had been liberated from through widowhood. For other widows, sex was something they missed, but they could not contemplate sex with anyone else. However, the two widowers in the sample both saw 'wanting sex' as a key determinant of their decision to remarry (one had been married twice, the other three times). This finding could partly be explained by the importance of maintaining masculinity through sexual 'performance'. It is also a finding that is likely to be very cohort-specific, as marriage now assumes far less importance as a context for sex than previously (Weeks 1985) and therefore highlights the dangers of generalizing research findings relating to sexual beliefs and behaviours between age cohorts.

Although this chapter provides useful insights into an area long neglected within studies of ageing, several limitations must be acknowledged (these are discussed more fully elsewhere: Gott and Hinchliff 2003). Two specific points need reiterating in relation to the content of this chapter. First, the sample exclusively self-defined as heterosexual, although this was not an intention of the study. Indeed, research into non-heterosexual ageing and sexuality is scarce and could provide valuable theoretical insights, as well as enabling the voices of this marginalized group of older people to be heard. Second, only 25 per cent of those initially contacted consented to participate in the study (and this figure was lower for women in the oldest age group). Although this does not challenge the 'logical generalizability' of our findings, it does indicate the potential for participation bias.

To conclude, this chapter has identified that sex and ageing is a gendered issue, in terms of both the sexual attitudes and behaviours of older people and the ways in which ageing impacts upon individual notions of sexuality. Key influences on the attitudes and behaviours of current cohorts of older people include the specific historical circumstances shaping their formative experiences, the individual experience of ageing and wider societal shifts in sexual attitudes and behaviours during their lifecourse. As McLaren (1999: 2) identifies, 'Sexuality has been remade by each generation and to understand such transformations necessarily requires placing its discussion in its social and cultural context.'

Acknowledgements

We would like to thank all staff at the general practice involved in the study and all participants for their time. This research was funded by an educational grant from Pfizer Ltd, Walton Oaks, Surrey, UK.

References

Askham, J. (1995) The married lives of older people. In S. Arber and J. Ginn (eds) *Connecting Gender and Ageing*. Buckingham: Open University Press.

Bretschneider, J. G. and McCoy, N. L. (1988) Sexual interest and behavior in healthy 80- to 102-year-olds, *Archives of Sexual Behaviour*, 17(2): 109–29.

Daker-White, G. and Donovan, J. (2002) Sexual satisfaction, quality of life and the transaction of intimacy in hospital patients accounts of their (hetero)sexual relationships, *Sociology of Health and Illness*, 24(1): 89–113.

Davidson, K. (2000) What we want: older widows and widowers speak for themselves, *Practice*, 12(1): 45–54.

Diokono, A. C., Brown, M. B. and Herzog, A. R. (1990) Sexual function in the elderly, *Archives of Internal Medicine*, 150(1): 197–200.

Doyle, J. A. (1983) *The Male Sexual Experience*. Dubuque, IA: William C. Brown.

Featherstone, M. and Hepworth, M. (1991) The mask of ageing and the post-modern life course. In M. Featherstone, M. Hepworth and B. S. Turner (eds) *The Body: Social Process and Cultural Theory*. London: Sage.

Feldman, H. A., Goldstein, I., Hatzichristou, D. G., Krane, R. J. and McKinlay, J. (1994) Impotence and its medical and psychosocial correlates: results of the Massachusetts Male Aging Study, *Journal of Urology*, 151: 54–61.

Foucault, M. (1979) *The History of Sexuality. Volume I: The Will to Knowledge*. London: Allen Lane.

Gannon, L. R. (1985) *Menstrual Disorders and Menopause: Biological, Psychological, and Cultural Research*. New York: Praeger.

Gannon, L. R. (1999) *Women and Aging: Transcending the Myths*. London and New York: Routledge.

Giddens, A. (1992) *The Transformation of Intimacy: Sexuality, Love and Eroticism in Modern Societies*. Cambridge: Polity Press.

Gilleard, C. and Higgs, P. (2000) *Cultures of Ageing: Self, Citizen and the Body*. Harlow: Prentice Hall.

Ginn, J. and Arber, S. (1995) 'Only connect': gender relations and ageing. In S. Arber and J. Ginn (eds) *Connecting Gender and Ageing: A Sociological Approach*. Buckingham: Open University Press.

Gott, M. and Hinchliff, S. (2003) How important is sex in later life? The views of older people, *Social Science and Medicine*, 56(8): 1617–28.

Gutmann, D. (1987) *Reclaimed Powers: Towards a New Psychology of Men and Women in Later Life*. New York: Basic Books.

Hawkes, G. (1996) *A Sociology of Sex and Sexuality*. Buckingham: Open University Press.

Hinchliff, S. and Gott, M. (in press) Intimacy, commitment and adaptation: Sexual relationships within long-term marriages, *Journal of Social and Personal Relationships*.

Johnson, A. M., Mercer, C. H., Erens, B., Copas, A. J., McManus, S. and Wellings, K. (2001) Sexual behaviour in Britain: partnerships, practices, and HIV risk behaviours, *The Lancet*, 358: 1835–42.

Jones, R. L. (2002) 'That's very rude, I shouldn't be telling you that': older women talking about sex, *Narrative Inquiry*, 12(1): 121–42.

LeMoncheck, L. (1997) *Loose Women, Lecherous Men: A Feminist Philosophy of Sex*. Oxford: Oxford University Press.

Lewis, J. (1984) *Women in England 1870–1950*. Routledge: London.

Ley, H., Morley, M. and Bramwell, R. (2002) The sexuality of a sample of older women:

myths and realities explored. In *Proceedings of the British Gerontology Society Annual Conference*. Birmingham: British Society of Gerontology.

Mcdaniel, S. (1988) *Getting Older and Better: Women and Gender Assumptions in Canada's Aging Society*. Toronto: Butterworths.

Mckee, K. J. (1998) The body drop: a framework for understanding recovery from falls in older people, *Generations Review*, 8: 11–12.

Mckee, K. J. and Gott, M. (2002) Shame and the ageing body. In P. Gilbert and J. Miles (eds) *Body Shame: Conceptualisation, Research and Treatment*. London: Routledge.

McLaren, A. (1999) *Twentieth Century Sexuality: A History*. Oxford: Blackwell.

Masters, W. H. and Johnson, V. E. (1966) *Human Sexual Response*. Boston: Little, Brown and Co.

Matthias, R. E., Lubben, J. E., Atchison, K. A. and Schweitzer, S. O. (1997) Sexual activity and satisfaction among very old adults: results from a community-dwelling medicare population survey, *The Gerontologist*, 37(1): 6–14.

Person, E. S. (1980) Sexuality as the mainstay of identity; psychoanalytic perspectives, *Signs*, 5: 605–30.

Pfeiffer, E., Verdwoerdt, A. and Davis, G. C. (1972) Sexual behaviour in middle life, *American Journal of Psychiatry*, 128(10): 82–7.

Ritchie, J. and Spencer, L. (1994) Qualitative data analysis for applied policy research. In A. Bryman and R. G. Burgess (eds) *Analyzing Qualitative Data*. London: Routledge.

Schiavi, R. C. (1999) *Aging and Male Sexuality*. Cambridge: Cambridge University Press.

Sinnott, J. (1986) *Sex Roles and Aging: Theory and Research from a Systems Perspective*. Basle: Karger.

Smith-Rosenberg, C. (1985) Puberty to menopause: the cycle of femininity in nineteenth-century America. In C. Smith-Rosenberg (ed.) *Disorderly Conduct*. New York: Knopf.

Sontag, S. (1978) The double standard of aging. In V. Carver and P. Liddiard (eds) *An Ageing Population*. London: Hodder and Stoughton.

Symons, D. (1979) *The Evolution of Human Sexuality*. Oxford and New York: Oxford University Press.

Tiefer, L. (2000) The social construction and social effects of sex research: the sexological model of sexuality. In C. Brown Travis and J. W. White (eds) *Sexuality, Society and Feminism*. Washington, DC: American Psychological Association.

Weeks, J. (1985) *Sexuality and Its Discontents: Meanings, Myths and Modern Sexualities*. Routledge: London and New York.

Weeks, J. (1986) *Sexuality*. Routledge: New York.

6

BRINGING OUTSIDERS IN: GAY AND LESBIAN FAMILY TIES OVER THE LIFE COURSE

Ingrid Arnet Connidis

> Ours is not an unusual story. Lesbians and gays come from families and are connected to those original families . . . We are daughters and sons, siblings, aunts and uncles, parents and grandparents. Like everyone else, most of us have continuing, complicated relationships with our families. We participate in negotiating the changing meanings, rituals, values, and connections that define kinship.
>
> (Laird 1996: 90)

Howard Becker's (1963) concept of 'outsiders' continues to apply to those who are gay or lesbian, both in society and in research on family ties across the life course. The aim of this chapter is to bring gay and lesbian adults into view in explorations of inter-generational and sibling relationships across the life course. The concept of ambivalence is central to this discussion because it encourages examinations of socially created contradictions and of negotiation as ongoing features of family relationships. Gender, age, time and place are considered as critical forces in shaping the extent and negotiation of ambivalence.

Terminology and parameters

The terms gay and lesbian are used to delineate the parameters of this discussion. Excluding other non-heterosexual orientations is a limiting but useful simplification that allows for comparisons based on one conceptual distinction: whether intimate ties are with the other or same sex.

How does one define families and family relationships that involve gay and lesbian adults? Thinking of families as constellations of relationships helps to avoid the exclusion and traditionalism that 'the family' evokes (Connidis 2001). The terms gay or lesbian families are inaccurate because not all members of a family are gay or lesbian (Stacey 1998). Usually, reference to gay or lesbian families really means gay or lesbian couples; other members of the family network may be gay, lesbian or straight. Thus, referring to the family ties of gay and lesbian adults is preferable.

The objective to bring in the other (outsider) leads to a focus on ties of gay or lesbian adults with straight members in the family of origin. Taking the perspective of both gay and straight family members enhances observing their *shared* affiliation to some dominant cultural views and the simultaneous exclusion of straight family members from the potential supports offered by gay and lesbian culture (Laird 1993; Allen 1999), making them the outsiders.

The implications of either being or having a gay or lesbian family member for ageing and old age are of particular interest. However, because this is relatively uncharted territory, first establishing a conceptual framework for including gay and lesbian adults in the study of family networks is essential to setting a foundation for future research. The reader is encouraged to consider the repercussions of the ideas discussed in this chapter for older persons and for ageing.

Bringing gay and lesbian adults into family networks

On the rare occasions when gay and lesbian adults are included in explorations of family ties, the usual focus is on same-sex relationships and parenting, including the legal and social right to form unions and have children (Rubenstein 1996; Milbank 1997; Carter 1998; Schwartz and Rutter 1998; Stacey 1998). However, spotlighting gay and lesbian individuals' relationships with one another or with dependent children tends to minimize their relationships with other family members (see Allen and Demo 1995). Marginalizing adult gay and lesbian sibling and inter-generational ties reinforces an exclusionary view of family membership that undermines our understanding of the significance to gay and lesbian adults of these family relationships, and, just as important, the significance of gay and lesbian family members to their siblings, parents and adult children.

Including gay and lesbian individuals in a broader range of family ties helps to offset the exclusiveness of assuming that sexual orientation is a family matter for only a small minority. Whatever the number of gay and lesbian individuals, many are likely to have had the personal experience of having a gay or lesbian family member (Laird 1993; Lehmann 2001). Being gay or lesbian is an experience that extends to the lives of a wide range of family members and requires their active involvement, even if that involvement means a conscious attempt at exclusion.

The current conception of family ties as relationships that *evolve over the life course* is rarely applied to studies of the ties between gay and lesbian individuals and members of their original family. Even examinations of the response by family members, especially parents, to coming out (O'Brien and Goldberg 2000) tend to treat this process as a one-time revelation that, once enacted, demarcates a 'before and after' in family ties. Yet coming out is typically the beginning of an ongoing process of renegotiating relationships with others. We know little of how relationships evolve over time when a child, sibling or parent happens to be gay or lesbian.

The HIV/AIDS epidemic has prompted some research on family support offered to gay men, primarily by mothers (Brown and Sankur 1998; Mullan 1998; Thompson 2000). Although important, this focus exemplifies a tendency to consider the gay or lesbian family member as someone who requires additional or unique attention, rather than as someone making his or her own important contribution to the lives of parents, siblings and other relations (Kimmel 1992).

Ambivalence and sexual orientation

Recently, ambivalence has been discussed as a fruitful concept for improving explorations of the dynamics of family ties, particularly inter-generational relations (Luescher and Pillemer 1998; Connidis and McMullin 2002a, b). The concept of ambivalence helps to avoid the normative trappings of earlier concepts such as solidarity and captures the coexistence of harmony and conflict in family relationships. Psychological ambivalence refers to the simultaneous experience of positive and negative sentiments in particular situations; for example, the contradictory feelings of some parents who love their gay or lesbian child but hold negative views about their child's status as gay or lesbian (Cohler and Beeler 1999).

A sociological conception of ambivalence emphasizes the significance of social structural arrangements for family ties. The apparently personal situation of a parent's response to a gay or lesbian child is linked to social structure because the ambivalence of our relationships is, in part, an outcome of social arrangements. At this level, ambivalence can be viewed as 'structurally created contradictions that are experienced by individuals in their interactions with others' (Connidis and McMullin 2002a: 559).

Ambivalence serves as a sensitizing concept, rooted in core ideas from symbolic interactionist and critical theory (Connidis and McMullin 2002a, b). Individuals are viewed as social actors who attempt to act on their own behalf – that is, with agency – while being constrained or facilitated by their position in the social structure according to gender, sexual orientation, class, age, ethnicity and race (Connidis and McMullin 2002a). Because sexual orientation is a principal basis for organizing family life in our culture, an openly gay or lesbian adult has less agency in attempts to assume parental responsibilities. Yet, as the growing number of gay and lesbian parents attests, social structure is not completely constraining, even among the relatively powerless and excluded.

State legislation in many countries dramatically illustrates how ambivalence in family ties that involve gay and lesbian adults is socially structured. In Canada, the USA and the UK, legislation regarding the rights to partner and parent and the related benefits and responsibilities of these relationships generally excludes people in gay and lesbian relationships. The coexistence of self-ascriptive definitions that affirm gay and lesbian family membership with legal definitions that do not (see Macdonald 2000) creates socially structured ambivalence in family ties that include a gay or lesbian adult. This ambivalence rests in the contradiction between the social practices of acting 'like family' while not having legal status as a spouse or parent; of exercising the responsibilities of family membership without being granted the full rights and benefits of family membership.

Although not directed at all family ties, laws concerning partnering and parenting do have repercussions for relationships with other family members. Oswald (2002: 379) argues that legalization of same-sex partnerships and the right to parent 'promotes resilience by bolstering relationships with economic supports. Also, to the extent that legalization enables network members and outsiders to recognize relationships are legitimate . . . legalization promotes social supports as well.' While a contentious issue (Weeks *et al.* 2001), the failure to accord same-sex partnerships the same legal status as straight marriages does heighten ambivalence in inter-generational and sibling ties because personal claims for recognition are not supported by formal definitions of family. For example, a lesbian may expect her parents and siblings to treat her partner as a daughter- or sister-in-law but the absence of legal confirmation of in-law status makes for an ambivalent relationship.[1]

Similarly, when parenting must coexist with state-imposed limits to the legal rights of gay and lesbian individuals as parents (Rubenstein 1996; Milbank 1997), ambivalence in other relationships is heightened. One might term this ambiguity, but the ambiguity lies in the state's stance on family membership, not in the relationship. Ambivalence results as parents, for example, attempt to reconcile their lesbian or gay child's demands for acceptance of a partner or partner's child as a full-fledged family member in the context of structured social relations that do not.

Ambivalence is a primary catalyst for action as family members try to *negotiate* or 'work out' (Finch 1989) the contradictions and paradoxes of their ties to one another. Changing circumstances, life transitions and new situations and players lead the extent of ambivalence to ebb and flow, making its negotiation an ongoing process over the life course. Our actions as individuals can alter social structure because the ways that family members negotiate their relationships can either reproduce current social arrangements or change them. At the same time, emphasizing the link between ambivalence and socially structured relations fosters a focus on social change as a solution to the personally experienced ambivalence of relationships.

Ambivalence and family ties involving a gay or lesbian adult

Gay and lesbian individuals occupy a marginalized status in relation to the idealized family of heterosexual parents and their straight, biological children and grandchildren. The stigmatized status of being gay or lesbian means facing the possibility of socially sanctioned estrangement, exclusion or rejection. Consequent attempts at securing acceptance, inclusion and support – by both a gay or lesbian person and members of his or her family – are more self-conscious and less taken-for-granted, making the processes of negotiating ambivalence more transparent. We can learn more about negotiating ambivalence in all family ties by studying those that involve a gay or lesbian adult. Placing these relationships in the context of ageing and later life underscores the continuous nature of negotiating relationships, partly in response to key life transitions.

While the legal right to adopt and the impact on young children of having gay or lesbian parents are the focus of much current work related to gay or lesbian parenting, for many older gay and lesbian adults, parenthood is an ongoing reality that began with a heterosexual relationship, usually marriage (Laird 1993). In these cases, it is parents coming out to adolescent or adult children that marks a significant transition in the evolution of the parent–child relationship.

Unlike other minority statuses, such as those based on race, being gay or lesbian is not typically a status shared with either parents or siblings (Laird 1993). Thus, sexual orientation as gay or lesbian creates a unique standing in one's family. Yet, because relationships cannot be negotiated independently, it is not only the gay or lesbian individual who must deal with his or her sexual orientation when coming out to others (Allen 1999). In turn, one family member's sexual orientation as gay or lesbian affects relationships among other family members, such as those between a mother and father, or between a parent and other children in the family (Crosbie-Burnett *et al.*, 1996).

Structured inequality, stigma and ambivalence

The structured inequalities of our society interact with one another and are evident in variations in the ability of gay and lesbian individuals to exercise agency in their relationships. Older gay and lesbian individuals confront the double invisibility of being old and gay/lesbian (Lee 1989; Grossman 1997). The more negative views of homosexuality when they were young often meant concealing their identity as gay or lesbian. Coming out may also be harder for members of ethnic minorities (Manalansan 1996) and the working class (Chapple *et al.* 1998). Those in lower status positions experience greater ambivalence in being gay or lesbian while attempting to pass as straight, creating more strain in their family relationships (Peplau *et al.* 1996). The dramatic impact of class and paid work on domestic inequality among gay and lesbian couples (Carrington 1999) shows how the cross-cutting of two domains of structured social inequality creates parallel power dynamics among *all* couples.

Managing stigma, or a spoiled identity (Goffman 1959, 1963), is a continuous challenge to gay and lesbian individuals in their interactions with others. But the stigma of being gay or lesbian is not confined to them. Family members may experience or fear a courtesy stigma (Goffman 1963) in which their individual and family identities or social standing become suspect because a child, sibling, parent or partner comes out as gay or lesbian. Thus, family members may have a corresponding need to manage stigma (Laird 1993), and this may be especially true of older family members, given the more negative view of gay and lesbian identities among their peers. Where does the concept of ambivalence take us that stigma does not? A key contribution of focusing on ambivalence is that the mutual need of the gay or lesbian individual and his or her family members to manage stigma is treated as a property of their *relationship*, not only of individual efforts to manage identity.

Ambivalence is heightened by the fact that the sexual orientation of a family member is not necessarily known in all social worlds. Gays and lesbians do not come out to everyone and everywhere at once. Often, friends are the first to know (Preston 1992) and, within the family, some know before others and some may never know (Miller 1996). The complexity of negotiating ambivalence is amplified by the restrictions or openness that family members may encourage regarding how private or public a gay or lesbian's sexual orientation should be. Even parents who are apparently accepting of their child's sexual orientation in their personal relationship with them may be reluctant to be public about it with their friends, co-workers and others in their family network, such as in-laws, parents or siblings (Laird 1993; Allen 1999). Thus, coming out and the subsequent negotiation of heightened ambivalence is a *process*, a series of decisions, negotiations and actions involving multiple players.

In sum, viewing the family ties of gay and lesbian adults from the vantage point of negotiating ambivalence provides a theoretical foundation that combines individual action (relationship negotiation), family processes and cross-cutting social structural arrangements. The next section considers the negotiation of ambivalence in the context of socially structured gender and age relations. Intertwined with age relations are multiple dimensions of time. Both time and place are likely to modify the degree of ambivalence and the pressure to resolve it; to influence negotiation strategies and processes; and to affect outcomes such as contact and support exchange.

Gender relations and family ties between straight and gay or lesbian adults

Gender also differentiates the family experiences of gay and lesbian individuals (Erera and Fredriksen 2001). While inter-related, gender and sexual orientation are two analytically distinct dimensions of socially structured relations. To be gay or lesbian does not mean escape from the power of gender and the power of gender can be undercut or enhanced by one's sexual orientation. Although views and practices of gender vary by sexual orientation, class, race and ethnicity – creating multiple masculinities and femininities – there is a pervasive view of masculinity and femininity that informs all men and women and is reproduced in all partnerships (Kimmel 2000). A critical difference between heterosexual and homosexual partnerships is that gay and lesbian couples involve two gendered men or women, rather than one of each. In Kimmel's (2000: 234) words, 'you have masculinity or femininity multiplied by two'. The coexistence of gender and sexual orientation as gay or lesbian represents a fundamental contradiction (see Connell 1995) that is likely to be one basis for ambivalence in relationships between gay or lesbian and straight family members.

This contradiction does not itself produce change, but its negotiation in relationships with others does so. The fact of shared gender between gay or lesbian partners sets the stage for more egalitarian relationships than is typical of straight couples (Connell 1995; Kimmel 2000; Weeks *et al.* 2001). Yet there are marked differences between lesbian and gay adults in their view of how same-sex relationships challenge the structured conventions of heterosexual partnerships (Weeks *et al.* 2001). Lesbians tend to emphasize the potential of their partnerships to make the traditional division of labour by gender irrelevant; gay men focus on challenging conventional masculinity by being more expressive and communicative.

How might the gendered lives of gay or lesbian individuals affect the negotiation of ambivalence in their ties to parents, adult children and siblings? Comparisons of gay and lesbian couples show gendered patterns in intimate relations, with lesbians more likely to form committed relationships while gay men are sexually active with more partners and more often (Kimmel 2000; for review see Connidis 2001). This means that lesbian couples tend to have relationships that more closely approximate the assumptions of traditional straight family life in terms of having longer-term, stable, monogamous ties with each other. Lesbian partners are also more likely than gay couples to be parents (Kimmel 2000). Providing a grandchild, niece or nephew may prove to be a great facilitator to negotiating ambivalence, especially if the child is biologically related (Hequembourg and Farrell 2001).

The patterns of 'doing gender' among lesbians may reduce the ambivalence of their ties with straight parents, grandparents and siblings. Meanwhile, gay men 'do gender' by having more independent and less conventional partnerships than is true of both lesbian and straight couples, potentially weakening ties to straight family members. These possibilities suggest that the gender and sexual orientation of family members combine to create variable relational dynamics.

The greater acceptance of difference, including homosexuality, by women than men and the greater closeness of mothers than fathers to their children (Rossi and Rossi 1990; Lynott and Roberts 1997) suggest the relevance of gender to negotiating family ties. Gendered patterns of parenthood may leave both gay sons and lesbian daughters better able to exercise agency in negotiations with their mother than father, aided for sons by virtue of the power of being men and, for daughters, by shared gender. This makes a renegotiated relationship with greater harmony more likely, a contention supported by the greater likelihood of gay and lesbian young people and adult children to disclose to mothers than fathers and to have a closer relationship with them (D'Augelli et al. 1998; Savin-Williams 1998).

The threat of being gay to dominant conceptions of masculinity may curtail the power of shared gender in interactions between straight fathers and gay sons or gay fathers and straight sons, and make conflict between them more likely. In contrast, lesbian daughters and mothers will have less agency in encounters with their straight fathers and sons by virtue of gender, but their sexual orientation may be less threatening. Somewhat distant ties between lesbian daughters and their straight fathers or lesbian mothers and their straight sons may be the most likely result of attempts at resolving ambivalence.

The greater egalitarianism and shared cohort membership of sibling ties may lessen the ambivalence of a relationship with a gay brother or lesbian sister by minimizing the impact of contrasting views of sexual orientation across time. There may also be greater acceptance by sisters than brothers of a gay or lesbian sibling, based on the greater acceptance of difference among women than men. These are, of course, all possibilities that need to be explored.

Age relations, ageing and the influence of time

Age is a central basis for structuring social relations (McMullin 1995) and is influential in the negotiation of ambivalence in family ties. With ageing, the relative power of each generation within a family shifts. So does the impact of other socially structured relations, such as those based on gender and sexual orientation. Working-age adults tend to have more power than either the old or young. Thus, gay and lesbian parents may have greater control in shaping their children's acceptance of their sexual orientation than adolescent or young adult children will have vis-à-vis their parents. However, members of the oldest generation in a family may have less power in their relationships with adult children and grandchildren (Dowd 1980), making them feel more reluctant either to come out or to be critical of the gay or lesbian sexual orientation of younger family members.

Closely tied to the issue of age relations are multiple dimensions of time. One significant dimension of time for negotiating the ambivalence of family ties involving gay and lesbian persons is the *timing of the relationship*. Like most ties in the family of origin, those with a gay or lesbian person begin at birth or in early childhood. However, coming out to family members alters the understanding of the relationship and marks the point at which family members have a spoken 'shared definition of the situation'.

The timing of coming out determines which players are involved at what age in negotiating ambivalence. Thus, timing is in part influential in negotiating ties between gay and straight family members because of its link to age relations. Consider some possibilities related to inter-generational ties between parents and children: an adolescent child comes out to a middle-aged parent; an adult child comes out to an ageing parent; a middle-aged parent comes out to an adolescent child; and an ageing parent comes out to an adult child.

Coming out in adolescence makes parents primary parties in renegotiating family relationships. Conversely, coming out in middle or later life may still involve parents as part of the social audience but also includes children for those who are parents themselves (Cohler *et al.* 2000). In general, whether disclosing or hearing the news, a parent may feel greater responsibility than a child for effectively negotiating the ambivalence that results. However, age will matter too, so that an adult child may feel considerably more responsible for an ageing parent's welfare than does an adolescent child towards middle-aged parents. Age brings with it changing relations between generations in a family.

Timing is also likely to be significant to siblings. Coming out in adolescence makes it probable that siblings will be at a point in their lives when grappling with sexuality is a central concern, potentially making the sexual orientation of a sibling as gay or lesbian more problematic. At the same time, being in the same age group heightens the probability of sharing similar views about sexual orientation and may also mean serving as allies in negotiations with parents. In turn, middle-aged and older parents may find siblings are important sources of support as they negotiate their relationship with a gay or lesbian child (see Connidis 1994). How siblings negotiate their ties with one another when one is gay or lesbian is likely to affect how they work out caring arrangements for their parents should the latter need support.

A profound implication of living longer is the lengthening of overlapping lives (Hagestad 1987; Connidis 2001). More years for all family members provide opportunities for renegotiating relationships and add to the significance of a second aspect of time, *duration*. How long a tie is *expected* to last and how long it *actually* lasts are both likely to affect the negotiation of this relationship. Extended shared time in inter-generational relationships has the potential for enhancing the negotiation of ambivalence in the long run. Ideally, this may mean that any estrangement or conflict that is the outcome of ambivalent ties with a gay or lesbian child is resolved by the time that older family members require support. For some parents, failure to negotiate ambivalence is likely to mean lost opportunities for support later in life. When coming out as gay is coupled with disclosing HIV or AIDS, anticipated duration is typically shortened. The outcome of a shorter anticipated duration is not obvious, however. It may increase pressure to negotiate ambivalence as quickly as possible, or soften this imperative and minimize the effects of failing to do so. For parents who are hostile to homosexuality, ambivalence is heightened by the coexistence of a social status that is a basis for rejection, being gay, and another that calls for help, being ill. Another component of anticipated duration is assuming that being gay or lesbian is a passing phase, in which case anticipated duration becomes a short-term mechanism for negotiating ambivalence that cannot be sustained in the long run.

Longer actual duration of family ties increases the significance of *change over time*. Regarding *cohort effects*, social change over time has altered the situation of being gay or lesbian and, accordingly, altered the impact of sexual orientation on negotiating family ties. Pivotal events include the Stonewall riots in the United States, movements in support of civil rights for various groups, including women, and the AIDS epidemic (Reid 1995). Coming out stories tend to conform to socially constructed scripts that reflect the views of a particular time or organization (Liang 1998; Cohler and Beeler 1999). Thus, they capture both personal and historical experience and are a helpful avenue for exploring the lives of older gay and lesbian persons.

Changes in gender relations should also be expected to affect gay and lesbian partnerships over time, as they do straight relationships. Current observations about the butch/femme characterization as a stereotype of gay or lesbian couples may reflect change over time. Like straight couples, older gay and lesbian couples may have had a 'man' and a 'woman' because partnerships ('marriages') in their day reproduced more traditional conceptions of masculinity and femininity (Ponse 1978; for review see Jacobson and Grossman 1996).

Change over time also relates to *ageing* itself. We tend to assume that negative views of homosexuality have softened across generations and, therefore, that older generations will be less accepting than younger ones of a gay or lesbian family member. However, the perspective of old age – the accumulated experience of ageing – may lead older parents to be more accepting of their gay or lesbian child over time. This possibility may make grandparents particularly receptive to the coming out of a grandchild, contrary to stereotypical notions of old age. Similarly, the fact that ageing brings with it greater self-confidence and self-acceptance among midlife lesbians may have positive effects on negotiating ambivalence with family members, although many are not openly lesbian with their family of origin (Kimmel and Sang 1995).

At the same time, new situations and transitions over the life course may rekindle ambivalence and require new negotiations for handling it. When older parents retire, are widowed or are ill, their shifting available time and need for support from their children are likely to include gay and lesbian children, even if previously estranged. A midlife lesbian couple's account of their ties with parents over time is an example: 'After each father died, the surviving mother turned to her daughter for emotional and/or practical support' (Raphael and Meyer 2000: 148). Later in life, the greater availability of lesbian and gay adult children *because* they do not have the competing commitments of conventional marriage or parenthood may enhance ties between them and old family members.

Time also incorporates the *social timing of key life events* across the life course (Settersten and Hagestad 1996). Public ceremonies accompany many life transitions, particularly for those who follow conventional paths. Such public events provide venues for exploring how ambivalent relationships with gay or lesbian family members have been negotiated. For example, a sibling's marriage or the arrival of a sister or brother's children extends the issue of accepting a gay or lesbian family member to a larger social audience and may uncover a variety of ambivalent family relations. Is a gay brother or uncle's partner invited to the wedding? If so, do they feel accepted as a couple who can engage in the celebration in the same way as heterosexual couples; for example, dancing together? When such situations arise, do family members agree or is there conflict among them? Are there differences based on gender, generation and age?

The influence of place

Closely linked to time are two dimensions of place: *co-residence* and *proximity*. Co-residence is used to distinguish between those who disclose their gay or lesbian identity when still living at home and those who do not. Many adults who identify as gay or lesbian were aware of their sexual orientation and came out while still living with their family of origin. However, many older gay and lesbian adults did not come out to their parents and/or siblings when still living with them, some because they considered themselves straight at the time (Cohler *et al.* 2000). The views of minority-group gays and lesbians about their home of origin probably apply to many gay and lesbian family members, as Weeks and his colleagues (2001: 79) report:

> For many ... family is a critical defensive element in resistance to a hostile world ... but if you are a minority within a minority, then your feelings are necessarily ambivalent ... Memories of first homes may be deeply ambivalent, with love of parents, siblings and other relatives mingling with suppressed desires and fears of rejection.

Co-residence may increase the ambivalence of ties with a gay or lesbian family member because there is a greater demand to be 'a family', a potentially heightened fear of a courtesy stigma due to closer association and the impossibility of ignoring that family member. At the same time, co-residence heightens the pressure to negotiate ambivalence to the point of establishing at least workable daily relations. Thus, co-residence may affect both the *extent of ambivalence* and the *pressure to manage it*. Making decisions about co-residence may also be a *mechanism* for negotiating ambivalence. Deciding to live with or apart from family members may be tactics for managing ambivalence. Although co-residence may heighten ambivalence in the short-term, the greater pressure to resolve it may result in less ambivalence in the long run.

A related feature of place is *proximity*. A critical facet of proximity is exploring the underlying reasons for living near to or far from family members. The treatment of geographic proximity as an aspect of solidarity implicitly suggests that distance from family is chosen and based largely on the nature of ties to family. Yet other factors often drive our location, an issue we rarely explore. Can one conclude that a gay son lives on the west coast of Canada or the USA or in Manchester or London because his family ties are strained? Not necessarily.

Maintaining distance may be a tactic for managing through avoidance the ambivalence in family relationships that is assumed will result from coming out (hence, moving before disclosing) or that actually occurs after coming out (moving after disclosure) (Weeks *et al.* 2001). However, because gay and lesbian communities often provide their own sense of family (Weston 1991), moving may be opportunity-seeking in the form of finding acceptance and a circle of family-like friends. Such pull factors may be far more significant than any possible push factors related to family ties. In either case, the long-term net effect for many gay or lesbian adults and their family members is to live far apart, threatening the potential support exchanges that greater proximity allows. Once again, this implication may be most strongly felt when old age reduces mobility and makes both giving and receiving care more problematic.

The relationship between proximity and ambivalence may be time sensitive. In the short run, living nearby may force unwanted or challenging interaction and heighten ambivalence. Accommodating a distant child's gay or lesbian identity as shared information within the family is quite different from accommodating a proximate child's openly gay or lesbian identity in the local community. In the long run, the opportunity and pressure to resolve ambivalence created by proximity may mean less ambivalence. Over time, changing circumstances may alter geographic proximity or co-residence and require the renegotiation of family ties between straight and gay or lesbian family members.

Assumptions about old age may make older family members the most likely never to be told about a family member being gay or lesbian. Even co-residing with an old parent who needs care may not mean coming out, as in the case of 'closeted lesbians' who continue to pose as single (unattached) persons while looking after their older mothers (Raphael and Meyer 2000). In the absence of knowing, sexual orientation is not negotiated directly, but unspoken understandings, complete ignorance and denial may be considered ways of managing the ambivalence that would result from disclosure.

Concluding comments

Applying the concept of ambivalence to family relationships involving gay or lesbian adults simultaneously heightens our appreciation of the unique contradictions inherent in these relationships and of the common challenges of all intergenerational and sibling ties. In turn, considering the variable circumstances of gay and lesbian adults underscores the significance of structured social relations, particularly gender and age, and of time and place to negotiating ambivalence. Conceiving of ambivalence as socially constructed contradictions highlights the significance of both individual action and social change.

The conceptual discussion in this chapter lays a foundation for studying the negotiation of ambivalence in ties involving gay or lesbian family members across the life course. Placed in the context of ageing, this framework applies to older persons who are gay or lesbian and to older individuals who are the straight parents, siblings or grandparents of a gay or lesbian family member. The complexity of family, age and gender dynamics demands that older men and women be included in explorations of how their own, or other family members', sexual identity as gay or lesbian is negotiated. Older family members may be uniquely poised to facilitate such negotiations and to suffer negative consequences if such negotiations fail.

The fact that most research on the family ties of gay and lesbian adults has focused on same-sex relationships and same-sex partners or gay/lesbian parenting may be indicative of another form of exclusion: an unspoken view that researchers of gay and lesbian family ties should themselves be gay or lesbian. Much like the isolation of straight family members from the potential support of gay and lesbian culture (Laird 1993; Allen 1999), straight researchers may be excluded from research involving gay and lesbian persons. Thus, a related but rarely discussed element of bringing outsiders in is the involvement of straight researchers in explorations of gay and lesbian adults' family ties. This issue echoes earlier debates about whether men should research gender and, more particularly, women.

Claims in support of exclusion are both methodological – the merits of having interviewers and study participants share similar standpoints – and ideological – the oppressor should not be studying the oppressed. But sharing sexual orientation does not guarantee openness; there may simply be differences in what constitutes the socially desirable thing to say. And, just as gay and lesbian family members are constrained in their attempts to be accepted as equal players in family relations, so too are straight individuals oppressed by a heterosexist society that makes forging their ties with loved gay and lesbian family members problematic. Such oppression is most likely among the old who grew up in a time when silence was the common response to being or having a gay or lesbian member of the family.

Note

1 In June 2003, same-sex marriages were legally sanctioned in Ontario, Canada and the federal government has claimed that it will not appeal this province's decision. Editorials and letters to the Editor in the wake of this ruling and of subsequent same-sex marriages show ongoing ambivalence at the societal level.

References

Allen, K. R. (1999) Reflexivity in qualitative analysis: toward an understanding of resiliency among older parents with adult gay children. In H. I. McCubbin, E. A. Thompson, A. I. Thompson and J. A. Futrell (eds) *The Dynamics of Resilient Families*. Thousand Oaks, CA: Sage.

Allen, K. R. and Demo, D. H. (1995) The families of lesbians and gay men: a new frontier in family research, *Journal of Marriage and the Family*, 57(1): 111–27.

Becker, H. S. (1963) *Outsiders: Studies in the Sociology of Deviance*. New York: Free Press.

Brown, D. R. and Sankur, A. (1998) HIV/AIDS and aging minority populations, *Research on Aging*, 20(6): 865–84.

Carrington, C. (1999) *No Place Like Home: Relationships and Family Life among Lesbians and Gay Men*. Chicago: University of Chicago Press.

Carter, D. D. (1998) Employment benefits for same-sex couples: expanding the entitlement, *Canadian Public Policy*, 24: 107–17.

Chapple, M. J. S., Kippax, S. and Smith, G. (1998) Semi-straight sort of sex: class and gay community attachment explored within a framework of older homosexually active men, *Journal of Homosexuality*, 35(2): 65–83.

Cohler, B. J. and Beeler, J. (1999) The experience of ambivalence within the family: young adults 'coming out' gay or lesbian and their parents. Working paper no. 1, International Network on Intergenerational Ambivalence, University of Konstanz Research Centre on Society and Family, and Cornell University Bronfenbrenner Life Course Centre.

Cohler, B. J., Galatzer-Levy, R. M. and Hostetler, A. (2000) Lesbian and gay lives across the adult years. In B. J. Cohler and R. M. Galatzer-Levy (eds) *The Course of Gay and Lesbian Lives: Social and Psychoanalytic Perspectives*. Chicago: University of Chicago Press.

Connell, R. W. (1995) *Masculinities*. Los Angeles: University of California Press.

Connidis, I. A. (1994) Sibling support in older age, *Journal of Gerontology: Social Sciences*, 49(6): S309–17.

Connidis, I. A. (2001) *Family Ties and Aging*. Thousand Oaks, CA: Sage.

Connidis, I. A. and McMullin, J. A. (2002a) Sociological ambivalence and family ties: a critical perspective, *Journal of Marriage and Family*, 64(3): 558–67.

Connidis, I. A. and McMullin, J. A. (2002b) Ambivalence, family ties, and doing sociology, *Journal of Marriage and Family*, 64(3): 594–601.

Crosbie-Burnett, M., Foster, T. L., Murray, C. I. and Bowen, G. L. (1996) Gays' and lesbians' families-of-origin: a social-cognitive-behavioral model of adjustment, *Family Relations*, 45: 397–403.

D'Augelli, A. R., Hershberger, S. L. and Pilkington, N. W. (1998) Lesbian, gay, and bisexual youth and their families: disclosure of sexual orientation and its consequences, *American Journal of Orthopsychiatry*, 68(3): 361–71.

Dowd, J. J. (1980) *Stratification among the Aged*. Monterey, CA: Brooks/Cole.

Erera, P. I. and Fredriksen, K. (2001) Lesbian stepfamilies: a unique family structure. In J. Lehmann (ed.) *The Gay and Lesbian Marriage and Family Reader: Analyses of Problems and Prospects for the 21st Century*. Lincoln, NE: Gordian Knot Books/University of Nebraska Press.

Finch, J. (1989) *Family Obligations and Social Change*. Cambridge: Polity Press.

Goffman, E. (1959) *The Presentation of Self in Everyday Life*. Garden City, NY: Doubleday.

Goffman, E. (1963) *Stigma: Notes on the Management of Spoiled Identity*. Englewood Cliffs, NJ: Prentice-Hall.

Grossman, A. H. (1997) The virtual and actual identities of older lesbians and gay men. In M. Duberman (ed.) *A Queer World: The Center for Lesbian and Gay Studies Reader*. New York: New York University Press.

Hagestad, G. (1987) Able elderly in the family context, *The Gerontologist*, 27(4): 417–22.

Hequembourg, A. L. and Farrell, M. P. (2001) Lesbian motherhood: negotiating marginal–mainstream identities. In J. Lehmann (ed.) *The Gay and Lesbian Marriage and Family Reader: Analyses of Problems and Prospects for the 21st Century*. Lincoln, NE: Gordian Knot Books/University of Nebraska Press.

Jacobson, S. and Grossman, A. H. (1996) Older lesbians and gay men: old myths, new images, and future directions. In R. C. Savin-Williams and K. M. Cohen (eds) *The Lives of Lesbians, Gays, and Bisexuals*. Toronto: Harcourt Brace.

Kimmel, D. C. (1992) The families of older gay men and lesbians, *Generations*, Summer: 37–8.

Kimmel, D. C. and Sang, B. E. (1995) Lesbians and gay men in midlife. In A. R. D'Augelli and C. J. Patterson (eds) *Lesbian, Gay, and Bisexual Identities over the Lifespan: Psychological Perspectives*. New York: Oxford University Press.

Kimmel, M. S. (2000) *The Gendered Society*. New York: Oxford University Press.

Laird, J. (1993) Lesbian and gay families. In F. Walsh (ed.) *Normal Family Processes*, 2nd edn. New York: Guilford Press.

Laird, J. (1996) Invisible ties: lesbians and their families of origin. In J. Laird and R. J. Green (eds) *Lesbians and Gays in Couples and Families: A Handbook for Therapists*. San Francisco: Jossey-Bass.

Lee, J. A. (1989) Invisible men: Canada's aging homosexuals. Can they be assimilated into Canada's 'liberated' gay communities?, *Canadian Journal on Aging*, 8(1): 79–97.

Lehmann, J. M. (ed.) (2001) *The Gay and Lesbian Marriage and Family Reader: Analyses of Problems and Prospects for the 21st Century*. Lincoln, NE: Gordian Knot Books/University of Nebraska Press.

Liang, A. C. (1998) The creation of coherence in coming out stories. In A. Livin and K. Hall (eds) *Queerly Phrased: Language, Gender, and Sexuality*. New York: Oxford University Press.

Luescher, K. and Pillemer, K. (1998) Intergenerational ambivalence: a new approach to the study of parent-child relations in later life, *Journal of Marriage and the Family*, 60: 413–25.

Lynott, P. P. and Roberts, R. E. L. (1997) The developmental stake hypothesis and changing perceptions of intergenerational relations, *The Gerontologist*, 37(3): 394–405.

Macdonald, R. A. (2000) All in the family, *Transition Magazine*, 30(2): 1–7 (http://www.vifamily.ca/tm/302/1.htm). Accessed 5 February 2000.

McMullin, J. (1995) Theorizing age and gender relations. In S. Arber and J. Ginn (eds) *Connecting Gender and Ageing: A Sociological Approach*. Buckingham: Open University Press.

Manalansan, M. F. IV (1996) Double minorities: Latino, Black, and Asian men who have sex with men. In R. C. Savin-Williams and K. M. Cohen (eds) *The Lives of Lesbians, Gays and Bisexuals*. Fort Worth, TX: Harcourt Brace.

Milbank, J. (1997) Lesbians, child custody, and the long lingering gaze of the law. In S. B. Boyd (ed.) *Challenging the Public/Private Divide: Feminism, Law, and Public Policy*. Toronto: University of Toronto Press.

Miller, J. (1996) Out family values. In M. Lynn (ed.) *Voices: Essays on Canadian Families*. Toronto: Nelson Canada.

Mullan, J. T. (1998) Aging and informal caregiving to people with HIV/AIDS, *Research on Aging*, 20(6): 712–38.

O'Brien, C. A. and Goldberg, A. (2000) Lesbians and gay men inside and outside families. In N. Mandell and A. Duffy (eds) *Canadian Families: Diversity, Conflict, and Change*. Toronto: Harcourt Brace.

Oswald, R. F. (2002) Resilience within the family networks of lesbian and gay men: intentionality and redefinition, *Journal of Marriage and Family*, 64(2): 374–83.

Peplau, L. A., Veneigas, R. C. and Campbell, S. M. (1996) Gay and lesbian relationships. In R. C. Savin-Williams and K. M. Cohen (eds) *The Lives of Lesbians, Gays, and Bisexuals*. Fort Worth TX: Harcourt Brace.

Ponse, B. (1978) *Identities in the Lesbian World: The Social Construction of Self*. Westport, CT: Greenwood.

Preston, J. (1992) *A Member of the Family: Gay Men Write about Their Families*. New York: Plume.

Raphael, S. M. and Meyer, M. K. (2000) Family support patterns for midlife lesbians: recollections of a lesbian couple 1971–1997. In M. R. Adelman (ed.) *Midlife Lesbian Relationships: Friends, Lovers, Children, and Parents*. Binghamton, NY: Harrington Park Press.

Reid, J. D. (1995) Development in late life: older lesbian and gay lives. In A. R. D'Augelli and C. J. Patterson (eds) *Lesbian, Gay, and Bisexual Identities over the Lifespan: Psychological Perspectives*. New York: Oxford University Press.

Rossi, A. S. and Rossi, P. H. (1990) *Of Human Bonding; Parent–Child Relations across the Life Course*. New York: Aldine de Gruyter.

Rubenstein, W. B. (1996) Lesbians, gay men, and the law. In R. C. Savin-Williams and K. M. Cohen (eds) *The Lives of Lesbians, Gays, and Bisexuals*. New York: Harcourt Brace.

Savin-Williams, R. C. (1998) Lesbian, gay, and bisexual youths' relationships with their parents. In C. J. Patterson and A. D'Augelli (eds) *Lesbian, Gay, and Bisexual Identities in Families: Psychological Perspectives*. New York: Oxford University Press.

Schwartz, P. and Rutter, V. (1998) *The Gender of Sexuality*. Thousand Oaks, CA: Pine Forge.

Settersten, R. A. Jr and Hagestad, G. O. (1996) What's the latest? Cultural age deadlines for family transitions, *The Gerontologist*, 36(2): 178–88.

Stacey, J. (1998) Gay and lesbian families: queer like us. In M. A. Mason, A. Skolnick and S. D. Sugarman (eds) *All Our Families: New Policies for a New Century*. New York: Oxford University Press.

Thompson, E. (2000) Mothers' experiences of an adult child's HIV/AIDS diagnosis: maternal responses to and resolution of accountability for AIDS, *Family Relations*, 49(2): 155–64.

Weeks, J., Heaphy, B. and Donovan, C. (2001) *Same Sex Intimacies: Families of Choice and Other Life Experiments*. London: Routledge.

Weston, K. (1991) *Families We Choose: Lesbians, Gays, Kinship*. New York: Columbia University Press.

7

SOCIAL NETWORKS AND SOCIAL WELL-BEING OF OLDER MEN AND WOMEN LIVING ALONE

Jenny de Jong Gierveld

Over the past decades, empirical research has pointed out striking differences in the social networks and social well-being of older adults in relation to their gender and marital status (Bradburn 1969; Gove 1972; Dykstra 1995; de Jong Gierveld 1998). This chapter focuses on social embeddedness, which is defined as the composition and the functioning of an individual's network of social relationships. Whether older adults are able to achieve social embedment and avoid or alleviate loneliness depends to a large extent on the personal and social resources at their disposal and the various restrictions they have to deal with. Health and age are frequently related to loneliness but participation in mediating social structures, such as the family and relationships with friends and non-kin, seems to be even more important. The extent to which these different factors can avoid or alleviate loneliness among Dutch older men and women living alone are analysed in this chapter.

Socio-demographic trends affecting the marital status and living arrangements of older adults

There is a link between gender and marital status and the type of living arrangements of older people. Most married people live in a household as a couple, either with or without their children. Never married or formerly married adults primarily live in one-person households. However, recent socio-demographic and socio-cultural changes have resulted in an increasing diversity of living arrangements, as well as more complex partner histories, than was formerly the case. More specifically, the distribution of older people according to marital and partner status has shifted as a result of the following changes:

1 The characteristics of succeeding cohorts entering old age have changed over the years – a higher percentage of recent cohorts of older adults survive until the age of 80 or above, and more older adults have never been married but have been in long-term consensual unions.
2 There have been striking transitions in marital and partner status after the age of 55: ageing together as a couple in a first marriage is not the only pattern; an increase in divorce rates is now also seen among older people. The proportion of people who make the transition from married to divorced after the age of 55 is low, but steadily rising (Uhlenberg *et al.* 1990; see Chapter 1). After losing a partner in old age through either death or divorce, some older adults start a new partner relationship; men more frequently than women, but the majority of people continue to live in a single-person household (de Jong Gierveld and Peeters 2002).

Because of gender-related differences in life expectancy, the absolute number of older men living alone is lower than the number of women. However, the number of men living alone is expected to increase in the near future because of the diminishing difference in male and female survival rates (van Poppel 2001).

Social embeddedness as related to living alone and partner history

Partner relationships and family relationships are major integrating structures in society. Individuals with a partner are less likely to be lonely than individuals without a (marital) partner (Peters and Liefbroer 1997). Thus, living with or without a partner is a central issue in investigating social well-being and loneliness among older adults. In addition, a network of kin and non-kin personal relationships can provide cohesion, a sense of belonging and protection against loneliness. There is a negative correlation between the degree of social embeddedness and the intensity of loneliness (Wenger *et al.* 1996). Older adults who live alone have a higher risk of loneliness because they are less likely to have a close relationship with someone and tend to have a smaller network than married older people (Dykstra 1995; Havens and Hall 2001).

Loneliness has been defined as the individual's perception of a situation in which he or she experiences an unacceptable, sometimes even distressing, lack of certain relationships and/or a lack of quality of certain relationships; in other words, situations where the number of relationships maintained is less than is considered desirable or acceptable by the individual or situations where the kind of intimacy the individual desires cannot be realized (de Jong Gierveld 1989). Weiss (1973) differentiated between loneliness resulting from *emotional isolation*, associated with the absence of a close partner (i.e. an attachment figure), and loneliness resulting from *social isolation*, stemming from the absence of a broader set of social contacts. Thus, having a heterogeneous network of ties that includes a close partner, children and friends, as well as maintaining social contacts, is thought to be a key step in reducing the likelihood of loneliness (de Jong Gierveld 1998). *The first question* addressed in this chapter is to compare the extent to which older men and women living alone participate in integrating structures on a regular basis and, in doing so, avoid or alleviate loneliness.

Drawing upon a life course perspective that emphasizes the continuing and cumulative influence of early experiences on later life (Elder *et al.* 1984), this chapter considers both *current partner* position and *partner history*. The partner history of older adults has not yet attracted much attention from scholars (Cooney and Dunne 2001). However, having ever been widowed or divorced deeply affects an individual's personal and social life. Following the death of a spouse, and even more so after divorce, social relationships are often disrupted (DeGarmo 1996). Many studies show that when older widowed adults need help, they tend to rely on family members. The family still provides most of the support needed (Grundy 1999). The first to help are the children. This is especially so for older bereaved parents who choose to continue to live independently in a single-person household (Lopata 1996; Roan and Raley 1996; Eggebeen and Adam 1998; Kendig *et al.* 1999; Kohli *et al.* 2000).

Divorced men are less likely than widowers to keep in touch and to have rewarding interactions with their adult children and other family members (Doherty *et al.* 1998; Amato 2000). This difference can be related to factors such as a non-resident parent's lack of involvement, the failure to pay child support and feelings of anger, particularly from children, towards the father who left (Cooney and Uhlenberg 1990; Uhlenberg *et al.* 1990; Strain and Payne 1992; Furstenberg *et al.* 1995). Consequently, the transfer of time, money and support between adult children and their father tends to be less after divorce than it is within intact marriages (Dykstra 1998). Divorce can have long-term consequences: poor relationships between divorced middle-aged fathers and young adult children do not seem to improve as the parents age (Kaufman and Uhlenberg 1998; de Jong Gierveld and Dykstra 2003). Sometimes children feel a moral obligation to stay in touch, but for others it is merely the prospect of an inheritance (Hagestad 1987). Rossi and Rossi (1990) found that adults whose parents had divorced show a lower sense of obligation towards parents than those who grew up in intact families.

Older men living alone who have never had a legal partner relationship may be expected to have a continuous series of social relationships. However, never married older men are less likely to have extensive social networks, partly because there is only one member in the household to access potential network members. In the Netherlands, never-married men and women have usually had different educational and socio-economic careers. The current generation of older never-married women are primarily highly educated, having had relatively successful careers, whereas never-married men have often had less successful careers, and therefore find themselves in a less favourable socio-economic position (Liefbroer and de Jong Gierveld 1995). It is to be expected that the relatively restricted socio-economic resources of never-married men will be reflected in the size and composition of their social networks, and differ from networks of never-married women. Thus, the partner history of older men and women living alone (never been in a partner relationship, widowed, or divorced) is expected to have consequences for social embeddedness, social well-being and the intensity of loneliness. This will be addressed by our *second research question*.

Living alone and LAT-relationships

In the context of partner history, special attention is devoted here to a minority group of older people living alone who are involved in Living Apart Together (LAT) relationships; that is, they are (heterosexual) intimate partners who do not share a household (see Chapter 4). In-depth interviews were conducted with 23 older men and women in the Netherlands who were involved in a LAT relationship to investigate their motives for embarking on this kind of relationship. The majority of older adults in a LAT relationship explicitly stated that alleviation of loneliness was a motive for starting this type of partner relationship. One of my interviewees (80-year-old man, living alone in a LAT relationship) said: 'I know many elderly who start a LAT relationship, simply for the sake of companionship. Most of them drink a cup of coffee together, share meals . . . to avoid feeling lonely. Weekends are awful for people who live alone.' A 68-year-old woman told me the following about recently starting a new partner relationship:

R: It wasn't a motive for me, it was for him . . . he kept on nagging about it.
Interviewer: And then you acted positively?
R: Yes, stupid enough . . . feeling sorry for someone, I think efface yourself a little . . . Because for men when they are alone, I think . . . In my opinion, it's always more difficult than for a woman, a woman can support herself much more.
Interviewer: How long were you a widow before you began this relationship?
R: Ehh, two years, but it never was my intention to get a man. But perseverance pays.

It is clear that older adults who start a LAT relationship to alleviate loneliness want to retain their autonomy, freedom of choice and a certain degree of flexibility by maintaining separate living arrangements. Returning to the dependence traditionally associated with marriage is not seen as an attractive option. Older men and women who value independence highly would be less likely to remarry and more likely to consider living alone. One of the interviewed men involved in a LAT relationship summed this up as follows:

> Nowadays everything is freer and more open, isn't it? But marriage was for me . . . not at any price . . . It does not mean everything in life . . . Too fond of my personal freedom and I don't want to deny someone else's freedom.

This is also illustrated in the following extract from an interview with an older woman involved in a LAT relationship:

> *Interviewer:* You spend a lot of time together, either you go over to see him or he comes round to your house. Why don't you move in together?
>
> *R:* No, I don't want that, we are both too stubborn. I don't think it would work if we were together 24 hours a day. Not only that, he gets up so early in the morning! He is always so busy, and I can't keep up with him, it's just too much for me. When I have been over to his place, helping him with all kinds of things, then I am always glad to be home so that I can stay in bed until 9.00 in the morning [laughing]. He tells me 'you can stay in bed here as well', but I don't want that. I find older people very stupid when they do that [move in together], they give up their homes and go and live together, but what if it doesn't work out, what happens then?

A key question to be answered is to what extent men and women in LAT relationships are less likely to be lonely in later life.

Gender and social embeddedness

Relationships with family members and feelings of loneliness differ between men and women according to their different positions before, during and after marriage. To the extent that each gender's relational needs differ, this will affect the size and composition of their social network. Chodorow (1978) argues that the relationship with the mother as primary care-giver provides a model for adult interpersonal relationships. In order to develop an independent sense of self, boys must separate themselves from their mother and suppress desires for intimacy, while girls can continue to identify with their mother and maintain a strong need for intimacy and attachment. Women, according to Chodorow, have more complex affective needs, in which 'an exclusive relationship to a man is not enough' (*ibid.*: 119). They are encouraged 'to look elsewhere for love and emotional gratification' (*ibid.*: 200).

More recently, Josselson (1996) argued that relatedness and connection are important to both men and women and are experienced along the same relational dimensions, but women tend to nuance their experiences of relatedness in a more multifaceted and complex way than men. Moreover, she argues that women tend to have more attachment figures, and larger social networks than men: 'The man who has only one attachment figure (usually his wife) is more dependent on her' (*ibid.*: 236). In line with these arguments, an earlier study also revealed gender differences in the factors associated with loneliness. The loneliness of male respondents was mainly associated with the perceived quality of one main relationship, namely that with their female partner. In contrast, the loneliness of female respondents was associated with the subjective evaluation of their network in general (Dykstra and de Jong Gierveld 2001). These findings fit in with the notion that men, socialized to be emotionally independent, prefer undemanding relationships.

The socio-emotional selectivity theory of Carstensen (1992, 1995) suggests that older adults strategically cultivate their social networks to maximize social and emotional gains, and minimize social and emotional costs. In this context, it is to be expected that, with increasing age, emotional affective ties – contacts with children and other family members – become important, in contrast with social interactions that take place with people who are not so close (Lang and Carstensen 1994). This proactive construction of a social world can be seen as a strategy to reduce loneliness in old age. This leads to the *third research question*: how do social relationships contribute to combating loneliness in older men and women living alone?

The research study

This chapter examines data from the NESTOR-Living Arrangements and Social Networks (LSN) survey (Knipscheer *et al.* 1995). In 1992, face-to-face interviews were conducted with 4494 respondents in the Netherlands, constituting a stratified random sample of men and women born between 1903 and 1937; that is, aged 55 to 89. The sample was selected from the registers of 11 municipalities: the city of Amsterdam and two rural communities in the west of the Netherlands, Oss and two rural communities in the south and Zwolle and four rural communities in the north-east of the country. The response rate was 62 per cent. The sample can be considered representative of the elderly population of the Netherlands (Broese van Groenou *et al.* 1995). The average age of respondents was 73 years. Most lived at home: 1298 (29 per cent) lived alone in a one-person household, 2582 (57 per cent) lived with a partner, 206 (5 per cent) lived in some other kind of multi-person household and 351 (8 per cent) lived in an institution such as a nursing home, home for the aged or psychiatric hospital. Only men and women living alone who provided information about their social network and about loneliness (*n* = 1190) are analysed in this chapter. Network and/or loneliness data are missing for respondents with serious health problems because they could only participate in a short version of the questionnaire.

Since this research used a life history perspective, respondents were asked to provide details about the start and dissolution of *partner relationships*, including remarriage, unmarried cohabitation and LAT relationships.

To delineate the respondent's *social network* the following question was asked: 'Name the persons with whom you are in touch regularly and who are important to you.' Only persons above the age of 18 could be nominated. Network members were classified in the following way: partner, children (including step-children) and their partners, siblings, other relatives, neighbours, persons from work, voluntary work, members of organizations (e.g. church congregations, political parties), friends and acquaintances. Contact frequency was measured on an ordinal scale, with response categories ranging from: 'never or almost never' to 'daily'. This chapter focuses on those network members with whom the respondents had contact at least once a week.

Health was assessed on the basis of four activities of daily living (ADL). Respondents were asked to what extent they could still walk up and down the stairs, walk outdoors for five minutes, stand up from and sit down in a chair and dress and undress. Answers for each item ranged from 'not at all' to 'without difficulty'. Answers to the ADL scale were coded from four (numerous problems) to 20 (no problems).

The instrument to measure *loneliness* consisted of 11 items, none of which used the word 'loneliness' (de Jong Gierveld and Kamphuis 1985). Six items are negatively formulated, such as 'I often feel rejected.' The five positively formulated items express feelings of social embeddedness, such as 'There are plenty of people I can rely on when I have problems.' Answers to these items are dichotomized: answers indicating some feeling of loneliness are assigned a score of one, while other answers are scored as zero. Loneliness scores are summed for each individual. The loneliness scale has a range of zero (not lonely at all) to 11 (extremely lonely). The scale has been used in several surveys and proves to be a robust, reliable and valid instrument (van Tilburg and de Leeuw 1991).

Following a description of the frequency of contact with network members, multiple classification analyses were conducted to investigate variations in loneliness among older adults living alone.

Embeddedness in the social network: weekly contact with network members

The mean network size for men living alone is 10.1, while that of women living alone is significantly larger, 12.3 ($F_{(1190,1)} = 16.7$, $p < 0.001$). Network members contacted on (at least) a weekly basis by those living alone can, to a certain extent, be seen as a substitute for a partner in the household in terms of exchanging feelings. About half (mean 5.1) of the 10.1 network members of men living alone were contacted at least weekly, whereas the mean for at least weekly network contacts is 6.4 for women. This difference between men and women living alone is significant ($F_{(1190,1)} = 19.3$, $p < 0.001$). In total, 54 per cent of the network members contacted (at least) weekly by men and 57 per cent contacted weekly by women are kin: children, children-in-law, siblings, brothers or sisters-in-law and other relatives. Compared to women living alone, men living alone have a significantly lower number of kin ($F_{(1190,1)} = 19.9$, $p < 0.001$) and non-kin network members contacted at least weekly ($F_{(1190,1)} = 4.1$, $p < 0.05$).

Table 7.1 provides information about the social network members contacted (at least) weekly for men and women, by partner histories. Among men living alone, the mean number of network members contacted at least weekly differs significantly according to partner history ($F_{(349,2)} = 5.1$, $p < 0.01$). Widowers have the highest mean numbers (5.6) and men who have never had a partner relationship have the smallest mean number of frequent contacts (3.6). Similarly, the differences between women living alone are also significant ($F_{(860,2)} = 3.9$, $p < 0.05$). Widows have the highest mean number (6.6) and women who have never had a partner relationship have the smallest mean number of frequently contacted network members (5.3).

Table 7.1 Mean number of network members contacted at least weekly and loneliness scores, by partner history of men and women living alone, aged 55 and over

	Men living alone			Women living alone		
	(Ever) Divorced (n = 73)	*Widowers (n = 218)*	*Never partnered (n = 52)*	*(Ever) Divorced (n = 114)*	*Widows (n = 656)*	*Never partnered (n = 77)*
Children and children-in-law	0.95	2.51	–	1.69	2.80	–
Siblings and siblings-in-law	0.34	0.56	1.02	0.52	0.72	1.03
Other kin	0.21	0.27	0.62	0.45	0.47	0.86
Total kin	*1.50*	*3.34*	*1.64*	*2.66*	*3.99*	*1.89*
Friends	0.53	0.23	0.23	1.16	0.54	0.91
Neighbours	1.12	1.39	1.15	0.88	1.32	1.53
Other non-kin	1.19	0.67	0.58	0.97	0.76	0.97
Total non-kin	*2.34*	*2.29*	*1.96*	*3.01*	*2.62*	*3.41*
Total kin and non-kin	*4.34*	*5.63*	*3.60*	*5.67*	*6.61*	*5.30*
Loneliness score[a]	3.81	3.78	4.29	3.32	3.14	2.53

[a] Range: 0 (no loneliness) to 11 (extreme loneliness).

Source: NESTOR (1992).

Kin and non-kin contacts, variation with partner history?

Children make up a major proportion of all the network members contacted on a weekly basis, except for older men and women who live alone and have never been partnered, who are usually childless. Differences related to gender and partner history (for those with children alive) are significant ($F_{(1080,3)}$ = 17.4, $p < 0.001$), with widows scoring highest, followed by widowers; both categories had a mean of more than 2.5 weekly contacts with children and/or children in law. In contrast, ever-divorced women had a mean of 1.69 contacts, while ever-divorced men had a mean of only 0.95 weekly contacts with their children (see Table 7.1).

Differences in the numbers of frequently contacted non-kin members are significant for women living alone ($F_{(860,2)}$ = 5.5, $p < 0.01$). Women who have never had a partner relationship have the highest number of frequently contacted network members other than kin (3.4). Friendship contacts, in particular, are an important discriminating factor: divorced women and women who have never had a partner relationship have far more frequent contacts with friends than widows. Among men living alone, the never married have the highest number of frequent contacts with siblings and siblings-in-law, and ever-divorced men have higher levels of contact with friends and other non-kin. However, the differences according to partner history are not significant for the men ($F_{(349,2)}$ = 0.4), mainly due to the smaller subsample size of men compared to women.

Gender, social embeddedness and loneliness

The mean loneliness scores for each of the three subgroups of older men are above 3.75, indicating moderate to severe loneliness (see Table 7.1). Men who have never had a partner relationship have the highest mean values of loneliness (4.29). The loneliness scores of the women range from 2.53 (women never in a partner relationship) to 3.32 (ever-divorced women). The differences in loneliness scores among women are not significant ($F_{(846,2)}$ = 1.76, $p = 0.173$), and similarly for men ($F_{(342,2)}$ = 0.71, $p = 0.494$). The loneliness scores are higher for men than for women, and this gender difference is significant ($F_{(1189,5)}$ = 4.3, $p < 0.001$). Controlling for differences in age and health does not change the level or rank of the loneliness scores of men or women who live alone, differentiated by partner history.

This section examines to what extent there are differences in loneliness among older adults living alone, when the characteristics of their social network and other variables (age, health, time alone since the loss of their partner, educational level and the number of children alive) are taken into account. The results of multiple classification analyses (Table 7.2) show that partner history in combination with information about LAT relationships (model 1) explains 11.4 per cent of the variance in loneliness of older men

Table 7.2   Prediction of loneliness based on multiple classification analysis of variables of social embeddedness; men and women living alone, aged 55 and over

	Men alone					Women alone				
		Model 1		Model 2			Model 1		Model 2	
	N =	Dev.^{a}	Beta	Dev.^{a}	Beta	N =	Dev.^{a}	Beta	Dev.^{a}	Beta
Partner status			0.14		0.06			0.06		0.07
(Ever) divorced	73	0.42		0.08		114	0.32		−0.03	
Widowed	218	−0.28		−0.11		656	0.00		0.08	
Never partnered	52	0.59		0.37		77	−0.47		−0.65	
LAT relationship?			0.15**		0.16**			0.08*		0.07*
No	302	0.15		0.16		824	0.04		0.03	
Yes	41	−1.14		−1.16		23	−1.33		−1.20	
No. children (in law) contacted weekly					0.19***					0.18***
0	140			0.44		232			0.50	
1	51			0.56		113			0.89	
2 or more	152			−0.60		501			−0.42	
No. siblings (in law) contacted weekly					0.10					0.06
0	246			−0.09		530			0.13	
1	53			0.62		161			−0.26	
2 or more	44			−0.27		155			−0.17	
No. other kin contacted weekly					0.06					0.08†
0	282			0.08		615			0.11	
1	39			−0.41		116			−0.07	
2 or more	22			−0.26		115			−0.53	
No. friends contacted weekly					0.08					0.12**
0	281			0.07		573			0.24	
1	38			−0.03		149			−0.42	
2 or more	24			−0.74		124			−0.58	
No. neighbours contacted weekly					0.11					0.04
0	162			0.23		382			0.12	
1	67			−0.58		161			−0.05	
2 or more	114			0.02		303			−0.12	

Table 7.2   Continued

	Men alone				Women alone				
		Model 1		Model 2			Model 1		Model 2	
	N =	Dev.[a]	Beta	Dev.[a]	Beta	N =	Dev.[a]	Beta	Dev.[a]	Beta
No. other non-kin contacted weekly					0.07					0.02
0	245			0.04		591			0.02	
1	44			−0.48		114			−0.11	
2 or more	61			0.18		156			0.09	
Network size					0.13					0.18***
0–10	216			0.28		424			0.51	
11–22	103			−0.43		332			−0.48	
23 or more	23			−0.69		82			−0.67	
Grand mean			3.85	3.85				3.11	3.11	
R^2 (%)			11.4	19.4				5.9	17.3	

[a] Deviation from the grand mean adjusted for the covariates (age, health, time alone, educational level and number of children alive) and the independent variables.
†$p < 0.10$, *$p < 0.05$, **$p < 0.01$, ***$p < 0.001$.

Source: NESTOR (1992).

living alone. Being in a LAT relationship ⋯⋯⋯ y decreased the loneliness scores of older men living alone ⋯⋯⋯ and divorced men have higher loneliness scores than wid⋯⋯ the relationship is not significant.[1] Partnership status and L⋯ (Model 1) explained only 5.9 per cent of the variance in t⋯ ⋯perienced by older women living alone, less than for men. T⋯ of older women with a LAT relationship are characterized by ⋯ ⋯wer levels of loneliness than their peers not in a LAT relation⋯ ⋯er history is not statistically significant for women living alone, but never married women have a lower loneliness score than widows and divorced women (even after controlling for differences in age, health and other variables).

Introducing characteristics of the social network in Model 2 (Table 7.2) increases the explained variance in loneliness to 19.4 per cent for men and 17.3 per cent for women. The increase is especially large for women: 66 per cent of all the variance explained is related to their network characteristics, as compared to 41 per cent for men. For both men and women living alone, loneliness is higher among adults who have no weekly contacts with their children or only contact with one child. Compared to contacts with children, the relationships with siblings and other kin contribute relatively less to social well-being. Loneliness is significantly greater for women who live alone and have less than weekly contacts with friends; for men this relationship is not significant, but the trends are parallel to those for women. Network size is an important factor for both men and women living alone: loneliness is higher among adults with a small network size and less loneliness is found for those with a network size of 23 or more.

In summary, this analysis has shown that taking into account the number and frequency of intimate and close social bonds furthers our understanding of loneliness among older men and women living alone. Non-kin bonds, particularly those with friends, partially supplement and substitute for the effect of close social bonds with a LAT partner, children and other kin, creating a sense of social well-being among older adult men and women living alone and alleviating loneliness.

Discussion

This chapter has investigated the factors associated with the social embeddedness and loneliness of older people living in a one-person household, comparing men and women who live alone. We started with an analysis of the network size and composition. In relation to the overall size of the social network, and the number of nominated network members contacted weekly, there are significant differences between men and women. Men living alone characteristically have smaller networks, and less weekly contact with kin and non-kin. A closer look at the frequency of network contacts reveals that the highest source of weekly contacts is with children, and it is this type of contact that varies most according to partner history for older adults alone. Widows and widowers see children and children-in-law on a weekly basis more than divorced men and women. This confirms the findings mentioned earlier in the chapter that older parents who have to deal with the death of their spouse can usually rely on their children for emotional and instrumental support, whereas divorced older adults have less contact with their children, particularly older divorced men.

Interestingly, the mean total number of network members – excluding children and children-in-law – contacted weekly does not differ significantly between men who are divorced, widowed or never had a partner. Thus, the social capacity of older men to start and maintain close relationships with people other than their children does not seem to be related to partner history in the Netherlands. This contrasts with women living alone, where there are significant differences in the mean number of network members (excluding children and children in law) contacted weekly. Women who have never had a partner have the highest number of weekly contacts, in particular contact with siblings, other kin and neighbours. This finding might be related to the positive self-concepts and the social resources of older women never involved in a partner relationship. The largest number of frequently contacted friends was found among older divorced women. The life choices of divorced women, and the prevalence of a strong desire not to become involved again in an intimate relationship with a man, could lead to divorced women being more inclined to form friendships with women.

Loneliness differs significantly between men and women living alone: men living alone are more likely to be lonely than women with similar partner histories. The most striking difference in loneliness scores is between men and women who have never had a partner; never married men have the highest, whereas never married women have the lowest loneliness scores. Liefbroer and de Jong Gierveld (1995) concluded earlier that these results were attributable to differences in socio-economic and social resources of never partnered men and women. However, the differences in loneliness scores are still recognizable, albeit not significantly, in the multiple classification analysis after controlling for educational level, age, health, time alone, and the number of children alive. The results obtained using multiple classification analysis demonstrate that having an intimate partner is very important for the social well-being of both men and women living alone. Older men's loneliness is to a large extent affected by the availability of a LAT relationship. The variance explained by partner history and LAT status (in Model 1) is much higher for men than for women living alone, and supports the finding that men's loneliness is strongly associated with the lack of an intimate bond with a female partner, whether in marriage or in a LAT relationship (Josselson 1996). This finding is also in line with the socio-emotional selectivity theory of Carstensen (1992, 1995), which postulates that, after the age of 50, emotionally satisfying ties will be selected and oriented mostly towards intimate and close relationships.

The contribution of (at least) weekly contacts with other close and less close network members is important for the social well-being and alleviation of loneliness of both older men and older women living alone. However, the data also show that lone women have a wider range of social resources, providing them with a 'buffer' against loneliness, more than is the case for men living alone. In line with Josselson (1996) and others, the social well-being of women is related to intimate, close and less close social bonds. The parameters for other kin and friends contacted weekly for men and women are similar to one another. This is in line with research by Dykstra (1995) that has shown that older adults – men and women – need a broad and varied social network of kin and non-kin to achieve social embeddedness and to alleviate loneliness.

Note

1 However, we need to take into account that, in society and consequently in this chapter, the absolute number of men aged 55 and over who live alone is much lower than the number of women living alone. This lower number of men affects the levels of statistical significance of the relationships found in the multivariate analysis for men compared to women.

Acknowledgements

This chapter is based on data collected in the context of the research pro-gramme NESTOR, 'Living arrangements and social networks of older adults'. This research programme is being conducted at the Departments of Sociology and Social Science Methodology, Faculty of Social Cultural Sciences of the Vrije Universiteit in Amsterdam, and the Netherlands Interdisciplinary Demographic Institute in The Hague. The research is supported by a pro-gramme grant from the Netherlands Programme for Research on Ageing (NESTOR), funded by the Ministry of Education and Science and the Ministry of Welfare, Health and Cultural Affairs. I want to thank Petronella Kievit-Tyson for her work on the English text, which has considerably improved its clarity.

References

Amato, P. (2000) The consequences of divorce for adults and children, *Journal of Marriage and the Family*, 62: 1269–87.
Bradburn, N. (1969) *The Structure of Psychological Well-being*. Chicago: Aldine.
Broese van Groenou, M., van Tilburg, T. G., de Leeuw, E. D. and Liefbroer, A. C. (1995) Data collection. In C. P. M. Knipscheer, J. de Jong Gierveld, T. G. van Tilburg and P. A. Dykstra (eds) *Living Arrangements and Social Networks of Older Adults*. Amsterdam: VU University Press.
Carstensen, L. L. (1992) Social and emotional patterns in adulthood: support for socioemotional selectivity theory, *Psychology and Aging*, 7(3): 331–8.
Carstensen, L. L. (1995) Evidence for a life-span theory of socioemotional selectivity, *Current Directions in Psychological Science*, 4: 151–6.
Chodorow, N. (1978) *The Reproduction of Mothering: Psychoanalysis and the Sociology of Gender*. Berkeley: University of California Press.
Cooney, T. M. and Dunne, K. (2001) Intimate relationships in later life, *Journal of Family Issues*, 22(7): 838–58.
Cooney, T. M. and Uhlenberg, P. (1990) The role of divorce in men's relations with their adult children after mid-life, *Journal of Marriage and the Family*, 52: 677–88.
DeGarmo, D. S. (1996) Identity relevance and disruption as predictors of psychological distress for widowed and divorced women, *Journal of Marriage and the Family*, 58: 983–97.
de Jong Gierveld, J. (1989) Personal relationships, social support, and loneliness, *Journal of Social and Personal Relationships*, 6: 197–221.
de Jong Gierveld, J. (1998) A review of loneliness: concept and definitions, deter-minants and consequences, *Reviews in Clinical Gerontology*, 8: 73–80.
de Jong Gierveld, J. and Dykstra, P. A. (2002) The longterm rewards of parenting: older adults' marital history and the likelihood of receiving support from adult children, *Ageing International*, 27(3): 49–69.
de Jong Gierveld, J. and Kamphuis, F. (1985) The development of a Rasch-type loneliness scale, *Applied Psychological Measurement*, 9: 289–99.

de Jong Gierveld, J. and Peeters, A. (2002) Partnerpaden na het vijftigste levensjaar [Partner paths after the age of fifty], *Mens en Maatschappij*, 77(2): 116–36.

Doherty, W. J., Kouneski, E. F. and Erickson, M. F. (1998) Responsible fathering: an overview and conceptual framework, *Journal of Marriage and the Family*, 60: 277–92.

Dykstra, P. A. (1995) Loneliness among the never and formerly married: the importance of supportive friendships and a desire for independence, *Journal of Gerontology, Social Sciences*, 50B: 321–9.

Dykstra, P. A. (1998) The effects of divorce on intergenerational exchanges in families, *Netherlands Journal of Social Sciences*, 33(2): 77–93.

Dykstra, P. A. and de Jong Gierveld, J. (2001) Gender differences in Dutch older adult loneliness. Paper presented to the IAG Conference, Vancouver, 1–6 July.

Eggebeen, D. J. and Adam, D. (1998) Do safety nets work? The role of anticipated help in times of need, *Journal of Marriage and the Family*, 60: 939–50.

Elder, G. H. Jr, Liker, J. K. and Jaworski, B. J. (1984) Hardship in lives: depression influences from the 1930s to old age in postwar America. In K. McCluskey and H. Reese (eds) *Life-span Developmental Psychology: Historical and Generational Effects*. New York: Academic Press.

Furstenberg, F. F. Jr, Hoffman, S. D. and Shrestha, L. (1995) The effect of divorce on intergenerational transfers: new evidence, *Demography*, 32(3): 319–33.

Gove, W. R. (1972) Sex, marital status and suicide, *Journal of Health and Social Behavior*, 13(2): 204–13.

Grundy, E. (1999) Intergenerational perspectives on family and household change in mid- and later life in England and Wales. In S. McRae (ed.) *Changing Britain: Families and Households in the 1990s*. Oxford: Oxford University Press.

Hagestad, G. O. (1987) Parent–child relations in later life: trends and gaps in past research. In J. B. Lancaster, J. Altmann, A. S. Rossi and L. R. Sherrod (eds) *Parenting across the Life Span: Biosocial Dimensions*. New York: Aldine de Gruyter.

Havens, B. and Hall, M. (2001) Social isolation, loneliness, and the health of older adults, *Indian Journal of Gerontology*, 14: 144–53.

Josselson, R. (1996) *The Space Between Us. Exploring the Dimensions of Human Relationships*. Thousand Oaks, CA: Sage.

Kaufman, G. and Uhlenberg, P. (1998) Effects of life course transitions on the quality of relationships between adult children and their parents, *Journal of Marriage and the Family*, 60: 924–38.

Kendig, H., Koyano, W., Asakawa, T. and Ando, T. (1999) Social support of older people in Australia and Japan, *Ageing and Society*, 19: 185–208.

Knipscheer, C. P. M., de Jong Gierveld, J., van Tilburg, T. and Dykstra, P. (1995) *Living Arrangements and Social Networks of Older Adults*. Amsterdam: VU University Press.

Kohli, M., Künemund, H., Motel, A. and Szydlik, M. (2000) Generationenbeziehungen. In M. Kohli and H. Künemund (eds) *Die zweite Lebenshälfte: gesellschaftliche Lage und Participation im Spiegel des Alters-Survey*. Opladen: Leske + Budrich.

Lang, F. R. and Carstensen, L. L. (1994) Close emotional relationships in late life: further support for proactive aging in the social domain, *Psychology and Aging*, 9(2): 315–24.

Liefbroer, A. C. and de Jong Gierveld, J. (1995) Living arrangements, socio-economic resources, and health. In C. P. M. Knipscheer, J. de Jong Gierveld, T. G. van Tilburg and P. A. Dykstra (eds) *Living Arrangements and Social Networks of Older Adults*. Amsterdam: VU University Press.

Lopata, H. Z. (1996) *Current Widowhood; Myths and Realities*. Thousand Oaks, CA: Sage.

Peters, A. and Liefbroer, A. C. (1997) Beyond marital status: partner history and well-being in old age, *Journal of Marriage and the Family*, 59: 687–99.

Roan, C. L. and Raley, R. K. (1996) Intergenerational coresidence and contact: a longitudinal analysis of adult children's response to their mother's widowhood, *Journal of Marriage and the Family*, 58: 708–17.

Rossi, A. S. and Rossi, P. H. (1990) *Of Human Bonding, Parent–Child Relations across the Life Course*. New York: Aldine de Gruyter.

Strain, L. A. and Payne, B. J. (1992) Social networks and patterns of social interaction among ever-single and separated/divorced elderly Canadians, *Canadian Journal on Aging*, 11(1): 31–53.

Uhlenberg, P., Cooney, T. M. and Boyd, R. (1990) Divorce for women after midlife, *Journal of Gerontology: Social Sciences*, 45: S3–11.

van Poppel, F. (2001) Gemiddelde levensduur: voorsprong vrouwen neemt af [Mean life expectancy: women lose position], *Demos*, 17: 64.

van Tilburg, T. and de Leeuw, E. (1991) Stability of scale quality under various data collection procedures: a mode comparison on the 'De Jong-Gierveld Loneliness Scale', *International Journal of Public Opinion Research*, 3(1): 69–85.

Weiss, R. S. (1973) *Loneliness: the Experience of Emotional and Social Isolation*. Cambridge, MA: MIT Press.

Wenger, C. G., Davies, R., Shahtahmasebi, S. and Scott, A. (1996) Social isolation and loneliness in old age: review and model refinement, *Ageing and Society*, 16: 333–58.

8

GETTING BY WITHOUT A SPOUSE: LIVING ARRANGEMENTS AND SUPPORT OF OLDER PEOPLE IN ITALY AND BRITAIN

Cecilia Tomassini, Karen Glaser and Janet Askham

Introduction

Research on gender has traditionally focused on how gender divisions in work and family life contribute to the disadvantages faced by women, neglecting the existence of gender differences in old age. Recently the balance has been redressed, with studies on gender differences in later life in relation to: retirement and poverty (Arber and Ginn 1995a; Ginn and Arber 1996); health (Kinsella and Gist 1998; Arber and Cooper 1999); social networks (Scott and Wenger 1995); and receipt and provision of care (Arber et al. 1988; Velkoff and Lawson 1998; Spitze and Ward 2000).

This chapter focuses on older people without a spouse, examining their living arrangements and receipt of help or care from informal networks and from formal services. This is an important issue since they lack the usual primary source of help and support in later life: a husband or wife. This group is also important because it comprises a large proportion of the older population in both Britain and Italy. Thus, among those aged 65 and over, in 1998 in Italy 60 per cent of women and 21 per cent of men, and in Britain 56 per cent of women and 28 per cent of men, were without a spouse. The higher proportion of men in Britain without a spouse is due to the combined effects of greater age gaps between spouses among Italian couples (that is, men in Italy are less likely to be widowed) and higher divorce rates in Britain. Although the proportion of older people without a spouse is currently declining slightly in both countries it is projected to rise again in Britain within the next twenty years largely because of increases in divorce (Shaw 1999, and see Chapter 1).

Several theoretical reasons can be proposed to help to explain gender differences in the living arrangements and flows of care between family members in different societies: (a) demographic characteristics, affecting opportunities for different kinds of behaviour, individual physical or mental health and financial or economic well-being; (b) characteristics of family relationships and networks; (c) the nature of social institutions of housing, social welfare and education in different societies; and (d) cultural factors, particularly beliefs and norms about family behaviour. Each of these is described more fully.

Demographic characteristics, health and financial resources

Whether older people live alone or not, and what type of help they receive, depends on key demographic variables that affect people's opportunities for living with other family members or receiving help from them: namely marital status, and the existence of children, siblings or other relatives. Health is also a key factor in both the choice of living arrangements and the likelihood of receipt of help. This suggests that there may be differences between older men and women, since women have higher levels of disability in late old age, and are therefore more likely to need (or to be seen to need) help (Arber and Cooper 1999). For example, women report a greater use of health services and receipt of home help than men, which may be due to the higher prevalence of poor health among women, or to their possible greater awareness of community or public service provision. Gender differences may also reflect the greater financial resources available to older men, which may increase the likelihood that they will live independently or purchase care.

Characteristics of family relationships and networks

There are well-documented gender differences in the structure of families and social networks, and exchanges within each of these spheres. Women are consistently reported to have larger and more multifaceted networks than men: they report more friends, and provide and receive more support from members of their network, than men. Men tend to maintain close, intimate relationships with only a few people, primarily their spouse. These gender differences in patterns of social exchange appear to be fairly consistent across the adult life span (Shye et al. 1995). As well as differential networks, patterns of family co-residence may be of importance (and possibly even of increasing importance) in influencing the provision of help to older people without a spouse. For example, in Italy the presence of an unmarried son reduces the probability of an unmarried older woman living alone (Tomassini 1998). American studies show that unemployed or divorced children are more likely to return to the parental home (DaVanzo and Goldscheider 1990), and this pattern may be increasing.

Exchanges between the generations in a family should also be considered. Help may be provided to older members as reciprocity for past care or material support or in anticipation of future benefit (such as a bequest). Therefore, it may be that older people with more resources receive more help from kin (Henretta *et al.* 1997), or that those who have invested more in their children (usually thought to be women) receive more help (Spitze and Logan 1990). Studies that have considered adult children's motivations in helping their mother or father have shown no significant differences in provision of care dependent on the gender of the parent (Silverstein 1995). Nevertheless, they have found that widowed mothers receive more instrumental help from adult children than widowed fathers. Studies also suggest that affection is a stronger predictor when mothers are recipients of support and that support for fathers is more likely to be influenced by instrumental or obligatory concerns (Lawton *et al.* 1994).

Nature of societal institutions

A very different, but key, element in the decision to live independently is the characteristics of relevant social institutions within different societies. For example, housing facilities and availability will affect whether people live alone or in inter-generational co-residence, the latter being more widespread in southern than in northern Europe partly because of the scarcity of housing benefits for young people (Iacovou 2000). The educational system may also be important; for example, through its impact on the age of transition to adulthood, sex roles within the family or the opportunities for independence available to women.

Another institution that will have an impact on older people's independence is the welfare state system. The use of public services differs among European countries, ranging from a maximum of 24 per cent of elderly people receiving public help in Finland to only 1 per cent in southern European countries (Kinsella and Velkhoff 2001). Home care for elderly people is still very rare in Italy, as are support services for care-givers, and there is great regional variability in the general provision of health and social services (Lamura *et al.* 1999), though recent legislation has been enacted to promote home services. In contrast to Italy and most southern European countries, Britain has a more developed system of social provision for older people in both personal social services and health services (Hugman 1994). There are few studies on the receipt of private paid help, though it is an increasing source of domestic, personal or nursing help for older people who can afford it (Pickard *et al.* 2002). The recent increase in immigration over the past decade in Italy has increased the potential labour pool of inexpensive care providers from the migrant community.

Cultural factors

The culture of the community is also a possible influence on gender, regional and societal differences in the living arrangements of older people and their receipt of help (Pampel 1992; Wolf 1995). The notion of the familistic culture has been used in the past to explain the strong family ties existing in southern Europe (Banfield 1958; Reher 1998). In a familistic society, personal utility and family utility are seen as the same: the structure of the family and the relationships among family members are influenced by the strong ties that link them together. For example, inter-generational co-residence tends to continue until children leave the parental home to get married; and even then they normally live close to their parents (Dalla Zuanna 2001). In Britain there is a stronger individualistic culture, involving looser and less geographically close family ties, more emphasis on voluntaristic relationships (for example, recent research has shown that friends are becoming more important in older people's 'personal communities': Phillipson *et al.* 2001) and greater preference for independent living. Indeed, an increasing percentage of older people are living alone (Sundström 1994), though in Italy the never married are less likely to do so than widowed or divorced older people (Tomassini 1998). Some of the changes responsible for this trend towards greater residential independence among older people, such as greater financial independence and possible improvements in health, are positive developments that may enable more older individuals to meet their aspirations for 'intimacy at a distance' rather than having to co-reside with family members (Rosenmayr and Köckeis 1963).

These four sets of theoretical explanations may be useful in helping to explain gender differences and similarities in older people's living arrangements and the sources of help received by older people without a spouse in Britain and Italy. They have informed the research aims outlined below. This chapter compares Britain and Italy because of the demographic and socio-economic differences (outlined above) between the two countries, and in particular because of the desire to examine whether a society with a strong familistic culture shows less difference between older men and women without a spouse than a culture in which relations between kin are primarily influenced by individualistic values and in which older people may therefore have to 'earn' their support from kin rather than receive it as of right.

Research aims

The aim of this chapter is to analyse gender differences in the household composition and sources of care received by older people without a spouse in Italy and Britain. At its simplest we are comparing whether men or women fare better when they are unpartnered in later life. Are unpartnered men or women more or less likely to be able to live independently? And if they need assistance are there gender differences in who is more likely to receive it? Our first aim is to examine gender differences in *living arrangements* among older unmarried people. Understanding the demographic, social and cultural factors influencing household composition is important, as living arrangements directly affect the exchange of help and support between older people and their kin. We examine the effect of selected socio-economic and demographic characteristics on the probability of living alone. It should be remembered, however, that the older people included in the analysis are a 'selected' group, i.e. they are the healthy non-institutionalized elderly living in the community, as extremely frail elderly people are likely to be institutionalized (especially in Britain). A further source of selection for this group arises from the higher remarriage rate of older men than women.

Our second aim is to examine gender differences in the patterns of *receipt of help* from different sources among unmarried older people. Family members, friends, private helpers and public providers constitute the care-giving network of older people who need assistance. The way older people negotiate their care-givers is the result of a complex process that takes into account the availability, desirability and willingness of each member as a provider of help. International studies have shown that family members continue to be the primary sources of care for older people in need: in the European Union family members provide two-thirds of the care received, compared to 13 per cent provided by the public sector and 11 per cent by the private sector (Walker 1993).

Data and methods

A key issue in cross-national research is to assess to what extent data sets and measures are comparable across countries. This study employs the following three datasets: the 1998 Italian Multipurpose Survey on Family and Childhood Conditions (IMF); the 1999 wave of the British Household Panel Survey (BHPS); and the British 1998 General Household Survey (GHS).

Italy. The IMF survey is based on a nationally representative sample of private households: the 1998 IMF has a sample size of 59,050 respondents, with 3285 unmarried people aged 65 and over.

Britain. The 1999 BHPS is used to examine gender differences in the *living arrangements* of older unmarried people in Britain. The BHPS is an annual longitudinal survey that began in 1991 and is based on a nationally representative sample of private households. The 1999 survey wave has a sample size of 15,625 individuals, with 1387 unmarried people aged 65 and over. The GHS is used to analyse gender differences in the *receipt of help* among older unmarried people in Britain. The GHS is a continuous household survey that started in 1971 (Bridgwood 2000). This chapter focuses on the 1998 GHS, which included a module of questions asked to people aged 65 and over concerning their living circumstances, health, ability to manage various self-care and domestic tasks and use of health and personal social services. The 1998 GHS has a total sample size of 15,853 people, with 1360 unmarried older people.

Dependent variables

Two dependent variables are analysed: living arrangements and receipt of help. A binary variable of the living arrangements of unmarried older people was based on the household information given in the 1998 IMF and the 1999 BHPS (1 = *living alone*, and 0 = *living with others*).

Receipt of help was more difficult to operationalize because of differences between the surveys. For Italy the choice of the dependent variable for help received was constrained by the nature of available data. As the Italian survey did not ask respondents about any help received from household members, it was necessary to focus exclusively on help received from outside the household. The Italian question on help received was asked at the household rather than the individual level. Respondents were asked if help was provided to all household members, and if not, which specific members were the major recipients. The questions on help received referred to: health assistance (injections, medications, and so on), help with activities of daily living (ADL) and instrumental activities of daily living (IADL) and domestic help. For the type of help that the respondents considered the most important, they were asked who provided that form of help. It is therefore important to keep in mind that the amount of help received in Italy may be underestimated, as the question focused only on what the respondent considered the most important type of help.

Based on the information concerning who from outside the household provided the most important type of help received, the following four dependent dichotomous variables were created: help from family members, help from formal sources (excluding private help), help from friends/neighbours and private paid help. Private help was measured at the household rather than the individual level, as respondents were asked about domestic help provided to all family members. Help from formal sources was also measured by an additional question concerning the receipt of public services (meals on wheels, home cleaning, nurse help, physiotherapist) by the family (or by the main recipient) in the 12 months before the interview.

For Britain, the 1998 GHS asked a set of questions of all adults aged 65 and over, concerning their ability to manage a series of activities and tasks. To retain comparability with the Italian survey the measures created only included those receiving help from outside the household, namely whether older people received assistance from someone outside the household for each ADL and IADL. Four dichotomous measures were created indicating whether individuals had received help with any ADL or IADL activity from family members living outside the household, friends/neighbours, social or health services or from paid private assistance. Those who reported that in the last month they had used a district nurse or health visitor, meals-on-wheels or a day centre for older people were also considered to have received help from social or health services. Respondents were also asked if they had used private domestic help in the past month.

Independent variables

The aim of this chapter is to examine gender differences within Italy and Britain rather than to compare gender differences between the two countries. Therefore, the variables used in our study are not necessarily similar in their scale, time reference or definition. However, we have tried to make them as comparable as possible.

The independent variables used in the analysis of *living arrangements* of older men and women without a spouse were age, marital status, number of children, education, housing tenure and health. Age was coded as 65 to 74, 75 to 84 and 85 and over, with the youngest group used as the reference category. Marital status and number of children were included because of the positive association between widowhood, number of children and co-residence among unmarried elderly people (Wolf 1994; Tomassini and Wolf 2000). Marital status was coded into two groups: the divorced, separated or widowed versus the never married. A binary variable indicated whether or not the older person had any living children.

Previous studies have shown that individuals with a higher education were more likely to live alone (Glaser and Tomassini 2000; Tomassini and Wolf 2000). In order to retain comparability, given differences in the educational systems of the two countries, individuals with higher educational levels were distinguished from those with lower levels. For Britain, those with no educational qualifications were grouped into the medium/low category, as were those in Italy with less than a high school diploma or no educational qualification. All others were in the higher category.

Housing tenure was included in the model because of its strong association with co-residence in Britain and Italy, as owner-occupiers in both countries are less likely to live alone than those in other housing tenures (Warnes and Ford 1995; Glaser and Tomassini 2000; Tomassini and Wolf 2000). In the two countries a dichotomy was created that distinguished owner-occupiers from those in other tenures (largely social sector tenants in Britain and private renters in Italy).

Health status was included in the models, as those who are in need of help have a higher probability of living with others and of receiving help (Glaser and Tomassini 2000). Both the British and Italian surveys contained questions on whether the respondent's health limited their daily activities.

The independent variables used in the analysis of *receipt of help* among older unmarried people were gender, marital status, age, living arrangements, social class, housing tenure and health. For older people the British GHS does not contain information on education or whether they have children. We used the socio-economic grouping based on the head of household's current occupation or, for those who were not in paid work, the last job held (Bridgwood *et al.* 2000). Respondents were divided into non-manual/manual socio-economic groups, with the former category as the reference group. With respect to health the GHS asked respondents if they had any long-standing illness, infirmity or disability and, if so, whether it limited their activities in any way.

Living arrangements

The percentages of unmarried older women and men living alone were 56 and 55 per cent respectively in Italy compared with 83 and 84 per cent respectively in Britain. Thus, no clear gender difference in household composition among unmarried elderly people was found. We used logistic regression models to investigate whether there were gender differences in the effects of the determinants of living arrangements among unmarried older men and women using data from the 1998 IMF and the 1999 BHPS. Following Arber and Ginn (1995b), we conducted separate models for men and women in order to examine gender differences in the effect of each independent variable on the probability of living alone.

Table 8.1 shows the effect of the explanatory variables (i.e. age, education, tenure, marital and health status and living children) on the probability of living alone. As the outcome measure is binary, taking the value 1 = *living*

Table 8.1   Logistic regression models of living alone, unmarried men and women aged 65 and over, Italy and Britain (odds ratios)

Variables	Italy		Britain	
	Men	Women	Men	Women
75–84 (v. 65–74)	1.27	1.03	1.77	1.45
85+ (v. 65–74)	0.80	0.64**	1.60	1.37
Low education (v. high)	0.75	0.62**	0.48*	0.52**
Other tenures (v. owner)	2.16**	2.69**	3.50**	3.59**
Divorced/separated/widowed (v. single)	2.75**	2.48**	3.07	1.53
Presence of limiting health problems				
(v. no health problems)	0.83	0.91	0.57	0.47*
Living children (v. none)	0.41**	0.33**	0.64	0.49*
N =	709	2576	355	980

Significance: *$p < 0.05$, **$p < 0.01$.

Source: Italian Multipurpose Survey on Family and Childhood Conditions (1998); and British Household Panel Survey (1999).

alone and 0 = *living with others*, the most appropriate statistical technique is logistic regression. Table 8.1 shows odds ratios that indicate how much more or less likely a person with each of the characteristics is to live alone, controlling for all the other factors in the model. For example, divorced, separated or widowed men in Italy had a nearly three times higher odds of living alone as compared with the never married. All the explanatory variables have the expected effect on the probability of living alone. In Italy, the determinants of living alone are the same for men and women, with the exception that being aged 85 and over and education were only significant for women. If we assume that education is a proxy for social status in Italy, these results suggest that higher social status women are more likely to live alone, although this is not a significant determinant of household composition for unpartnered Italian men. Both men and women aged 85 and over were more likely to live with others, especially women over 85. This finding is likely to reflect co-residence associated with increasing frailty in advanced old age.

In Britain, similar factors are associated with living alone for men and women. For example, unpartnered men and women with high education and those in largely social sector housing were more likely to live alone. In addition, women with a health condition that restricted their activities and who had children were less likely to live alone. Unlike in Italy, the data suggest that the probability of living alone among older unmarried individuals increases with rising age (although the association between age and the probability of living alone was not statistically significant in Britain). Although we found no gender differences in the probability of living alone in either country, some variables (e.g. age and education in Italy, and health and number of living children in Britain) were significant only for women.

Receipt of help

In Italy 29 per cent of unmarried older men and 27 per cent of unmarried older women received help from outside the household, whereas the percentages were 43 and 55 per cent respectively in Britain. Table 8.2 presents the sources of help received from outside the household for people aged 65 and over. Italian women received slightly more help than men from all the sources considered, except for private help. There is little difference between the percentages who received help from family members (14 per cent) and from private providers (13 per cent); however, women were slightly more likely to receive help from the former, whereas men were more likely to receive help from the latter.

Table 8.2 shows the proportion of older unmarried men and women receiving help in Britain. In contrast to Italy, British respondents were more likely to report receiving help from the public sector (17 per cent). There were high levels of help from family members reported by 32 per cent of women and 20 per cent of men. Gender differences appear to be more accentuated in

Table 8.2   Percentage receiving different sources of care from outside the household, unmarried men and women aged 65 and over, Italy and Britain

	Help from family members	Help from friends	Public help	Private help	Any help	N =
Italy						
Men	13.6	3.9	1.0	14.5	29	2576
Women	14.3	4.3	2.0	12.3	27	709
Total	14.1	4.2	1.8	12.7	27	3285
Britain						
Men	20.1	6.3	15.0	11.6	43	379
Women	32.2	8.7	17.9	13.1	55	980
Total	28.8	8.0	17.1	12.7	52	1359

Source: Italian Multipurpose Survey on Family and Childhood Conditions (1998); General Household Survey (1998).

Britain, especially with regard to help provided by family members, but women also received more of the other three sources of help. However, differences between men and women in the sources of help received shown in Table 8.2 may be confounded by other demographic or socio-economic characteristics that vary between the two groups, such as age, marital status and health.

We now analyse factors that may influence the receipt of help from the family and private paid help in both countries, in addition to public help in Britain, in order to try to explain gender differences in the receipt of help observed in Table 8.2. Table 8.3 shows the results of the logistic model for receiving help from family members or from paid carers in Italy. The relationships between receiving help from family members and the explanatory variables were as expected: being older than 75, and especially older than 85, increased the probability of receiving help, as did being less educated and having health problems that limited daily activities. As expected, living alone increased the probability of receiving help from kin living outside the household. In Italy, gender did not have a significant effect on the probability of receiving help from family members outside the household.

Table 8.3 shows similar relationships between receiving private paid help and the explanatory variables, except for education. Education, which is usually a good proxy for the respondent's social status and income, is positively associated with private help, as people who are better off economically are more likely to be able to afford private domestic help. Home ownership (another proxy for social status) is also positively related to receiving private help.

For Britain, Table 8.4 shows the results of the logistic model based on the GHS data. For help provided by family members, the explanatory variables

Table 8.3 Logistic regression model of receiving family and private paid help from outside the household, unmarried people aged 65 and over, Italy (odds ratios)

Variables	Family help	Private paid help
Women (v. men)	1.01	0.90
Widow and divorced (v. single)	1.05	0.94
75–84 (v. 65–74)	1.54**	1.54**
85+ (v. 65–74)	2.10**	2.14**
Low education (v. high education)	2.18**	0.18**
Other tenures (v. owner)	1.23	0.77*
Not living alone (v. living alone)	0.32**	0.64**
Presence of limiting health problems (v. no health problems)	3.39**	2.92**

Significance: *$p < 0.05$; **$p < 0.01$.
$n = 3285$.

Source: Italian Multipurpose Survey on Family and Childhood Conditions (1998).

Table 8.4 Logistic regression model of receiving family, public and private help from outside the household, unmarried people aged 65 and over, Britain (odds ratios)

Variables	Family help	Private paid help	Public help
Women (v. men)	1.79**	1.01	1.00
Widowed (v. single)	4.05**	0.49**	0.62*
Separated/divorced (v. single)	2.28*	0.36**	0.67
75–84 (v. 65–74)	1.52**	1.89**	3.06**
85+ (v. 65–74)	2.55**	3.54**	6.38**
Manual (v. non-manual)	1.95**	0.53**	1.05
Other tenures (v. owner)	1.74**	0.61*	1.72**
Not living alone (v. living alone)	0.13**	0.42**	0.44**
Presence of limiting health problems (v. no health problems)	3.56**	2.22**	3.56**

Significance: *$p < 0.05$, **$p < 0.01$.
$n = 1292$.

Source: General Household Survey (1998).

have similar effects to those found in Italy, apart from gender and marital status. Widowed and divorced older people were more likely to receive help from family members compared to the never married, but were less likely to receive private paid help. However, there was no significant difference according to marital status in the receipt of public help, although there was a suggestion of higher rates of receipt by the never married. In contrast to our earlier analysis of living arrangements, gender has a significant effect on the receipt of help from family members: older unpartnered women received more help than men from family members living outside of the household (odds ratio = 1.8), even after controlling for age, social status, living arrangements and health. Using the BHPS we found that there were no significant gender differences among older unmarried individuals in the likelihood of having living children once age and marital status were controlled for. Thus, the fact that unmarried older women in the GHS were more likely to receive family help than men was not due gender differences in having living children. For the other two types of help, the results were as expected, and gender was not a significant determinant of either private or public help.

Discussion and conclusions

Italy and Britain show large differences in the proportion of unmarried older people living alone (e.g. 55 per cent in Italy compared with 84 per cent in Britain). Both countries, however, show similar levels of living alone by gender. Although our findings showed no gender differences in the probability of living alone in *either* country, some variables were significant only for women. In Italy, education and age were only significantly associated with living alone for women. Education may be a significant determinant for women and not for men in Italy, as education serves to increase both material resources, which enable residential independence, and options in living arrangements. In Britain, poor health and the presence of living children significantly decreased the likelihood of living alone among older unmarried women but not men, suggesting that women may be more likely to use co-residence as an option when health problems occur and when they have children. These results support previous research that has shown no gender differences in living arrangements among older unmarried individuals (de Jong Gierveld *et al.* 2001).

With respect to the receipt of care in Italy, there were no gender differences in receipt of help from any sources from outside the household. Older Italian men and women were equally likely to receive help from family members. On the other hand, in Britain, older unmarried women were more likely to receive help from family members outside the household, while there were no statistically significant gender differences in the receipt of private or public help. Receipt of private help in both countries is not gender driven, even though studies have suggested that financial resources are unevenly distributed between older men and women.

Our findings showed no gender differences in the receipt of help in Italy, whereas in Britain women were more likely to receive family help. In Italy, the family may be performing the helper role regardless of the sex of the older person receiving the assistance. These results are in line with the familism perspective, which hypothesizes that family members consider their own well-being and their family's well-being to be the same, so that help is provided to each member of the network regardless of the individual characteristics of the person receiving the help (Dalla Zuanna 2001). In Italy, parents and adult children continue to have a strong relationship, even when the latter move away in order to form their own families. The 1998 IMF shows that 95 per cent of elderly people with children have at least weekly contact with them, and the percentages are almost identical for men and women. The same picture emerges when contacts with siblings are considered. Since children are more likely to be their parents' carers, a family system that provides strong connections between generations is less likely to create privileged dyads between carer and cared for.

Gender differences in the receipt of family help in Britain may reflect men's decreased involvement in family life, which reduces the likelihood of receiving help in old age. Several studies show that, for example, divorced and widowed men have significantly less contact with their children than their female counterparts (Goldscheider 1994; Silverstein 1995; Goldscheider and Lawton 1998). Other hypotheses could include the fact that older unmarried women may be more likely to ask for help or their larger social networks may enable greater exchanges of assistance (Shye *et al.* 1995). Therefore, a family system largely based on individual relations may encourage interaction between particular dyads, e.g. the mother–daughter dyad. It is well known that among family carers, daughters are most likely to provide help. Furthermore, older women are more likely to have contacts with children and siblings than men (Jarvis 1993). British older unmarried women are more likely to receive help perhaps because they are more involved in help exchanges within the family. Moreover, in our sources of data, the questions on help focused on problems with ADL/IADL, where relatives are often the privileged helpers: it is possible that for other types of help, gender differences may be weaker. The evidence of no gender differences in the receipt of public help shows that men and women are equally likely to receive help from the public system. This suggests that women are not more likely to use public services than men because they have greater knowledge of the services offered.

This chapter shows no evidence to suggest that unpartnered older women are more or less able to cope with living alone than comparable men, as they were neither more nor less likely to live alone or to receive public or private help. In Britain we found a gender difference in receiving help from family members living outside the household, which is most likely to reflect women's greater and earlier investment in family life. If gender differences in help received by older people continue, and if individualism – as opposed to familism – develops further in northern Europe (or indeed in southern Europe), then the care of older men without a spouse may become an increasingly problematic issue, as the willingness of relatives to provide assistance may decrease.

Acknowledgements

This research is part of an Italian Ministry for University and Scientific Research funded project entitled 'Gender and Demography in Developed Countries'. We are grateful to Professor Antonella Pinnelli, coordinator of the project at the University 'La Sapienza', and to the other project members for their help and advice.

The BHPS and GHS data used in this chapter were made available through the Data Archive, University of Essex. The GHS data were collected by the Social Survey Division of the Office for National Statistics (ONS), and the BHPS data were originally collected by the ESRC Research Centre on Microsocial Change at the University of Essex (now incorporated within the Institute for Social and Economic Research). Neither the original collectors of the data nor the Archive bear any responsibility for the analyses or interpretations presented here.

References

Arber, S. and Cooper, H. (1999) Gender differences in health in later life: the new paradox?, *Social Science and Medicine*, 48: 61–76.

Arber, S., Gilbert, G. N. and Evandrou, M. (1988) Gender, household composition and receipt of domiciliary services by elderly disabled people, *Journal of Social Policy*, 17: 153–75.

Arber, S. and Ginn, J. (1995a) Gender differences in the relationship between paid employment and informal care, *Work, Employment and Society*, 9: 445–71.

Arber, S. and Ginn, J. (eds) (1995b) *Connecting Gender and Ageing: A Sociological Approach*. Buckingham: Open University Press.

Banfield, E. (1958) *The Moral Basis of a Backward Society*. Chicago: Free Press/University of Chicago.

Bridgwood, A. (2000) *People Aged 65 and Over*. London: Office of National Statistics.

Bridgwood, A., Lilly, R., Thomas, M., Bacon, J., Sykes, W. and Morris, S. (2000) *Living in Britain: Results from the 1998 General Household Survey*. London: The Stationery Office.

Dalla Zuanna, G. (2001) The banquet of Aeolus: a familistic interpretation of Italy's lowest low fertility, *Demographic Research*, 4: 133–61.

DaVanzo, J. and Goldscheider, F. K. (1990) Coming home again: returns to the parental home of young adults, *Population Studies*, 44: 241–55.

de Jong Gierveld, J., de Valk, H. and Blommesteijn, M. (2001) Living arrangements of older persons and family support in less developed countries. In *Living Arrangements of Older Persons: Critical Issues and Policy Responses*, Special issue nos 42/43. New York: United Nations.

Ginn, J. and Arber, S. (1996) Gender, age and attitudes to retirement in mid-life, *Ageing and Society*, 16: 27–55.

Glaser, K. and Tomassini, C. (2000) Proximity of older women to their children: a comparison of Britain and Italy, *The Gerontologist*, 40: 729–37.

Goldscheider, F. K. (1994). Divorce and remarriage: effects on the elderly population, *Reviews in Clinical Gerontology*, 4: 253–9.

Goldscheider, F. K. and Lawton, L. (1998) Family experiences and the erosion of support for intergenerational coresidence, *Journal of Marriage and the Family*, 60: 623–32.

Henretta, J. C., Hill, M. S., Soldo, B. J. and Wolf, D. A. (1997) Selection of children to provide care: the effect of earlier parental transfers, *Journal of Gerontology: Series B, Special Issue*, 52B: 110–19.

Hugman, R. (1994) *Ageing and the Care of Older People in Europe*. New York: St. Martin's Press.

Iacovou, M. (2000) The living arrangements of elderly Europeans. Working paper 9, European Panel Analysis Group (EAPG), Institute for Social and Economic Research, University of Essex.

Jarvis, C. (1993) Family and friends in old age, and the implications for informal support: evidence from the British Social Attitudes Survey of 1986. Working paper 6, Age Concern Institute of Gerontology, London.

Kinsella, K. and Gist, Y. J. (1998) *Gender and Aging. Mortality and Health*, International Brief IB/98–2. Washington, DC: US Department of Commerce, Bureau of the Census.

Kinsella, K. and Velkoff, V. A. (2001) *An Aging World: 2001*. Washington, DC: US Government Printing Office.

Lamura, G., Melchiorre, M. G. and Mengani M. (1999) Caring for the care-givers: challenges for Italian social policy. In *Ageing in a Gendered World: Women's Issues and Identities*. Santo Domingo: UN-INSTRAW.

Lawton, L., Silverstein, M. and Bengtson, V. (1994) Affection, social contact, and geographic distance between adult children and their parents, *Journal of Marriage and the Family*, 56: 57–68.

Pampel, F. C. (1992) Trends in living alone among the elderly in Europe. In A. Rogers (ed.) *Elderly Migration and Population Redistribution: A Comparative Study*. London: Belhaven Press.

Phillipson, C., Bernard, M., Phillips, J. and Ogg, J. (2001) *The Family and Community Life of Older People*. London: Routledge.

Pickard, L., Wittenberg, R., Comas-Herrera, A., Darton, R. and Davies, B. (2002) Community care for frail older people: analysis using the 1998/9 General Household Survey, mimeo, Personal Social Services Research Unit, University of Kent.

Reher, D. (1998) Family ties in Western Europe: persistent contrasts, *Population and Development Review*, 24: 203–34.

Rosenmayr, L. and Köckeis, E. (1963) Propositions for a sociological theory of aging and the family, *International Social Science Journal*, 15: 410–26.

Scott, A. and Wenger, G. C. (1995) Gender and social support networks in later life. In S. Arber and J. Ginn (eds) *Connecting Gender and Ageing: A Sociological Approach*. Buckingham: Open University Press.

Shaw, C. (1999) 1996-based population projections by legal marital status for England and Wales, *Population Trends*, 95: 23–32.

Shye, D., Mullooly, J. P., Freeborn, D. K. and Pope, C. R. (1995) Gender differences in the relationship between social network support and mortality: a longitudinal study of an elderly cohort, *Social Science and Medicine*, 41: 935–47.

Silverstein, M. (1995) Stability and change in temporal distance between the elderly and their children, *Demography*, 32: 29–45.

Spitze, G. and Logan, J. (1990) Sons, daughters, and intergenerational social support, *Journal of Marriage and the Family*, 52: 420–30.

Spitze, G. and Ward, R. (2000) Gender, marriage, and expectations for personal care, *Research on Ageing*, 22: 451–69.

Sundström, G. (1994) Care by families: an overview of trends. In *Caring for Frail Elderly People. New Directions in Care, Volume 14*. Paris: OECD Social Policy Studies.

Tomassini, C. (1998) La tipologia familiare delle donne anziane: mutamenti demografici o scelte individuali? Doctoral thesis in demographics, University of Padova.

Tomassini, C. and Wolf, D. (2000) Stability and change in the living arrangements of older Italian women: 1990–1995, *Genus*, 56: 203–19.

Velkoff, V. A. and Lawson, V. A. (1998) *Gender and Aging: Caregiving*. Washington, DC: Bureau of the Census.

Walker, A. (1993) *Age and Attitudes: Main Results from a Eurobarometer Survey*. Brussels: Commission of the European Communities.

Warnes, A. and Ford, R. (1995) Migration and family care. In I. Allen and E. Perkins (eds) *The Future of Family Care for Older People*. London: HMSO.

Wolf, D. A. (1994) The elderly and their kin: patterns of availability and access. In L. G. Martin and S. H. Preston (eds) *Demography of Aging*. Washington, DC: Academy Press.

Wolf, D. A. (1995) Changes in the living arrangements of older women: an international study, *The Gerontologist*, 35: 724–31.

9

SHARING THE CRUST? GENDER, PARTNERSHIP STATUS AND INEQUALITIES IN PENSION ACCUMULATION

Debora Price and Jay Ginn

People over state pension age are on average much poorer than those under state pension age, and most people over state pension age are women. The predominance of women among pensioners is in part because of the historic inequality in the state pension age between men (65) and women (60), but is mostly the result of men's higher mortality rates, so that women are more likely to survive into old age than men. The 2001 UK Census (Office for National Statistics 2002a) shows that while the ratio of women to men in their sixties is 1.07, this rises to 1.29 in their seventies, 1.91 in their eighties, and 3.46 in their nineties.

With growing privatization of the pension system in the UK over the past thirty years, relative poverty or wealth in later life has been increasingly linked to participation during the working life in pension schemes designed to supplement the basic state pension: additional state schemes, occupational or other private pension schemes. This is because the full basic state pension (£75.50 per week for a single person in 2002/3) now pays far less than the minimum for means tested benefits (£98.15), and has declined in value in real terms since 1980, when it was indexed to prices rather than growth in average earnings. Since women have much lower employment participation rates than men and are far more likely than men to work part-time and/or for low pay (Kingsmill 2001), women have been disadvantaged in these supplementary pension schemes. The UK also has the highest gender pay gap in Europe, and even when human capital and other relevant variables are held constant, women working part-time earn much less per hour than both men and women working full-time (Anderson *et al.* 2001; Harkness 2002).

Further, employed women are much less likely than men to have access to an occupational pension scheme (Ginn and Arber 1993, 2000).

Despite major social changes since the 1940s, when Beveridge's welfare state was predicated on the assumption that men would be the breadwinners and women would perform unpaid work as housewives and mothers (Beveridge 1942), women still provide the bulk of unpaid family caring. Since financial status in later life in the UK is so closely linked with employment and earnings, it is also inextricably linked to women's family roles across the life course, in particular their maternal and partnership history, which impact heavily on their participation in paid work.

This chapter is concerned with the ways in which changing patterns of partnership formation, especially increases in the proportion of people who are separated or divorced, have implications for gender differentials in pension income. We first review trends in divorce and cohabitation and the likely pension consequences for later life, and then present analyses of employment participation and pension arrangements of men and women by partnership status, and maternal status of women.

Trends in partnership formation and dissolution

Many changes in patterns of family formation and dissolution are taking place. The average age of first marriage is increasing, as is the average age at which mothers have their first child. Marital status has become more diverse, with more people choosing not to marry, many people cohabiting before or instead of marrying and an increase in people marrying more than once. Almost a third of all children are born to cohabiting couples who are not formally married (Office for National Statistics 2002b). Cohabiting relationships, however, rarely last more than a few years, ending either in marriage or dissolution (Ermisch and Francesconi 2000). For those who do marry, the rise in the divorce rate is well known: it is estimated that four out of every ten marriages entered into in the UK in 1996 will end in divorce (Shaw 1999), the highest rate in the EU (Barlow et al. 2002). In the early 1970s, the proportions of widows and of separated and divorced women heading lone mother households was approximately equal, but divorce is now the main route to single motherhood (Haskey 2002). Remarriage after divorce has 'declined dramatically' over the past 25 years, with large increases in cohabitation among divorcees (Haskey 1999: 19). In short, the likelihood of individuals having multiple changes in partnership status over the life course has grown, and for women the age of childbearing has become less predictable.

The various categories of 'marital status' impose different structural and normative constraints on men's and women's abilities to accumulate pensions. For example, women caring for children or a disabled partner can be credited by the government with pension contributions to state pensions. State pension income varies according to marital and partnership status, legal rights to assets and income may be acquired and obligations may be conferred only on formal marriage or legal divorce, and workforce issues and childcare constraints vary according to partnership status and the age and number of children in a family. Cultural norms about childrearing and couples' beliefs about the appropriate relationship between each partner's employment effort and earnings vary widely in the population. The way men and women share household money or apportion household expenditure may depend on their marital status. Further, the extent to which women might reasonably expect to be financially dependent on a man in retirement is influenced by their marital status at any given time. Thus a woman might participate in paid work, but decide she need not belong to a private pension scheme since her husband has a good pension.

Living alone and income in later life

In Chapter 1, the anticipated changes in the divorced population were discussed, showing the estimated rapid ageing of this group as a whole, and increases in the proportions over 60 who are divorced. The growth in the proportion of older divorced people makes it urgent to consider how pension incomes vary with marital status. Bardasi and Jenkins (2002) highlight the substantially higher risk of poverty for women over 60 who live alone compared with other older people, particularly if they are divorced. Divorced men and women forgo the possibility of a survivor's pension, even if this had been an expectation while married. Ginn (2001) showed that in 1998 divorced and separated women over 65 had a median income of only £89 per week, compared with £112 for never married single women and £100 for widows. Among men aged over 65 in the mid-1990s, divorced men had a slightly lower average income than other men, and a high proportion, 17 per cent, relied on Income Support. At this time, over twice the proportion of older divorced women were in receipt of Income Support (37 per cent), compared with 15 per cent of older women who had never married (Ginn and Price 2002).

Pension income is an important indicator of financial well-being for older people, but tends to be lowest among women living alone (Department for Work and Pensions 2002: Chapter 6). Almost 40 per cent of women aged 65 to 74 and 60 per cent of women aged over 75 live alone, whereas for men the percentages are only 19 and 33 per cent respectively (Walker *et al.* 2001).

Divorced and separated women must generally rely on their own pension income in retirement. Recent changes in divorce law permitting pension sharing on divorce are not likely to make much difference to the vast majority of divorcees (Price 2003). In contrast, a widow may have a survivor's pension in addition to her own pension. A survivor's pension is typically only half of the deceased spouse's pension. Even this income may be reduced due to the trend in the developed world away from occupational defined benefit (DB) pension schemes to defined contribution (DC) pension schemes. DB schemes are generally based on the employee's final salary and almost always include a survivor's pension. DC schemes invest pension contributions in a fund that is used to buy an income for life (an annuity) from an insurance company on or after retirement. Apart from a small element required by law to replace the inherited portion of the state second pension, the person buying the annuity can choose whether to make provision for a widow or widower after his or her death, but if he or she decides to do this, then the pension during his or her lifetime is smaller. Because of this trade-off, retirees may decide not to make any such provision for a surviving spouse after their death. In this way, widows may suddenly find their husband has left them with no additional pension, apart from that replacing the state second pension. Some countries (for example, Canada and the USA) require a husband to buy a pension for a surviving spouse unless his wife has formally signed a waiver agreeing to forgo the benefit, but this is not the case in Britain. The Pickering Report (2002) recommends that survivors' benefits be phased out even for DB occupational pension schemes, although this proposal is not likely to be adopted. The trend from DB to DC pensions with smaller survivor benefits makes women's acquisition of their own independent pensions increasingly important.

Data and methods

This chapter examines how full-time employment and the pension acquisition of working age women and men differ according to their partnership status (whether married, cohabiting, divorced/separated or single), focusing on to what extent maternal status (for women) and occupational class interact with partnership status, leading to different outcomes. We analyse three years of the British General Household Survey (GHS) combined: 1993–4, 1994–5 and 1995–6 (OPCS 1996, 1997, 1998). The GHS is a cross-sectional probability sample survey of about 9000 households per annum and in the mid-1990s had a response rate of about 80 per cent (Walker et al. 2001: Appendix B); the three combined years yield a sample of over 14,000 men and 17,000 women aged 20 to 59. Marital histories are available for men and women, allowing classification of those who are cohabiting according to whether they have ever been married. Those who were divorced or separated are grouped together for most of the analyses. Widows and widowers ($n =$ 480) and same-sex cohabitants ($n = 51$) have been excluded from the analysis because of their small numbers.

The variables included in the analysis were coded in the following way. Occupational class is based on the individual's current or last occupation and grouped into three categories: professionals, managers and employers; intermediate and routine non-manual; and manual occupations. 'Employment' and 'employed' include the self-employed, and full-time employment means those undertaking paid work for 31 or more hours per week. Children in the family unit include children under 16 and those aged under 18 who are still in full-time education or training. Individuals are described as contributing to pension schemes if they are paying contributions out of their earnings, or the government pays a National Insurance rebate into their private pension schemes or their employers contribute to their pension schemes as part of their employment package.

Measuring levels of pension saving

Since this chapter is concerned with the extent to which pension entitlements are being accumulated, we group individuals according to their level of pension saving:

1 *Basic state pension*. Those not in paid employment or on low earnings – below the 'lower earnings limit'[1] – are currently building at best only a basic state pension. Because the basic pension is very low and declining over time, individuals who only have this source of household income in retirement will qualify for means tested benefits in later life.[2]

2 *Compulsory second tier*. Those earning above the lower earnings limit must contribute to a second pension.[3] They may contribute to the State Earnings Related Pension (SERPS), now renamed the State Second Pension (S2P), or choose to contract out of the second-tier state pension and into a private pension. If individuals have only the basic pension and this compulsory minimum level of second-tier pension in retirement, they are likely to qualify for means tested benefits[2], either at retirement or subsequently (Falkingham and Rake 2001).

3 *Voluntary additional pension provision: third-tier pensions*. People can choose to pay additional contributions into a personal or occupational pension scheme, and some employers contribute extra to an employee's personal pension scheme. Theoretically, not all occupational pension schemes have to provide a better pension than SERPS/S2P but the vast majority do, and for the purposes of this analysis, this has been assumed. In these ways, pension contributions are being made above the statutory minimum, potentially building a good level of entitlements for the individuals concerned, so that they are the least likely to require means tested benefits in retirement.

For much of this analysis, the first two groups have been combined to focus on those individuals contributing to what we refer to here as 'third-tier pensions'. Research has shown that these third-tier pensions are the largest source of income inequality among pensioners (Johnson and Stears 1995) and are largely responsible for income differentiation according to gender and previous occupational class (Ginn and Arber 1991, 1999; Ginn 2003).

Gender, paid work and marital status

Women are less likely than men to be employed or earning enough to contribute to a pension scheme. Women comprise two-thirds of those aged 20 to 59 who are not earning and 80 per cent of those earning below the lower earnings limit, mostly part-timers. These women are not accumulating any pension provision apart from, at best, the basic state pension (see note 1). Gender differences in employment, hours of work and earnings have important implications for participation in third-tier pension schemes. Whereas 56 per cent of men aged 20 to 59 are in an occupational scheme or making voluntary contributions to a personal pension, the corresponding proportion for women is only 31 per cent (authors' analysis).

Partnership status also influences levels of pension saving, but in different ways for men and women. Partnership and maternal status affect women's hours in employment, reflecting highly gendered roles in breadwinning, home-making and childrearing (Yeandle 1999). Part-time working reduces occupational scheme membership largely because of differential availability of such schemes according to type of job and occupational sector (Ginn and Arber 1993). Differences in employment status are illustrated in Figure 9.1, which shows the percentages of men and women working full-time according to partnership status and age group.

Figure 9.1 shows that married men in each five-year age group are the most likely to be working full-time. Almost 90 per cent of married men are in full-time work from age 25 to 49. Men who cohabit are more likely to be employed full-time in all age groups over 25 than are divorced/separated men or those who have never married. Divorced and separated men are far less likely than married or cohabiting men to be working full-time, despite few caring for small children (only 3 per cent for a child under 11 and 6 per cent for a child under 18). Apart from the age group 30 to 34, the proportion of divorced or separated men working full-time never rises above 70 per cent, drops to below 60 per cent after age 45 and finally falls to around 30 per cent after 55. Their low employment rate is very similar to that of single men.

A different pattern is evident for women. The groups least likely to be caring for young children – never married women and never married cohabitants – are the most likely to be working full-time until age 50. Among married women, only around 40 per cent in their twenties work full-time, falling further to 30 per cent in their thirties and rising slightly among those in their forties. Married women are the least likely of all women to work full-time after the age of 45. Married women's low full-time employment rate, fewer than 40 per cent across all age groups over 25, illustrates their vulnerability to an inadequate pension of their own if they divorce or are widowed.

Divorced/separated women's full-time employment rate is lower than that of any other group among women in their twenties. From age 30 to 44 their rate of full-time employment resembles that of married women, despite the difficulties of combining full-time employment with lone parenthood.

Figure 9.1 Percentage in full-time work (at least 31 hours per week), by marital/ partnership status and age group, men and women aged 20 to 59.

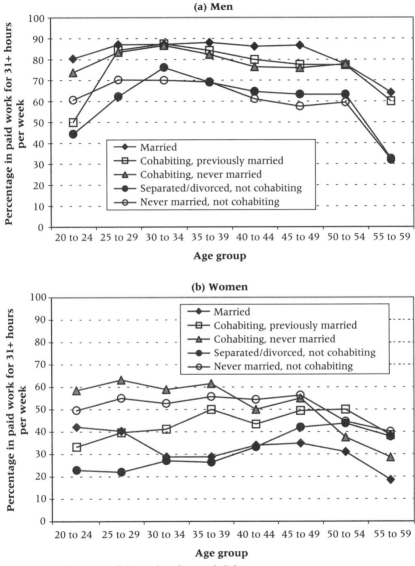

Widow(er)s and same-sex cohabitants have been excluded.

Source: General Household Survey (1994–6), authors' analysis.

In contrast, the full-time employment of cohabiting women who were previously married is closer to that of never married cohabiting and single women from age 30 to 44. Formerly married women (whether living alone or

Figure 9.2   Percentage in full-time work (31 hours per week), according to marital/partnership status and age of the youngest dependent child in the family unit, women aged 20 to 59.

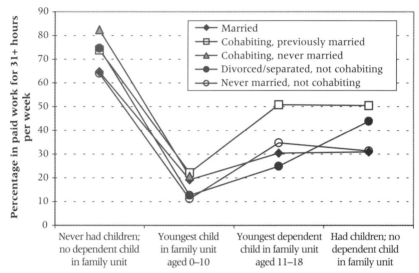

Widow(er)s and same-sex cohabitants have been excluded. Data are not shown for never married cohabitants with children aged 11 to 18 or no longer dependent (*n* < 20).
Source: General Household Survey (1994–6), authors' analysis.

cohabiting) become progressively more likely to work full-time from age 40 to 54, unlike married and never married women. These trends highlight that the labour force participation of women is related to their marital history, as well as their current partnership status.

Women's employment, dependent children and partnership status

The gendered patterns of full-time employment described above reflect women's role in childcare as well as their partnership status. This is illustrated in Figure 9.2, which shows the percentage of women working full-time according to their maternal history within each partnership category. The impact of having children is clear from the very steep downward slope between the first group (never had a child, and no dependent children in the family unit) and the second (youngest child in family unit aged 0 to 10). Where the youngest child is under 11, women divide into those who are cohabiting or married on the one hand, with about 20 per cent employed full-time, and those who are lone mothers, among whom only 10 per cent are employed full-time. While the well known structural difficulties for lone mothers in taking full-time employment (Paull and Taylor 2002) may explain their low rate of full-time employment, the rates remain very low for partnered mothers as well. Given the relatively high risk of partnership breakdown, the pension position of all these mothers is cause for concern.

A clear differentiation in full-time employment by partnership status only emerges among women with older children, among whom previously married cohabiting mothers are the most likely to be employed full-time and divorced/separated mothers least likely, with married and never married mothers falling in between. The difference between cohabiting and married mothers might reflect a greater perception of financial security among married than cohabiting mothers, with the latter perceiving that they are at greater risk of relationship breakdown than married women. It might also reflect different systems of allocating money within married and cohabiting households. These interpretations are supported by the maintenance of the full-time employment differential between married and cohabiting women after children are no longer dependent, and hence less likely to influence full-time work status.

The full-time employment rates for never married lone mothers rise steeply (from 11 to 35 per cent) when their children reach secondary school, as do the rates for previously married cohabiting mothers (from 21 to 50 per cent). The employment rates for separated/divorced and married mothers show a smaller rise (from 12 to 23 per cent, and 20 to 30 per cent respectively). It is notable that never married mothers appear to return to full-time work on average sooner than those who have been through separation or divorce. This might be because they have, on average, fewer children.

Even where all children are no longer dependent, the proportion of married mothers and never married mothers employed full-time does not increase, whereas that of divorced/separated mothers does, whether they are cohabiting or not. These latter groups are more likely than married women to have a financial need to support themselves, both currently and in retirement. While never married mothers of older children may also perceive this need, they are disproportionately likely to have low educational qualifications and to work in manual jobs (results not shown). There may be little or no financial benefit to them in taking a job if their potential wages are very low.

Women's pension scheme participation, dependent children and partnership status

Women's full-time employment is highly correlated with their likelihood of third tier pension saving, but the strength of association varies according to partnership category. For example, among those working full-time, 68 per cent of married women with no dependent children contribute to third tier pensions compared with 75 per cent of divorced/separated women with no dependent children. Among mothers working full-time who have a child aged 11 to 18, only 58 per cent of those who are married contribute to third-tier pensions, compared with 70 per cent of divorced/separated mothers and 76 per cent of never married mothers (authors' analysis).

The influence of family circumstances on women's participation in third-tier pension schemes is shown in Figure 9.3. Among those who have never had a child, divorced/separated women are the most likely to make third-tier pension contributions, whether cohabiting or not. Divorce or separation is likely to have highlighted long-term financial issues for women, making savings for pensions more salient. But divorced/separated mothers with children under 11, like other lone mothers, are the least likely to contribute to third-tier pension schemes, reflecting their low full-time employment rates (Figure 9.3). Despite divorced women's awareness of pension issues, it is likely that constraints relating to childcare reduce ability to work full-time. Among those in employment, access to an occupational pension scheme may be rare if they work part-time. Moreover, even those with access to an occupational scheme may be too financially stretched to join: they are likely to be the sole supporters of their children, as relatively few fathers pay child support (Marsh *et al.* 2001). However, once children are no longer dependent,

Figure 9.3 Percentage in third-tier pension schemes, according to marital/partnership status and age of the youngest dependent child in the family unit, women aged 20 to 59.

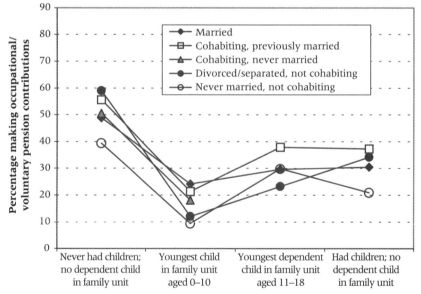

Widow(er)s and same-sex cohabitants have been excluded. Data are not shown for never married cohabitants with children aged 11 to 18 or no longer dependent (*n* < 20).

Source: General Household Survey (1994–6), authors' analysis.

formerly married women – both cohabiting and divorced/separated – are the most likely to contribute to third-tier pension schemes. Notably, though, participation rates in occupational and/or voluntary additional private pensions do not rise above 40 per cent for any group of mothers, and only 10 to 30 per cent of women with a child under 11 at home are contributing to third-tier pensions.

Thus, motherhood restricts employment and pension building, but more severely for lone than partnered mothers. There is also an indication that cohabiting women are more aware of the need for financial independence than married women. The low rates of third-tier pension coverage among women who raise children show that, given current policies to reduce state pensions, the majority of these women will retire with an independent pension income that is near to or below the level of means tested benefits.

Gender, pensions and occupational class

Our broad consideration of the gendered division of pension accumulation has so far tended to treated women (and men) as homogeneous within categories of marital and maternal status. Yet the income and receipt of pensions from private sources by men and women in later life shows differentiation according to previous occupational class (Arber 1989; Ginn and Arber 1991). Private pensions tend to perpetuate class inequalities arising during working life, in contrast to state pensions, which have a levelling effect on retirement income. There are signs that among working age women a sharper differentiation – or polarization – is emerging in mother's full time employment (McRae 1993; Glover and Arber 1995). With dramatic improvements in the educational levels of women, and inroads made by women into occupational strata previously occupied almost exclusively by men, the experience of women, while still gendered, is increasingly diverse (Crompton and Harris 1998; Warren 2000; Blackburn et al. 2001; Elliot et al. 2001).

Thus, the financial effects of separation and divorce are expected to vary with the qualifications, experience, social background, social environment, cultural assets and networking abilities of individuals. The minority of women in high status jobs have the advantage that such jobs are likely to pay more, giving more options for childcare, enabling job retention and making third-tier pension provision more affordable. These jobs are also more likely to offer an occupational pension scheme.

The experience of men is also diverse: class divisions among men have long been the focus of political and sociological analyses, and in recent years men have also faced increasing employment risk and competition from women. However, in considering occupational class differentiation among men and women, it is important to recognize that despite the recent occupational advances by women, women are still concentrated in certain less well paid social classes. Indeed, the very large degree of sex segregation in the British labour force is widely thought to be one of the important factors supporting the persistence of the gender pay gap (Walby 1997; Equal Pay Task Force 2001).

Figure 9.4 shows how for married and formerly married men and women aged 20 to 59, the level of pension saving is influenced by their occupational class (defined by current employment, or last employment for those not currently in paid work). About a third of men are professionals, employers or managers, compared with only 13 per cent of women. More than half of women are intermediate or junior non-manual workers,[4] compared with only 16 per cent of men. The remaining 50 per cent of men and 37 per cent of women are skilled, semi-skilled or unskilled manual workers. However, within this broad manual grouping, men and women have different types of jobs, with women disproportionately employed, for example, in the cleaning, catering and caring industries.

In each class category, men are far more likely to make pension provision than women (the two grey sections in the bar charts). Men show a consistent pattern according to partnership status. Married men have the highest third-tier pension coverage, formerly married cohabitants slightly lower rates, separated much lower rates and divorced men the lowest rates. A lack of pensions saving due to non-employment or earnings below the lower earnings limit (white sections in the bar charts) is most likely for divorced men, especially for manual workers, where over half of divorced men are currently accumulating only the basic state pension or less. Even among men who are professionals, employers and managers, the proportion lacking pension saving is over 30 per cent for those who are divorced, compared with just over 10 per cent of comparable married men.

Among women, there is a larger differential than for men in levels of pension saving according to occupational class, and the impact of marital/ partnership status is least in the highest class category. Among women who are professionals, managers or employers (13 per cent of married or previously married women), over half participate in third-tier pensions, with no statistically significant differences according to partnership status.

The low rate of third-tier pension saving among women who are manual workers is striking. For manual workers, separation and divorce are associated with even lower rates of third-tier pension savings than among married women. Yet divorced and separated women have no current expectation of financial support from a partner in retirement. Thus a large proportion face relying on means tested benefits in retirement.

Our analysis has shown that occupational class has a somewhat greater effect on women's level of private pension saving than on men's. For men, divorce is associated with a lack of pension saving in all class categories, but for women class and partnership status interact, with divorced and separated women in non-manual occupations showing little or no pension disadvantage relative to married, while their manual worker counterparts are the group with the poorest pension saving level.

Figure 9.4 Pension saving level according to occupational class and marital/partnership status; married or formerly married men and women aged 20 to 59.

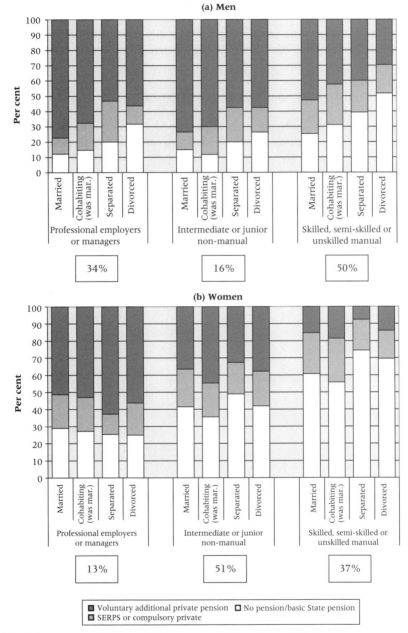

Widow(er)s, same-sex cohabitants and those never married have been excluded.

Source: General Household Survey (1994–6), authors' analysis.

While divorced professional/managerial women are the most likely group of women to be contributing to third-tier pensions, the divorced men in this occupational class are the least likely, meaning that among divorced professionals/managers women have a similar pension saving profile to men. Apart from this specific group, large gender differentials in pension scheme participation remain in each partnership status/class grouping.

Multivariate analysis of pension saving

The social factors underlying third-tier pension scheme participation are clearly complex. To elucidate which are most important, a multivariate logit analysis is presented in Table 9.1. The odds are shown of having third-tier pension coverage, relative to a reference category for which the odds have

Table 9.1 Odds ratios of third-tier pension contributions to an occupational pension scheme or private pension, men and women aged 20 to 59. ($N = 28, 524$)

	Model 1	Model 2	Model 3
Sex and marital/partnership status	†	†	†
Men, married	1.00	1.00	1.00
Men, cohabiting, previously married	0.61***	0.59***	0.66***
Men, cohabiting, never married	0.72***	0.56***	0.73***
Men, never married	0.47***	0.29***	0.70***
Men, divorced/separated	0.38***	0.30***	0.61***
Women, married	0.24***	0.20***	0.67***
Women, cohabiting, previously married	0.28***	0.24***	0.65***
Women, cohabiting, never married	0.47***	0.30***	0.66***
Women, never married	0.41***	0.25***	0.72***
Women, divorced/separated	0.20***	0.18***	0.57***
Age group	†	†	†
20–24	0.36***	0.42***	0.24***
25–34	0.87***	1.08	0.59***
35–44	1.06	1.31***	0.86**
45–54	1.00	1.00	1.00
55–59	0.45***	0.43***	0.83**
Age of youngest dependent child in family unit		†	†
No dependent children in family unit		1.00	1.00
Youngest 11–18 (still dependent)		0.66***	0.82**
Youngest 0–10		0.45***	1.04
Occupational class		†	†
Professional, managers, employers		1.00	1.00
Intermediate/junior non-manual		0.80***	1.31***
Skilled, semi-skilled or unskilled manual		0.37***	0.63***

Table 9.1 Continued

	Model 1	Model 2	Model 3
Highest educational qualification		†	†
Degree, diploma, professional		1.38***	1.22***
One or more A levels		1.00	1.00
Qualification at 16/apprenticeship		0.76***	0.91
No qualifications		0.47***	0.73***
Work hours and earnings per week			†
Works 31+ hours per week, earns £300+			1.00
Works 1–30 hours per week, earns £300+			0.43***
Works 31+ hours per week, earns £100–299			0.35***
Works 17–30 hours per week, earns £100–299			0.21***
Works 1–16 hours per week, earns £100–299			0.12***
Works 31+ hours per week, earns £1–99			0.06***
Works 17–30 hours per week, earns £1–99			0.05***
Works 1–16 hours per week, earns £1–99			0.01***
No earnings from paid work			0.00***
–2LL ratio	35,949	68,175	21,094
Change in –2LL ratio	–3205	–3150	–11,705
Change in degrees of freedom	–13	–7	–8

Significance of difference from the reference category: **$p \leq 0.01$, ***$p \leq 0.001$.
Significance of variable in improving model †$p \leq 0.001$.

Source: General Household Surveys (1994–6), authors' analysis, widow(er)s and same-sex cohabitants excluded.

been defined as one. In Model 1, odds ratios are shown according to sex and marital/partnership status, with married men as the reference category, and controlling for age group. Married men are the most likely to contribute to third-tier pensions, divorced/separated women the least. In Model 2, the age of the youngest dependent child in the family unit is included as a control variable, as are occupational class and highest educational qualification. Other analyses (not shown) found that once the age of the youngest child had been included in the model, controlling for educational level and social class had little effect on the odds ratios according to partnership status. Model 3 additionally controls for work status and earnings.

Model 1 highlights the differences among women, with cohabiting never married women the most likely to have third-tier pensions once age is controlled, but even here the odds ratio is only 0.47 relative to a married man. In contrast with married men, who are the most likely to be contributing to third-tier pensions, married women are less likely to contribute than never married or cohabiting women, with an odds ratio of only 0.24. Only divorced/separated women are less likely than married women to contribute to third-tier pensions, odds of 0.20 relative to married men.

All models show the large pension advantage of married men and highlight the substantial disadvantage of those who are separated/divorced. The odds of a divorced or separated man making third-tier pension contributions are only 0.38 of those for married men. Therefore, divorced and separated men are worse off than never married women.

After taking account of parental status and of measured differences in human capital, divorced/separated men have a low odds ratio of third-tier pension saving, 0.30, similar to never married men at 0.29 (Model 2). Divorced/separated women have an even lower odds ratio, 0.18, lower than any other group of men or women. Even after including employment and earnings in the model, both men and women who are divorced/separated have relatively low odds ratios of third-tier pension saving, 0.61 and 0.57 respectively (Model 3). Although the difference from married men is partly explained by these labour market variables, a residual pension disadvantage remains for men who are divorced/separated.

The relatively high likelihood of third-tier pension saving among never married cohabiting women (odds ratio of 0.47) can be partly explained by childlessness and higher educational qualifications/social class among this group of women (Model 2): once maternal status, social class and educational qualifications are controlled, the odds ratio decreases to 0.30. They are still the most likely third-tier pension participants among women, but in a far worse position than married men. Married women and separated/divorced women are almost equally unlikely to contribute to third-tier pensions, after controlling for the age of the youngest dependent child, class and education, with odds ratios of 0.20 and 0.18 respectively. This is perhaps surprising considering that divorced/separated women have the disadvantage of being lone mothers, but may reflect their greater perception of the need for an independent pension, compared with married women. Previously married women who are cohabiting have an odds ratio of only 0.24. Controlling for children in the family explains far more of the variation among women of different marital/partnership status than it does among men.

Controlling for work hours and earnings greatly reduces the pension inequality between men and women (Model 3), indicating that women's pension disadvantage is mainly due to inequalities in employment participation and earnings, rather than to educational level or occupational class. Married men retain their pension advantage even when earnings and work hours are controlled. The disadvantage of divorced/separated men and women is reduced, but the odds remain about 0.60 of the odds for married men.

Men and women of differing marital status tend to vary in age and parental status. Never married women are on average younger than other groups (analysis not shown) and the logit analysis shows that they are less likely to have dependent children and more likely to be highly educated and/or in a higher occupational class than other women, since when these three variables are included in Model 2 the odds ratio decreases from 0.41 to 0.25. Married and formerly married women have much in common, being more likely than the never married to have dependent children, lower hours of work and pay and, in due course, lower pensions.

For men, whether they are currently living with a wife or partner has more bearing on their employment participation and pensions than whether they have formerly been married. Married men are the most likely to be in full-time employment and contributing to a third-tier pension scheme. Cohabiting men are far more likely to be employed full-time than divorced/separated or single men. Divorced/separated men who are not cohabiting have much lower levels of pension scheme participation than other men, and are surprisingly similar in this respect to divorced/separated women, other things being equal.

For women, the explanation for the disadvantaged pension position of those whose marriage has broken down lies largely (but not wholly) in the financial implications of caring for children, especially as a lone parent, and gender disadvantages in the paid workforce, but for men the explanation is less clear. It is not possible with these data to identify the reason for their lower probability of saving in a third-tier pension scheme. In a longitudinal study of male unemployment where the correlation between divorce and unemployment in men was noted, Lampard (1994) found that in some cases unemployment precedes divorce and in others divorce precedes unemployment. Thus, there are three types of causal explanation here. First, men may have characteristics making them more likely to become both non-employed and divorced, e.g. poor health, or particular personality characteristics. Second, unemployment may place sufficient stress on a relationship to cause its breakdown, or lead to higher divorce rates where there is no financial advantage to staying married. Third, divorce may cause deterioration in mental health, difficulty in coping with work or an unwillingness to work to avoid paying child and spousal maintenance.

Issues relating to divorced men's disadvantageous employment, earnings and pensions position have hardly been addressed in sociological analyses, where the emphasis following divorce has been on the problems of lone motherhood rather than male unemployment. However, employment issues are important for an understanding of the social implications of divorce and separation for men and their families, and for the pension accumulation of divorced men.

Conclusion

Differences in marital and partnership status impact significantly on pension scheme participation. The way in which this happens varies over the life course according to gender and social circumstances. Changes in partnership and family formation, changes in patterns of childbearing, periods of lone parenthood and financial disadvantages or unemployment associated with periods of separation and divorce are essential parts of the explanation for financial inequalities in later life.

Men provide relatively well for themselves under the current pension system in Britain compared with women. Their greater full-time participation in the labour market and higher earnings mean that more than half of working age men were making some third-tier pension provision for themselves through an occupational scheme and/or voluntary pension contributions in the mid-1990s. This contrasts with only a third of women aged between 20 and 59 who were making such provision.

The gender division of labour in the breadwinner/homemaker family model, even in the mid-1990s, is reflected in the large gap in pension scheme participation between married men and married women – a fourfold difference in the odds of third-tier pension participation, which persists even when there are no longer dependent children in the family unit. Married women continue to depend heavily on their husbands for pension provision. In the past such unequal distribution would have been experienced almost entirely in the private sphere between partners. With the much higher risk now of divorce or separation, this financial inequality has public policy implications, since an increasing proportion of women will have neither adequate pensions of their own in later life, nor financial support from a partner.

Pension participation histories are deeply gendered and culture bound. Most British married women are dependent on either a man or the state for pension provision, whereas most men, once married, participate in additional pension schemes as part of their 'breadwinning' role. Given the low level of the basic state pension and second-tier pensions in Britain, most working age women risk individual poverty in retirement through lack of participation in third-tier pensions. Even for those who participate at some stage in voluntary additional pension schemes, the time period during which they do this may only be a fraction of their working lives, on relatively low earnings, either at a young age prior to childbearing or at an age relatively close to retirement when investments have not long to grow. For women who do not remain married, or have many changes in marital or partnership status, this general disadvantage is compounded.

For men, the pension differences according to partnership status are also substantial. While few divorced or separated men care for dependent children, the very high rates of non-employment irrespective of social class among this group of men have a significant adverse effect on pension accumulation. Even for those in paid work, men's participation in third-tier pensions is markedly lower among the separated and divorced. While this might be in part because lower paid men are more likely to become separated/divorced, this lower level is possibly also due to other calls on their income, such as maintenance payments or divestment of capital as a result of the divorce itself (for example, the transfer of a house to a former wife), or because of difficulties in coping or failing health. While these men may well re-partner, and higher pay may make them more likely to re-partner, the rates of third-tier pension contributions among cohabiting formerly married men remain lower than those of married men.

In sum, divorced and separated people are at particularly high risk of poverty in later life. For divorced/separated women this matches the individual poverty and lack of independent pension building of married women – a situation from which they find it difficult to recover if they are caring for young children and in the part-time labour force. The impact of marital and partnership status in the lives of men has been little researched in terms of later life financial inequalities, but this chapter shows that changes in society associated with the increase in divorce and cohabitation may have far-reaching consequences. Financial circumstances in later life can no longer be considered independently of previous family formation and partnership history, for both men and women.

Acknowledgements

We are grateful to the Office for National Statistics for permission to use the General Household Survey data, to the Data Archive, University of Essex, for access to the data and to the Economic and Social Research Council for funding the research. The analysis is our responsibility alone.

Notes

1 The lower earnings limit is a government-defined threshold below which the basic state pension and second pensions are not compulsorily accumulated. In the years examined here, the lower earnings limits for employees were £56–58 per week. Accordingly, those classified into this category may not be building any pension at all. They may, however, be acquiring credits to the basic state pension, if they can claim certain 'deemed credits' at times of unemployment or sickness, or through 'Home Responsibilities Protection' for certain carers. The GHS does not differentiate these various individuals, and these distinctions are not made here.

2 Individuals may be disqualified if they have savings exceeding an exempt amount (£6000 in 2003). They may also be disqualified by their partner's income/savings.

3 The government now credits those earning between the lower earnings limit (currently £3900 per annum) and the lower earnings threshold (currently £10,800 per annum) with contributions to both the basic state pension and the State Second Pension.

4 This category combines occupations that might be viewed as quite different: junior non-manual workers include office staff, whereas intermediate non-manual workers include teachers, nurses and local government officers, for example. The latter are more likely to carry occupational pension schemes as part of their remuneration package.

References

Anderson, T., Forth, J., Metcalf, H. and Kirby, S. (2001) *The Gender Pay Gap*. London: Women's Equality Unit.

Arber, S. (1989) Class and the Elderly, *Social Studies Review*, 4(3): 90–5.

Bardasi, E. and Jenkins, S. (2002) *Income in Later Life: Work History Matters*. Bristol: Policy Press.

Barlow, A., Duncan, S., James, G. and Park, A. (2002) Just a piece of paper? Marriage and cohabitation. In A. Park, J. Curtice, K. Thomson, L. Jarvis and C. Bromley (eds) *British Social Attitudes: Public Policy, Social Ties. The 18th Report 2001/2002*. London: Sage.

Beveridge, Sir W. (1942) *Social Insurance and Allied Services*, Cmd 6404. London: HMSO.

Blackburn, R. M., Brooks, B. and Jarman, J. (2001) Occupational stratification – the vertical dimension of occupational segregation, *Work, Employment and Society*, 15(3): 511–38.

Crompton, R. and Harris, F. (1998) Gender relations and employment: the impact of occupation, *Work, Employment and Society*, 12(2): 297–315.

Department for Work and Pensions (2002) *Households Below Average Income 1994/5–2000/01*. Leeds: Corporate Document Services.

Elliot, J., Dale, A. and Egerton, M. (2001) The influence of qualifications on women's work histories, employment status and earnings at age 33, *European Sociological Review*, 17(2): 145–68.

Equal Pay Task Force (2001) *Just Pay: A Report to the Equal Opportunities Commission*. Manchester: Equal Opportunities Commission.

Ermisch, J. and Francesconi, M. (2000) Cohabitation in Great Britain: not for long, but here to stay, *Journal of the Royal Statistical Society Series A – Statistics in Society*, 163: 153–71.

Falkingham, J. and Rake, K. (2001) Modelling the gender impact of British pension reforms, in J. Ginn, D. Street and S. Arber (eds) *Women, Work and Pensions*. Buckingham: Open University Press.

Ginn, J. (2001) Pensions for women of all ages. In *All Our Tomorrows*. London: Eunomia Publications.

Ginn, J. (2003) *Gender, Pensions and the Lifecourse*. Bristol: Policy Press.

Ginn, J. and Arber, S. (1991) Gender, class and income inequalities in later life, *British Journal of Sociology*, 42(3): 369–96.

Ginn, J. and Arber, S. (1993) Pension penalties: the gendered division of occupational welfare, *Work, Employment and Society*, 7(1): 47–70.

Ginn, J. and Arber, S. (1999) Women's pension poverty: prospects and options for change. In S. Walby (ed.) *New Agendas for Women*. London: Macmillan.

Ginn, J. and Arber, S. (2000) Personal pension take-up in the 1990s in relation to position in the labour market, *Journal of Social Policy*, 29(2): 205–28.

Ginn, J. and Price, D. (2002) Do divorced women catch up in pension building?, *Child and Family Law Quarterly*, 14(2): 157–73.

Glover, J. and Arber, S. (1995) Polarisation in mothers' employment, *Gender, Work and Organisation*, 2(4): 165–79.

Harkness, S. (2002) *Low Pay, Times of Work and Gender*. London: Equal Opportunities Commission.

Haskey, J. (1999) Divorce and remarriage in England and Wales, *Population Trends*, 95: 18–22.

Haskey, J. (2002) One-parent families – and the dependent children living in them – in Great Britain, *Population Trends*, 109: 46–58.

Johnson, P. and Stears, G. (1995) Pensioner income inequality, *Fiscal Studies*, 16(4): 69–93.

Kingsmill, D. (2001) *Report into Women's Employment and Pay*. London: Cabinet Office/ DTI/DfES.

Lampard, R. (1994) An examination of the relationship between marital dissolution and unemployment. In D. Gallie, C. Marsh and C. Vogler (eds) *Social Change and the Experience of Unemployment*. Oxford: Oxford University Press.

McRae, S. (1993) Returning to work after childbearing: opportunities and inequalities, *European Sociological Review*, 9(2): 125–37.

Marsh, A., McKay, S., Smith, A. and Stephenson, A. (2001) *Low Income Families in Britain. Work, Welfare and Social Security, DSS Research Report No. 138*. Leeds: Corporate Document Services.

Office for National Statistics (2002a) *Census 2001 Demographic Data* (http:// www.statistics.gov.uk/census2001/demographic_uk.asp). Accessed 17 December 2002.

Office for National Statistics (2002b) *Social Trends*. London: The Stationery Office.

OPCS (1996) *General Household Survey, 1993–1994*. Computer file. Colchester: The Data Archive.

OPCS (1997) *General Household Survey, 1994–1995*. Computer file. Colchester: The Data Archive.

OPCS (1998) *General Household Survey, 1995–1996*. Computer file. Colchester: The Data Archive.

Paull, G. and Taylor, J. (2002) *Mothers' Employment and Childcare Use in Britain*. London: Institute of Fiscal Studies.

Pickering, A. (2002) *A Simpler Way to Better Pensions: An Independent Report by Alan Pickering*. London: Department for Work and Pensions.

Price, D. (2003) Pension sharing on divorce: the future for women, in C. Bochel, N. Ellison, and M. Powell (eds) *Social Policy Review 15*. Bristol: The Policy Press.

Shaw, C. (1999) 1996-based population projections by legal marital status for England and Wales, *Population Trends*, 95(Spring): 23–32.

Walby, S. (1997) *Gender Transformations*. London: Routledge.

Walker, A., Maher, J., Coulthard, M., Goddard, E. and Thomas, M. (2001) *Living in Britain: Results from the 2000/01 General Household Survey*. London: The Stationery Office.

Warren, T. (2000) Women in low status part-time jobs: a class and gender analysis, *Sociological Research Online*, 4(4): 113–137.

Yeandle, S. (1999) Women, men and non-standard employment: breadwinning and caregiving in Germany, Italy, and the UK. In R. Crompton (ed.) *Restructuring Gender Relations and Employment*. Oxford: Oxford University Press.

10

RE-EXAMINING GENDER AND MARITAL STATUS: MATERIAL WELL-BEING AND SOCIAL INVOLVEMENT

Sara Arber, Debora Price, Kate Davidson and Kim Perren

The marital status of older people reflects their prior life course as well as their current social situation. Widows and widowers, for example, have had and lost a marital partner. The death of a companion, confidante and major source of emotional and practical support can represent a profound loss to men and women (Askham 1994; Davidson 1999), but their family ties, social networks and material situation will in turn reflect that they were married, often for most of their lives. Divorcees, on the other hand, may have disrupted family relationships. Older divorced men particularly are likely to have weak contacts with children and grandchildren (see Chapters 7 and 11) and to report less practical and emotional support from family and friends than married men (Solomou *et al.* 1999). They may have suffered significant financial hardship during their working lives associated with marital breakdown, particularly as many divorced women become lone mothers, and many divorced men experience unemployment (see Chapter 9).

Older people who never married may have particular characteristics that led them not to marry and are unlikely to have had children, and their work patterns and social contacts may reflect both these things. Many single men, and some single women, remained living in their parental home. Never married women from these generations are more likely than married women to have been 'career' women, with formal marriage bars operating on civil servants and teachers until the mid-1940s, and strong social norms operating against married women working in the years immediately after the Second World War. Despite some never married men being well educated, they are on the whole more likely to be socially and educationally disadvantaged. Thus, in later life, material wealth and pension accumulation, inheritance and patterns of family and friendship all reflect the life lived to date. The present material circumstances and social relationships of older people can only be understood by reference to their past, both present and past being reflected in the categorization of current marital status.

This chapter examines marital status in relation to inequality, focusing on the differences between older men and women. Inequality is viewed here from two perspectives, material inequality and social involvement.

Material inequality in later life

Material inequality can take many forms. Three are examined here: income, car ownership and home ownership. Income in later life is largely linked to the accumulation of pensions during the working life, and then whether pensions are inherited on the death of a spouse. A sufficient income is necessary for engagement in society – it determines the ability to socialize outside the home, visit friends, buy presents for family members and go on holiday. Inequality between rich and poor pensioners, linked to class and gender, has grown over the past 30 years, as the UK pension system has been increasingly privatized (Ginn and Arber 1999). A third of men have no private pension provision in retirement – manual workers are far less likely than professionals and managers to have had occupational pensions. But for women the differentials are even more stark: older women on average have much lower personal income than men, and two-thirds of women over 65 have only state pensions (Ginn and Arber 1999, 2001). Price and Ginn (Chapter 9) show that pension accumulation during working life is sharply differentiated by gender and partnership status – inequalities that lead directly to income differences among older people according to marital status.

Car ownership too is differentiated by marital status, class and gender. While car ownership indicates that a household has sufficient material resources to own, run and maintain a car, it represents far more than that to many people. For men, it may represent masculinity, and for both men and women it may symbolize and indicate independence – the ability to shop, visit friends, enjoy leisure facilities, help with grandchildren, attend hospital appointments and so forth. Yet older cohorts of women, particularly those over 70, came from generations where it was unusual for them to obtain a driving licence (Dale 1986). Women thus depended on their husband for transport by the 'household' car, whether for social contact, shopping or accessing health care facilities. Even when they are able to drive, research has shown that older women tend to cease driving at a younger age than men, despite similar physical and mental disabilities (Rabbitt *et al.* 1996). Thus, for women, widowhood or divorce may represent more than the loss of a breadwinner and partner – it may include the loss of mobility.

Even where public transport is available, frailty and disability may make public transport difficult or impossible. Older people also have more fear of public safety, and the absence of a household car may lead to more socially isolated lives (Gilhooly *et al.* 2002). Whether through having insufficient financial resources to own a car, or through the inability to drive because of lack of a driving licence or failing health, having no car in the household represents a clear material disadvantage.

Like car ownership, home ownership is an indicator of material inequality. Over the past twenty years in the UK, government policy to promote private home ownership has led to the 'residualization of council housing' (Pickvance 1999: 416). Housing tenure has increasingly come to represent a social divide, with rented accommodation being disproportionately found in socially and economically deprived neighbourhoods. These neighbourhoods are also more likely to have problems of safety and security, adversely affecting social relations with friends and neighbours. While home ownership may represent a drain on financial resources because of the costs of maintaining a property, if older people own their home, then this is an asset from which they can potentially release capital, and will provide a source of inheritance for their families. Home ownership is associated generally with greater capital wealth.

Social involvement in later life

The ability to form and maintain social relationships is in many ways connected with marital status and material resources. Social contact with family members and with friends is also critical for health and for well-being (Cohen 1988; Umbersen 1992), providing buffers and emotional support in times of stress (Cooper *et al.* 1999). Umbersen (1992) found that spouses affected the health behaviour of each other, with women more likely than men to have a positive influence on the health behaviour of their partner. De Jong Gierveld (Chapter 7) shows how older people living alone are less likely to report loneliness where they have more contact with both family and friends, and Farquhar (1995) and Bowling (1995) have both identified relationships with family and friends as of key importance to the quality of life of older people.

Social relationships may take the form of family relations, relationships with friends and contact with neighbours, each of which contributes in a different way to quality of life (Phillipson *et al.* 2001). Social contact and activity for older people varies widely and also includes involvement in social organizations (Perren *et al.* 2003a). Davidson *et al.* (Chapter 11) suggest that older men in general, and divorced or never married men in particular, often socialize in public settings such as pubs and clubs rather than in their own home or the home of others. However, social interactions of older people mainly take place in the private sphere of the older person's own home or in the home of relatives or friends, or with neighbours. We follow de Jong

Gierveld (Chapter 7) in using the term 'social embeddedness' to refer to an individual's network of social relationships.

Neighbours can be an important source of social contact for older people, since they spend more time in their local area than people of working age. Neighbourhood interaction may vary from fairly brief standardized greetings to more lengthy interactions and possibly exchange of favours between neighbours (Perren *et al.* 2003b). Chatting with neighbours therefore provides another indicator of the degree of social embeddedness of older people, and provides the potential for reciprocity, including the provision of support by neighbours to older people in times of illness or other crises.

Should an older person become physically frail or disabled and unable to provide for their own activities of daily living, such as getting their shopping, they will either require assistance from family, friends or neighbours in order to remain living in the community, or need to rely on state, voluntary or privately paid provision of support services. If support is not available, an older person may enter residential care at a lower threshold of disability than older people who can easily obtain such functional support. Social relationships are important to a variety of aspects of well-being and independence in later life, yet are clearly differentiated by age, gender, marital status and material circumstances.

Data and methods

The aim of this chapter is to examine how gender and marital status interact for older people in relation to inequalities in material well-being and social embeddedness. We link these two indicators of quality of later life by analysing to what extent differential levels of social contacts between men and women according to marital status can be explained by differences in material resources and level of physical disability.

Our analysis is based on the General Household Survey (GHS), which is a nationally representative survey of about 10,000 households per year. All adults aged 16 and over in the household are interviewed, with a response rate of around 80 per cent in the mid-1990s (Walker *et al.* 2001). For the analysis of material circumstances, five years of the GHS are combined – 1993–6 and 1998 (there was no GHS conducted in 1997) – yielding a sample of nearly 18,000 men and women aged 65 and over. The GHS only asks questions about contacts with family, friends and neighbours periodically. For the analyses of these social relationships, two years of GHS data (1994 and 1998) were combined. The data sets used in this chapter are therefore sufficiently large to provide reliable estimates for small subgroups, such as never married older women and divorced older men. Less than 1 per cent of people aged 65 or over were cohabiting and they are combined with the married; similarly, the separated and divorced have been combined.

The GHS is a sample of people living in the community, and therefore omits people living in residential or nursing homes. The likelihood of entering a care home increases with advancing age, and reached 26 per cent of women and 15 per cent of men over age 85 at the 1991 census (Arber and Ginn 1998). Entry into residential care is strongly differentiated by marital status and gender. The never married were most likely to be in a care home, and the married were least likely (Arber and Ginn 1998). The widowed and divorced fell between these two extremes, with widowers under 80 more likely to be in residential care than widows. For married people, however, in each age group married women were more likely to be residents than men. Thus, when analysing older people according to marital status using the GHS, it is important to recognize that those remaining in the community are a selected group, and that the selection criteria differ by marital status.

The analysis in this chapter uses logistic regression models to compare the differential effects of marital status for women compared to men. Marital status is based on four categories: the married/cohabiting; the widowed; the divorced and separated, and those who have never married. We control for age in five year groups (ages 65 to 69, 70 to 74, 75 to 79, 80 to 84 and 85 or over). This is necessary because, as shown in Table 10.1, age is closely linked with the likelihood of being in each marital status, so that on average widows are older than married women, and divorced women are younger. Thus, controlling for five-year age groups provides a more accurate assessment of the relative material and social well-being of each gender/marital status group.

Table 10.1 Marital status by age group and gender, age 65 and over

	65 to 74 %	75 to 84 %	85 and over %	65 and over %
Men				
Married	78	66	45	72
Widowed	11	26	50	18
Divorced/separated	5	3	1	4
Never married	6	5	4	6
N =	4757	2334	463	7554
Women				
Married	54	30	10	42
Widowed	35	59	78	47
Divorced/separated	5	4	2	4
Never married	6	7	10	7
N =	5659	3500	1040	10,199

Source: General Household Survey (1993, 1994, 1995, 1996, 1998), authors' analysis.

Marital status and gender in later life

The gender and marital status profile of older people in the mid-1990s (from the five-year GHS data set) is shown in Table 10.1. Marriage remains normal for men throughout the life span: nearly three-quarters of men over 65 are married and even over the age of 85 nearly half of men are married. This contrasts markedly with women, among whom only 42 per cent of those over 65 are married, and this reduces to one in ten of those over 85. There are parallel increases in widowhood for women, the proportions reaching nearly four-fifths of women over 85. The chances of being a widow or widower versus remaining married in later life are sharply differentiated by gender.

Being divorced is a minority experience for the current generation of older people, especially for the oldest cohorts. Five per cent of women and men aged 65 to 74 are divorced but only 1–2 per cent among those over 85. However, as outlined in Chapter 1, divorce rates have increased rapidly over recent years. Therefore, any material or social disadvantages found for the current small cohorts of older divorced men and women are likely to become more salient as the proportion of older divorcees increases. Experiencing later life having never married is also a minority experience, and for women has decreased from 10 per cent above age 85 to 6 per cent aged 65 to 74. The proportion of men who are never married varies from 6 per cent among men aged 65 to 74 to 4 per cent aged 85 or over.

Material well-being in later life

This section examines how gender and marital status impact on the material well-being of older people. We examine three dichotomous household-based measures of material disadvantage, namely low household income, renting (rather than owning) a home and not having a car available within the household.

In Figure 10.1 we present three sets of logistic regression analyses, one for each measure of material disadvantage, in which married men are defined as the reference category with odds of 1.00, and age is controlled in five-year groups. The odds of falling into any other category are then contrasted by examining the odds ratios relative to married men. Any gender/marital status category with an odds ratio higher than 1.00 has a greater likelihood of being in disadvantaged material circumstances than married men; any with an odds ratio below 1.00 has better material circumstances. The asterisks indicate where the odds ratio for a particular category is significantly different from that for married men (* represents $p < 0.05$, and ** represents $p < 0.01$). Where there are no asterisks, this should be interpreted as indicating no statistically significant difference between the material circumstances of married men and that category.

Figure 10.1   Material circumstances by gender and marital status, odds ratios, age 65 and over.

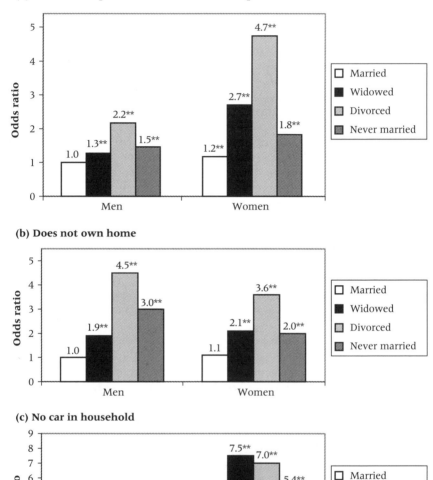

(a) Household equivalized income in lowest quartile of those 65 and over

(b) Does not own home

(c) No car in household

Odds ratios calculated after controlling for five-year age groups (65 to 69, 70 to 74, 75 to 79, 80 to 84, 85 and over); reference category is married men, with odds defined as 1.00. Household income adjusted for household composition using the McClements Scale. Significance of difference from the reference category, $*p < 0.05$, $**p < 0.01$.

Source: General Household Survey (1993–6, 1998).

Household income

Among older people there is considerable income inequality. We examine who falls into the lowest quartile (25 per cent) of the income distribution of those over 65. All income levels have been adjusted to 1998 values using the Retail Price Index. It is cheaper to live in a household containing two or more persons than to live alone, since many household running costs vary little irrespective of the number of people in the household (e.g. heating and lighting), and it is relatively cheaper to shop and prepare meals for two than for one. Therefore, household income has been adjusted for the older person's household composition, using the McClements income equivalizing scales (Department of Work and Pensions 2002). The incomes presented represent equivalent living standards rather than money. Using equivalized household income, we can directly compare the living standards of older people according to marital status.

On this basis, older people with equivalized income in the lowest quartile would have had, at 1998 levels, less than £138 per week per couple, or £84 as the equivalent for a person living alone. At this time, the minimum means tested benefit payable for a pensioner couple with no dependents was £110–118 per week, or £70–77 for a single pensioner. Those in the lowest quartile of the distribution therefore have a living standard either below or close to the level of means tested benefits. Where we refer to income in this chapter, we mean household equivalized income, and households in the bottom quartile of the 'over 65' income distribution are characterized as living in poverty.

Older women are on average poorer than older men. Almost a third of women live in households in poverty, compared with 19 per cent of men. The chances of having such low income are also sharply differentiated by marital status. So while only 16 per cent of married men live in poverty (the lowest probability of any group), almost half (48 per cent) of divorced and separated women do. Figure 10.1a shows that divorced women are the group who are most likely to be poor in later life, with an odds ratio of poverty of 4.7 compared with married men. The next most financially disadvantaged group are widows, with odds 2.7 times higher than the odds for married men and 2.3 times higher than the odds for married women. This disadvantage is particularly salient, as almost half of older women are widows. The household income of widowers is not very different from that of married men, showing that among men there is little financial penalty attached to widowhood. Divorced men stand out as the most financially disadvantaged group of men. Their odds of being in the lowest 25 per cent of the income distribution are 2.2 times higher than those for married men, but their income level is still much higher than that of divorced women.

The odds ratio for married women is close to 1 only because their husband's (usually much higher) individual income has been pooled with theirs to calculate household income. Of women living without a partner, never married women are the least likely to be living in a household in poverty.

Most never married women have been in the labour market throughout their working life and are the group of older women most likely to have accumulated their own occupational pension. That they are poorer than married and never married men reflects sex discrimination in occupational status, pay rates and the opportunity to join occupation-related pension schemes.

Our analysis of financial resources suggests that while there are household income differences between older men, with divorced men being the most disadvantaged, there are much larger income differences among older women, and between women and men, according to marital status. As we shall see next, the differences between older men and women are also substantial on the other two measures of material well-being.

Home ownership

Our analysis of home ownership focuses on the odds of older people not owning their home (Figure 10.1b). There are very large differences in home ownership among both men and women according to marital status. Married men and women are the most advantaged, and divorced men and women are the most disadvantaged; that is, have the highest odds of renting compared to married men. Divorced men over 65 have an odds ratio of 4.5 of renting their home, which is even higher than the odds for divorced women (3.6). This differential possibly reflects divorce settlements where a marital home (which was owned) was transferred to the wife in order to house dependent children of the marriage, leaving men renting accommodation. However, the very high odds ratio for renting among divorced women (odds ratio 3.6) also reflects their very disadvantaged financial circumstances in later life.

Never married men have much higher odds of renting in later life than married men (odds ratio of 3.0). Many never married men remain in their parental home for much of their life, and have to move to rented accommodation when the parent dies and their parent's 'family home' is sold to be subdivided with other siblings as inheritance. It is interesting to note that the housing situation of never married women (odds ratio of 2.0) is better than that of never married men, suggesting selection into the group of well educated 'career women' as compared with men who never married.

There is little difference in the housing position of widows and widowers: both have an odds ratio of living in rented accommodation of around 2.0 compared to the married (odds ratio of 1.0). This suggests that during widowhood, some older people move into rented accommodation, because they cannot afford the upkeep of an owned home, to move nearer other family members or to move into sheltered accommodation. Renting is associated with widowhood *per se*, since there are no clear differences by gender.

Car ownership

The pattern of car ownership varies fundamentally by gender; all groups of women without a partner are much less likely to have access to a car in the household than married women or men (see Figure 10.1c). This reflects the absence of driving skills or the cessation of driving by older women due to failing health, and the very disadvantaged financial position of previously married women described above. The greatest differential is for widows, with odds of not having a car 7.5 times higher than the odds for married men. The odds ratio for divorced women is 7.0 and for never married women is 5.4. Thus, loss of a partner for women, whether by widowhood or divorce, has a profound impact by restricting their mobility through removing access to a car in the household. Never married women are less disadvantaged, probably because they were more likely to have learnt to drive and owned a car when younger, as well as being relatively better off and more likely to be able to afford to run a car in later life. We can expect the gender division of car ownership to lessen for future cohorts in later life, since more younger women now learn to drive.

There is also a strong gradient in car ownership among men according to marital status. Married men are the most likely to have a car, followed by widowers (odds ratio of 2.0). Never married men are least likely to have a car (odds ratio of 4.2), with divorced men also disadvantaged (odds ratio of 3.5). The lower level of car ownership for divorced men may partly reflect their low household income (shown in Figure 10.1a), but for never married men is likely to relate to other aspects of their life course; possibly fewer were car drivers earlier in adult life.

Summary on material resources

On all three measures of material household well-being, older married people are highly advantaged. This gender similarity of the advantage of married older men and women must be tempered by the recognition that almost three-quarters of older men are married (Table 10.1), whereas the advantaged material state associated with marriage (including the assumed pooling of resources with their husbands) is the province of only a minority of older women. Widows, constituting about half of all older women (the largest group) have about twice the odds of both living in poverty and renting their home than their married counterparts. In terms of transportation and mobility, widows face major restrictions, with odds of not having a house-hold car that are 7.5 times higher than married men. There are less striking differences in the material well-being of the smaller group of widowed men compared to the majority group of married older men.

On all measures, the proportionately small groups of older divorced women and men are very disadvantaged. Divorcees are most likely to rent their home; divorced women have the lowest household income of any group, and divorced men the lowest among men. Because the divorced older population is currently relatively small, policy-makers may consider these stark differences in material well-being to be of minor importance. However, as discussed in Chapter 1, there is projected to be a major increase in the proportion of older divorcees, with as many divorced men as widowers projected by 2020. Thus, if the societal mechanisms that have led to the material disadvantage of the current cohort of older divorcees continue over the next twenty years, there will be a very substantial sector of the older population of both men and women living in significantly disadvantaged material circumstances.

The meaning of being never married differs markedly by gender in later life. The routes to remaining single among this cohort of older people are quite dissimilar, and the consequences of these divergent routes lead to gender differences in material well-being in later life. Never married women are in an advantaged material situation in later life compared to other women without a partner: they are less likely to have a low income, more likely to have a car and more likely to own their home. This contrasts with never married men, who are the least likely to own a car, and are much less likely to own their home than widowers, but more likely to do so than divorced men.

We conclude that analyses of material well-being in later life should examine the intersection between gender and marital status in order to show the interaction of these two critical determinants of material well-being, rather than treating them as separate (additive) variables. It is clear that being married is beneficial for both older men and women in terms of material well-being. We now turn to examine another source of well-being in later life: social embeddedness with family, friends and neighbours.

Contacts with relatives, friends and neighbours in later life

We examine three measures of social embeddedness, namely the extent to which older people say they *host* relatives or friends in their own home, *visit* relatives or friends and *chat* to neighbours. In each case, we focus on those who say they host, visit or chat to neighbours less than monthly or never, which we characterize as 'rarely'. Thus, we examine older people who are relatively isolated from social interactions in their own home and in the homes of relatives or friends, and rarely interact with neighbours. Older people with this limited amount of social contact have less ability to call on relatives, friends or neighbours to provide support or assistance should the need arise. This analysis of networks of social relationships is restricted by the questions asked in the GHS, which relate solely to contacts in the private sphere and the neighbourhood, and exclude social contacts in public settings, such as pubs or restaurants.

Our analysis of these three measures of social contact uses logistic regression models as in the previous section on material well-being. Age is controlled in five-year age groups, and each gender/marital status group is compared to the reference category of married men (with an odds ratio set to 1.00). There is much greater variation in the extensiveness of social contacts among men according to marital status than among women (see Figure 10.2). These findings differ markedly from those for material well-being.

Examining variations among men first, married men are the most likely to *host* friends and relatives in their home, while married men and widowers are equally likely to *visit* others. In relation to both *hosting* and *visiting* relatives and friends, those with the least social contact on average are never married, followed by divorced older men. When looking at who rarely *hosts* relatives and friends, never married men have odds 5.4 times higher than married men, and divorced men an odds ratio of 4.3 (Figure 10.2a). The odds of widowed men rarely hosting relatives and friends are almost twice as great as for married men. These sharp differences suggest that men living without a partner are much less likely to entertain others in their home than married men, indicating that their wives may be the major instigators of such home-based social interactions.

Among older men, the relative differences in *visiting* relatives and friends by marital status are more muted than for *hosting* visits. There is no difference in *visiting* between married and widowed men, suggesting that widowers are invited to the homes of family members and friends to the same extent as married men (Figure 10.2b). Never married men are the group least likely to visit relatives and friends, with an odds ratio of 2.3, followed by divorced men (odds ratio of 1.8). These two groups of older men appear to be relatively socially isolated from relatives and friends, which may lead to loneliness and/ or lack of access to potential sources of social and instrumental support.

There is no association between a woman's marital status and her likelihood of *visiting* relatives or friends (Figure 10.2b). However, there are differences in relation to *hosting* relatives and friends, the chances of which are significantly lower for never married women (odds ratio of 2.5) than either married or widowed women (odds ratios of about 1.0).

Chatting with neighbours is more the province of older men than women, particularly married and widowed men (Figure 10.2c). Again, there is a sig-nificant difference among men according to marital status, with a division between married men and widowers on the one hand, and divorced men and never married men on the other. Divorced men are least likely to speak to neighbours (odds ratio of 3.1), followed by never married men (odds ratio of 1.8). These findings suggest that these two groups of older men are relatively isolated from neighbours, as well as from relatives and friends. Among women, there is little difference according to marital status in the odds of rarely chatting to neighbours (odds ratios vary from 1.3 for married women to about 1.7 for all other groups of women).

This section has shown strong differences in the extent of social contacts of older people with relatives and friends in the home, and with neighbours, indicating that divorced and never married men are the groups least likely to

Figure 10.2   Social contact less than monthly by gender and marital status, odds ratios, age 65 and over.

(a) Hosts relatives or friends less than monthly

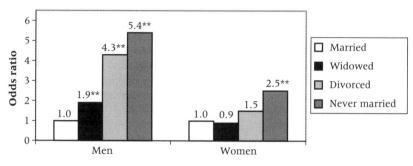

(b) Visits relatives or friends less than monthly

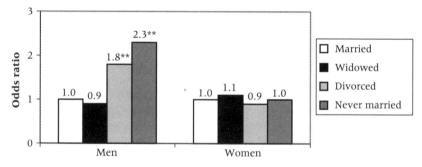

(c) Chats to neighbours less than monthly

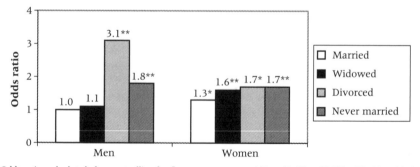

Odds ratios calculated after controlling for five-year age groups (65 to 69, 70 to 74, 75 to 79, 80 to 84, 85 and over); reference category is married men, with odds defined as 1.00. Significance of difference from the reference category, $*p < 0.05$, $**p < 0.01$.

Source: General Household Survey (1994, 1998).

be involved in such social relationships, and therefore most vulnerable to social isolation. They are potentially most likely to lack access to functional social support from others in order to remain living in the community should they become physically impaired. In the next section, we examine whether these differences in levels of social contact by gender and marital status can be explained by differences in resources.

The impact of resources on levels of social contact

Visiting relatives and friends is likely to be influenced by an older person's material resources, particularly whether they have access to a car in the household, and also by their health and physical mobility. In this section, we examine whether less frequent social contact with relatives, friends and neighbours might be explained by lower material resources and/or higher levels of disability. There is extensive evidence that older women are more likely than older men to have physical impairments that restrict their activities of daily living (Arber and Ginn 1991; Arber and Cooper 1999). Therefore, we would expect that older women's pattern of visiting relatives and friends might be lower because of mobility restrictions, as well as lack of car ownership.

It is important to note two things here. First, disabled married people are more likely than other groups to remain living in the community and therefore be sampled within the GHS (as discussed earlier). Married women may therefore appear to be more disabled and never married women less disabled in the GHS, particularly as they get older. Second, car ownership and health are correlated. Poor health may well cause a driver to give up a car, and severe disability is certainly likely to do so. In addition, low income may also mean lack of access to a car, and a propensity to poorer health (Arber and Cooper 2000).

Degree of disability is measured by a scale based on whether the older person can undertake six activities of daily living, namely cutting their own toenails, walking down the road, getting up and down stairs, getting around the house, washing or bathing and getting in and out of bed. If the person can undertake the activity without difficulty, it is coded 0, if undertaken only with difficulty the activity is coded 1 and if they cannot do the activity it is coded 2. These six items are summed to form a scale in which a score of 6 means that the person has severe disability and is likely to require assistance on a daily basis to remain living in the community (Arber and Cooper 1999). These scores have then been recoded into four categories: no disability, slight disability, moderate disability and severe disability.

We examine the extent to which car ownership and housing tenure, as well as the older person's level of disability, influence *hosting* and *visiting* relatives and friends, and *chatting* with neighbours. Logistic regression models are used to predict those who rarely *host* and *visit* relatives and friends, or *chat* to neighbours (Table 10.2). Model 1 included gender and marital status, while controlling for age in five-year age groups. (These are the same odds ratios as displayed in Figure 10.2.) Model 2 additionally controlled for car ownership, housing tenure and level of disability. However, housing tenure did not have an independent significant effect on any of the three measures of social contacts, so was omitted from the final models.

In relation to *hosting* relatives or friends in their own home, there were no significant effects of age, car ownership or degree of disability once marital status and gender were in the model (and therefore the results are not presented in Table 10.2). Therefore, the very low level of hosting of relatives and friends by divorced and never married men cannot be explained by any differences in age, lack of car ownership, disadvantaged housing tenure or differences in level of physical disability.

When we turn to *visiting* relatives and friends and compare the two models in Table 10.2a, the measure of disability is strongly related to the extent of visiting. Those with a severe level of disability have an odds ratio of rarely visiting relatives and friends that is over seven, compared with those with no disability (odds ratio defined as 1.0), and those with moderate disability have an odds ratio of 2.5. Thus, when an older person has physical disabilities this leads to a diminution in their ability to visit others, and thus in their social embeddedness. Car ownership is also strongly related to visiting others, with the odds of rarely visiting relatives or friends over twice as high for those without a car than for those with a car, after controlling for disability.

Contrasting the odds of *visiting* by gender/marital status categories in Models 1 and 2 shows that in each case the odds decrease relative to the reference category of married men, once car ownership and disability are controlled in Model 2. This is especially the case for non-partnered women. These findings reveal that restrictions associated with physical disability and not having a car adversely affect the ability of all groups of women to visit friends and relatives, and also restrict the visiting patterns of divorced and never married men. Never married men still have a lower level of visiting relatives and friends than married men (odds of 1.8), but once disability and car ownership are controlled, divorced men do not have a significantly lower level of visiting than married men. This means that for divorced men, the low odds ratio in Model 1 is largely a result of their material disadvantage and possibly greater disability, but for never married men, their lower level of social embeddedness is to a far greater extent independent of these factors.

Once women's higher level of physical disability and lower likelihood of owning a car are controlled, each group of women is far more likely to *visit* relatives and friends than married men, and divorced women are the most likely to do so (Table 10.2a). These findings confirm that women are more socially embedded than men in terms of visiting relatives and friends, but in later life they are more restricted in undertaking these social activities by their higher levels of physical impairment and lack of car ownership.

Table 10.2   Odds ratios of rare social contacts, controlling for resources, age 65 and over

	(a) Visits relatives and friends		(b) Chats to neighbours	
	Model 1	Model 2	Model 1	Model 2
Age	†††	†††	†††	n.s.
65 to 69	1.00	1.00	1.00	
70 to 74	1.34**	1.20*	0.91	
75 to 79	1.92**	1.39**	1.10	
80 to 84	2.91**	1.64**	1.45**	
85 and over	5.60**	2.59**	1.89**	
Gender and marital status	†††	†††	†††	n.s.
Men				
Married	1.00	1.00	1.00	1.00
Widowed	0.93	0.80	1.12	1.11
Divorced	1.84**	1.28	3.05**	2.81**
Never married	2.33**	1.83**	1.84**	1.79**
Women				
Married	0.98	0.79*	1.29*	1.18
Widowed	1.12	0.61**	1.58**	1.38**
Divorced	0.89	0.46**	1.73*	1.48
Never married	1.04	0.65*	1.74**	1.65**
Car in household		†††		n.s.
Yes		1.00		
No		2.38**		
Disability[a]		†††		†††
No disability		1.00		1.00
Slight disability		1.34**		1.28*
Moderate disability		2.49**		2.23**
Severe disability		7.23**		3.22**
Δ LLRatio	370.7	689.1	101.7	142.8
Δ Degrees of freedom	11	4	11	3
N =	6515		6513	

(a) Visit relatives or friends less than once a month or never, and (b) chat to neighbours less than once a month or never. Housing tenure was not statistically significant in either model, and therefore was omitted from Model 2.

[a] Disability was measured based on difficulty of doing, or inability to do, six activities of daily living (see text).

Significance of difference from the reference category (married men): *$p < 0.05$, **$p < 0.01$. Significance of variable in the model: ††† $p < 0.001$.

Source: General Household Survey (1994, 1998), authors' analysis.

Our earlier analysis showed that divorced older men were the group least likely to chat to neighbours (Figure 10.2c). Model 2 (in Table 10.2b) shows that an older person's level of disability is strongly related to whether they interact with neighbours. The odds of an older person with a severe level of disability rarely chatting to neighbours are three times higher than for someone without disability. Age differences in chatting to neighbours are shown by Model 2 to be entirely explained by increased disability with advancing age. However, controlling for level of disability (in Model 2) has very little effect on the high odds of divorced men and never married men rarely talking to neighbours, compared to married men. Never married women are also less likely to be involved in neighbourly relationships than most other groups of older people, when compared with those of similar age and level of disability.

This section has shown that the lack of home-based and neighbourhood relationships of older divorced and never married men is not solely due to their poorer material resources (measured by car ownership and housing tenure) or their level of physical disability. Qualitative research is required to understand fully why these groups of older non-partnered men have such low levels of contact with others in their home and their neighbourhood. The next chapter draws on qualitative interviews with older men to provide insights into some of the reasons for our quantitative findings.

Discussion and conclusions

This chapter has used British data from the 1990s to illustrate how marital status is linked to material disadvantage and to social roles in complex and gender-differentiated ways. Older married men are the most advantaged group, in terms of both material circumstances and social interaction with relatives, friends and neighbours. It is important to recognize that this advantaged position is the province of the vast majority of older men, since nearly three-quarters of men are married in later life, and most remain married until they die. Married older women are also advantaged in their household material circumstances and social interactions, but being married is a minority experience for older women, especially above age 75, when under a third are married.

Widowhood is the norm for women in later life. We have shown that widows are materially disadvantaged compared to married women, and in particular are far less likely to have access to a car, so their geographical mobility may be highly restricted. However, widows are similar to married women in their level of contacts with relatives, friends and neighbours. Widowers, while less likely to *host* relatives or friends in their own home, are also equally likely to *visit* relatives and friends and chat to neighbours.

The numerically small group of divorced men are particularly disadvantaged both materially and in their lack of home-based social contacts with relatives, friends and neighbours. Divorced older women are severely disadvantaged materially in terms of low household income, renting accommodation and low car access, but unlike divorced men, they are almost as integrated into social networks of relatives, friends and neighbours as married women and widows. Given the projected growth in the proportions of older people who will be divorced over the next decade (see Chapter 1), it is particularly important to assess the implications of larger groups of divorced older men and women who may be so materially disadvantaged.

The groups most likely to lack social contacts with relatives, friends and neighbours are divorced and never married older men. Their lack of social embeddedness makes them more vulnerable to social isolation and to lacking the receipt of instrumental support that might help them remain living in the community should they become disabled. They are therefore more vulnerable to entry into residential care at an earlier level of physical disability.

Among non-partnered women, those who have never married are more materially advantaged in terms of income, housing and car ownership. They have equivalent levels of social contact in terms of *visiting* friends and relatives, but are less likely to *host* friends and relatives in their own home and to chat to neighbours. If their mobility becomes restricted by physical disability, therefore, their options for social contact will be more limited, and may lead to social isolation.

This chapter has shown that it is important to treat marital status as an analytic variable when analysing women *and* men in later life. It is timely to draw together what have usually been treated as separate fields of study, namely the analysis of material well-being in later life and the analysis of social embeddedness. We have shown that married men and widowers are both materially and socially advantaged, but divorced and never married men tend to be disadvantaged on both dimensions, and are therefore more vulnerable in later life. This contrasts with older women, who are generally socially connected with relatives, friends and neighbours, irrespective of their marital status. When transport becomes unavailable through lack of a car or disability, those groups for whom most social contact is by visiting friends and relatives may face difficulties. Non-partnered women, especially divorcees, experience greatest material disadvantage in later life.

Acknowledgements

We are grateful to National Statistics for permission to use General Household Survey data, and to the UK Data Archive and Manchester Computing Centre for access to the data. The material presented in this chapter is based on research supported by the Economic and Social Research Council under the Growing Older Programme, grant no. L480 25 4033.

References

Arber, S. and Cooper, H. (1999) Gender differences in health in later life: a new paradox?, *Social Science and Medicine*, 48(1): 61–76.

Arber, S. and Cooper H. (2000) Gender and inequalities in women's health across the life course. In E. Annandale and K. Hunt (eds) *Gender Inequalities in Health*. Buckingham: Open University Press.

Arber, S. and Ginn, J. (1991) *Gender and Later Life: A Sociological Analysis of Resources and Constraints*. London: Sage.

Arber, S. and Ginn, J. (1998) Health and illness in later life. In D. Field and S. Taylor (eds) *Sociological Perspectives on Health, Illness and Health Care*. Oxford: Blackwell.

Askham, J. (1994) Marriage relationships of older people, *Reviews of Clinical Gerontology*, 4: 261–8.

Bowling, A. (1995) The most important things in life, *International Journal of Health Sciences*, 5(4): 169–75.

Cohen, S. (1988) Psychological models of the role of social support in the etiology of physical disease, *Health Psychology*, 7: 269–97.

Cooper, H., Arber, S., Fee, L. and Ginn, J. (1999) *The Influence of Social Support and Social Capital on Health: A Review and Analysis of British Data*. London: Health Education Authority.

Dale, A. (1986) A note on differences in car usage by married men and married women, *Sociology*, 20: 91–2.

Davidson, K. (1999) Marital perceptions in retrospect. In R. Miller and S. Browning (eds) *With this Ring: Divorce, Intimacy and Cohabitation from a Multicultural Perspective*. Stamford, CT: JAI Press.

Department of Work and Pensions (2002) *Households Below Average Income*. London: Department of Work and Pensions.

Farquhar, M. (1995) Elder people's definitions of quality of life, *Social Science and Medicine*, 41(10): 1439–46.

Gilhooly, M., Hamilton, K. and O'Neill, M. (2002) *Transport and Ageing: Extending Quality of Life for Older People via Public and Private Transport*. Final End of Award report to the ESRC. Swindon: Economic and Social Research Council.

Ginn, J. and Arber, S. (1999) Changing patterns of pension inequality: the shift from state to private sources, *Ageing and Society*, 19: 319–42.

Ginn, J. and Arber, S. (2001) A colder pension climate for British women. In J. Ginn, D. Street and S. Arber (eds) *Women, Work and Pensions: International Issues and Prospects*. Buckingham: Open University Press.

Perren, K., Arber, S. and Davidson, K. (2003a) Men's organisational affiliations in later life: the influence of social class and marital status on informal group membership, *Ageing and Society*, 23(1): 69–82.

Perren, K., Arber, S. and Davidson, K. (2003b) Neighbouring in later life: the influence of socio-economic resources, gender and household composition on neighbourly relationships, Mimeo, University of Surrey, Guildford.

Pickvance, C. (1999) Housing and housing policy. In J. Baldock, S. Millers and S. Vickerstaff (eds) *Social Policy*. Oxford: Oxford University Press.

Phillipson, C., Bernard, M., Phillips, J. and Ogg, J. (2001) *The Family and Community Life of Older People: Social Support and Social Networks in Three Urban Areas*. London: Routledge.

Rabbitt, P., Carmichael, A., Jones, S. and Holland, C (1996) *When and Why Older Drivers Give up Driving*. Manchester: University of Manchester, AA Foundation for Road and Safety Research.

Solomou, W., Richards, M., Huppert, F. A., Brayne, C. and Morgan, K. (1998) Divorce, current marital status and well-being in an elderly population, *International Journal of Law, Policy and the Family*, 12: 323–44.

Umbersen, D. (1992) Gender, marital status and the social control of behaviour, *Social Science and Medicine*, 34(8): 907–17.

Walker, A., Maher, J., Coulthard, M., Goddard, E. and Thomas, M. (2001) *Living in Britain: Results from the 2000/01 General Household Survey*. London: The Stationery Office.

11

EXPLORING THE SOCIAL WORLDS OF OLDER MEN

Kate Davidson, Tom Daly and Sara Arber

This chapter examines the influence of partnership status on the social networks and social relationships of older men, focusing on both friendship and family involvement. Research has identified that marriage can exert a protective effect on men's physical and psychological well-being, with women taking primary responsibility for monitoring the health of family members and maintaining social networks (Kulik 2002). Among current cohorts of older people, the majority of men live with a spouse; however, as a result of rising divorce rates and decreasing remarriage rates, larger numbers of older men will experience solo living in the twenty-first century (OPCS 2002). Although women will continue to outnumber men in later life, demographic trends show that an increasing proportion of men over the age of 65 will live alone in their latter years: almost one in four at present, which is projected to rise to one in three over the next generation (Davies *et al.* 1998).

A commonly rehearsed theme within social gerontology is the disadvantaged position of lone older men, who are particularly likely to experience isolation and loneliness (see Chapters 7 and 10). Allied to this is the recognition that lone older men often fail to frequent facilities designed to provide company or practical support (Davidson *et al.* 2003). This lack of social embeddedness has been attributed to the pivotal role of women in establishing and maintaining social networks.

Patterns of gender role congruence in domestic and caring responsibilities in later life have been investigated in recent decades (Keith 1994) and it has been argued that these factors contribute to a perceived 'feminization' of older men (Thompson 1994a). This is particularly relevant for older men who live without a partner and who need to take on domestic tasks traditionally carried out by women. This chapter examines how the marital histories of older men are reflected in their lifestyle, their well-being and their social networks. Men carry the legacy of their marital history into later life; consequently, differences in the social worlds and related behaviours of partnered and lone older men cannot be understood as merely being a function of their current partnership status.

Gender and social networks

Until comparatively recently, the significance of marital status to the lives of older men has been largely overlooked in social investigation (Thompson 1994b). Even less attention has been paid to the meanings of social interaction for men in later life, and how notions of gender and self-identity influence choices around such interaction. It is well documented that women, regardless of marital status, are more likely to have a wider network of kith and kin relationships than men (Scott and Wenger 1995). Although both men and women benefit from the social support that accompanies marriage in a couple-oriented social world (Goldman *et al.* 1995), older men in particular face distinct challenges in maintaining social networks on the dissolution of their marriage, whether from death or divorce (Burgoyne *et al.* 1987).

There is substantial evidence that women have a primary role in maintaining family relationships, and this may be increasingly salient in later life as family ties are tested by dissolution of marriage through death or divorce. Research indicates that older lone men have an elevated risk of social isolation (de Jong Gierveld 1998), but there is little recognition of the way in which marital histories lead to the growth or attenuation of family bonds.

Accounts of male and female patterns of friendship suggest that men and women 'do friendship' differently (Pleck 1975; Miller 1983; Seidler 1989; O'Connor 1992). Chodorow (1991) argues that gender differentiation in friendships can be explained in terms of the child's initial relationship with its mother. The female child is 'connected' to a caretaker of the same sex, whereas during adolescence the male child 'separates' himself from a caretaker of the opposite sex. Thus, she says, 'The basic feminine sense of self is connected to the world, the basic masculine sense of self is separate' (Chodorow 1991: 169). Consequently, we suggest these self-identities are reflected in the contrasting characteristics of male and female friendship (developed from O'Connor 1992), as shown in Table 11.1.

Webster argues that women's sense of self-identity is enmeshed in, and oriented towards, intimate social relationships:

> ... it has been advanced that women define themselves in terms of reciprocal interpersonal relationships in which understanding and nurturance are integral components. Women's 'different voices' develop as a

function of verbal exchange, that is, of talking, hearing and empathizing with an intimate.

(Webster 1995: 101)

This caring, expressive orientation contrasts with an instrumental, autonomous identity that is more characteristic of men. For men, Webster argues, identity precedes intimacy; for women, they are coincidental. Miller (1983: xi) in his preface notes that 'Most men . . . will admit they are disappointed in their friendships with other men . . . [these] are generally characterized by thinness, insincerity, and even wariness.' Pleck (1975: 233) noted the distinction between the emotional 'intimacy' of female friendship and the 'sociability' of male relationships: 'Male sociability is closely connected with male sex-role training and performance and is not characteristically a medium for self-exploration, personal growth or the development of intimacy.' The findings of these two American researchers are confirmed in the UK by Seidler (1989: 7), who suggests that 'masculinity is an essentially negative identity learnt through defining itself against emotionality and connectedness'.

Hess (1982) discusses friendship patterns of men and women across the life course. She found that in general, cultural norms, differential socialization and social structural constraints lead to gender differences in the range of friendships, particularly in the degree of self-disclosure and intimacy. Hess suggests that although young adult men report a greater range of acquaintances and friends than women, their relative lack of disclosure is adaptive for work-role performance and the competitive climate for promotion within the workplace. However, this 'learned incapacity' for intimacy can be deleterious for emotional health, particularly in later life. Conversely, the expressiveness and intimacy of female relationships, which may hamper competitive employment advancement in young adulthood, become an invaluable resource in later life.

Interview data collected for the Berkeley Older Generation longitudinal study (1968/9 and 1982/3) on friendships among young old (60 to 74) and old old (75 or over) men and women found more continuity than change in the amount of contact with friends (Field 1999). However, activities with casual friends occurred primarily in group settings in the public sphere. Activities with close friends were more often concerned with exchanging

Table 11.1   Gendered characteristics of friendship

Women's friendships are characterized by connectedness	*Men's friendships are characterized by* separateness
Intimacy – face to face	Sociability – side by side
Mutual disclosure	Self-disclosure rare
Focus on *talk*	Focus on *activity*
Context: home	Context: pub/sports club, etc.

confidences, sharing interesting experiences and thoughts, and helping each other, frequently in the domestic setting. Although there was a small difference in friendship patterns between men and women aged 60 to 74, above the age of 75 men, but not women, showed a marked decrease in the range of casual *and* close friendships. As men aged, they tended not to replace lost friends, and there was a reduction in the desire for close friendships and reduced interest in social involvement apart from family activities. These factors were not reported by women in either age group.

Most research on friendship throughout the life course has concentrated on the experience of women; consequently, the markers of what constitute 'meaningful' relationships are set through a female 'lens'. Francesca Cancian (1987) writes about romantic relationships, but her findings have relevance to older men's relationships, whether family or romantic.

> Part of the reason that men seem so much less loving than women is that men's behavior is measured with a feminine ruler. Most research considers only the kinds of loving behavior that are associated with the feminine role, such as talking about personal troubles, and rarely compares women and men on masculine qualities such as giving practical help.
>
> (Cancian 1987:74)

She goes on to report that in a marriage counselling session, it was suggested to a husband that he might show more affection to his wife. He went home, and washed her car. In doing so he demonstrated affection in the way he considered appropriate, by carrying out a task he knew his wife disliked. Cancian reported that his wife did not interpret his action as one of affection.

Duncombe and Marsden (1998) analysed 'emotion work' in the context of heterosexual relationships, drawing on research literature. They found that there is a widespread assumption that women play a primary role in doing the emotion work to sustain heterosexual relationships, while men lead what are often termed 'hollow' emotional lives. Their analysis of the literature, however, suggests that there are individual variations and that some individuals may derive a sense of gendered self-identity precisely by conforming to gendered rules concerning emotion work. In other words, women may feel they hold the high moral ground as a result of their superior communication skills, but men's sense of machismo is underpinned by the denial of any 'need' for intimacy.

This chapter focuses on how older men themselves view their social relationships and to what extent this differs by current and former marital status. We examine how partnership status influences social interaction with both friends and family members and how this links to the notion of masculinity and autonomy if men no longer have (or never had) a heterosexual relationship. Experience of ageing has to be seen in the context of the life course, so the chapter takes account of how the social roles in later life are linked to men's earlier lives in the public and private spheres.

Methods

A multi-method approach was used, which comprised quantitative and qualitative data collection and analysis.

Secondary analysis of a survey data set

Data were analysed from the General Household Survey (GHS), a national probability-based cross-sectional survey, published annually, which included questions on social relationships in 1994 and 1998 (OPCS 1997, 2000). We also analysed data from the 1995 GHS (OPCS 1998), which had a question on length of residence in the same house.

Qualitative interviews

In-depth interviews were conducted with 85 older men over the age of 65, who were married, widowed, divorced and never married, focusing on the meanings attached to their experience of later life. The sample was identified principally through the age–sex registers of two large group general practices, but also through flyers and posters distributed in social organizations, sports and leisure centres and other general practices. The majority of the interviews took place in the respondent's home, and lasted between two and three hours. They were tape recorded and fully transcribed. Comprehensive field-notes were made immediately following the visit. These notes and trans-criptions were entered into *NVivo*, a qualitative software program, and coded categories were identified, from which emerged themes used for the research analysis. All names were anonymized. The respondents were largely self-selected and, as such, no claim for generalizability can be made. However, the analysis revealed common themes among men within age and marital status groups.

Older men's social relationships

We analysed the 1994 and 1998 GHS in which men were asked about their social contacts outside the immediate family; that is, with friends, neighbours and other relatives. Figure 11.1a shows the percentage of men over the age of 65 who hardly ever – that is, less than once a month or never – *host* friends or relatives by marital status, and it can be seen that single men are least likely to entertain people in their home. The men most likely to entertain in their home were, not unsurprisingly, married. Widowed men entertained more in their home than divorced men.

Figure 11.1b examines older men who hardly ever or never *visit* friends and family by marital status. Once again, there is an increasing gradient between

Figure 11.1 Percentage of men aged 65 and over who rarely (less than once a month) or never (a) host friends/relatives, (b) visit friends/relatives, (c) chat to neighbours, by marital status.

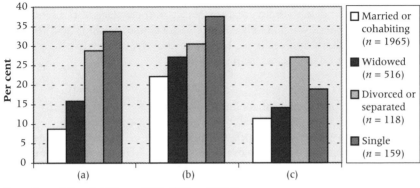

Source: General Household Survey (1994, 1998, combined).
p < 0.001 for (a), (b) and (c).

Figure 11.2 Percentage of older men who have lived in the same house for fewer than five years by age and marital status.

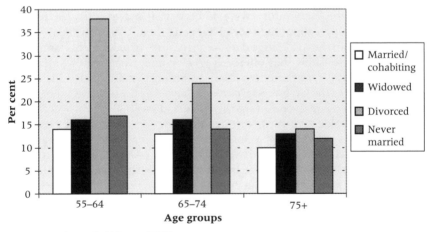

Source: General Household Survey (1995).

married, widowed, divorced and single men. Over a third of never married men hardly ever or never paid visits to friends or relatives. Figure 11.1c shows that married and widowed men are more likely, and divorced men least likely, to chat to neighbours. Therefore, in terms of neighbourhood involvement, divorced men appear to be the least engaged.

One possible explanation for the more restricted social contact patterns of divorced men is because of a shorter length of residence in the neighbourhood. Figure 11.2 goes some way in explaining why older divorced men are less likely to chat to neighbours (as identified in Figure 11.1c). It often takes some time to establish relationships within a neighbourhood and, as demonstrated above, divorced men between the ages of 55 and 74 are most likely to have moved home in the previous five years. Never married men, on the other hand, who demonstrate greater stability in their place of residence, are the group consistently least likely to have social contact within their home or the home of friends and relatives. However, they are somewhat more likely than divorced men to interact with neighbours.

Men's perception of social involvement

The above analysis, together with the findings in Chapter 10, suggests, on initial impression at least, that older men who are divorced or never married engage in considerably less social interaction than married and widowed older men. Consequently, it could be argued, they are more likely to be susceptible to social isolation and loneliness in their later years (as discussed in Chapter 7). In order to gain better insight into older men's social relationships, we conducted qualitative research to elicit their perceptions of the importance of social networks and neighbourhood involvement. A total of 85 men (30 married, 33 widowed, 12 never married and 10 divorced) over the age of 65 and living in the community were interviewed and encouraged to talk, among other things, about their social lives and friendship networks.

Emerging from the qualitative data were accounts of older men's family and friendship relationships that offered a greater understanding of differential meanings of social involvement to them, according to marital status. The married men reported the largest social circles, followed by the widowed men, while the divorced men and the never married men had the smallest circle of friends.

Analysis revealed that men, throughout their life course, may have had reduced opportunity to pursue intimate relationships, which include close and extended family, local and workplace relationships. For ever married men, a principal theme to emerge from the data was the importance attached to occupational status and the masculine imperative to provide for the family. Regardless of socio-economic status, this often necessitated long hours working outside of the home. Childrearing was carried out principally by their wife, who, even if she was in paid employment, organized her routine around her maternal and domestic responsibilities; in other words, 'women's work'. Retirement, for the majority of men, often required a renegotiation of these domestic responsibilities (Cliff 1993).

New skills and old in the domestic sphere

One issue raised from the interviews was the difference in attitude towards cooking and cleaning. Most of the men who were or had been married reported having done some cooking during their marriage, and enjoyed it.

Two of the married men had taken over sole responsibility for cooking since their retirement. Widowed men in particular were extremely proud of their culinary skills, although they admitted they were unable to produce meals 'quite like' their late wife. However, they frequently qualified this by saying 'some of the best chefs are men', thus lending credibility to the latterly imposed 'female' skill in which they took great pride. However, the beneficiaries of the new skill, besides the self-esteem it offered, tended to be the family – adult children and grandchildren when they visited – rather than friends or neighbours.

Less enthusiasm was expressed about housework. Not one married or previously married man said he enjoyed doing housework and some of the homes of lone men we visited were quite neglected, untidy and dirty. Where it could be afforded, the widowed (and divorced) men often paid for a regular cleaner. Several previously partnered men said they did not keep the house 'to her standards'. Our analysis suggests that for widowed and divorced men, sometimes their lower standard of tidiness and cleanliness acted as a deterrent to asking people inside. This, we suggest, is another example of men who had lived with women, measuring the condition of their home with the 'feminine ruler', which stipulates that it should be clean, neat and tidy for visitors. Never married men, on the other hand, tended to be well organized at keeping a tidy home, but still did not invite people in socially.

Private and public socializing

There is a distinction between interaction within the home and social involvement in public, and the balance of activities in each sphere differed by marital status. Married men socialized at home with friends and family, as well as belonging to a wide variety of social organizations outside the home. Widowed men socialized at home, mainly with family members, and belonged to a variety of organizations outside the home. The divorced men had little social contact within their home but were more likely to socialize outside the home. The most isolated were never married men who had the least friend and family social contact both within and outside the home. This section examines private and public socializing among married and widowed men, while later sections focus on the reasons for the lack of social interaction in the private sphere among divorced and never married older men.

Married older men met with friends, usually couples, together with their wife, inside their respective homes. They were also more likely than men who lived alone to carry out voluntary work, or belong to organizations that supported voluntary work, such as the Rotary and Lions Clubs, which kept them in contact with a variety of people outside their marital kith and kin networks. In doing so these men maintained post-employment routines based on a pre-retirement model. That is, they made a regular commitment, were being useful and enjoyed the self-esteem that accompanied doing 'good works'. As long as they had good, or reasonably good, health, married men continued to be active outside the home, in a variety of settings.

Widowers went out frequently to public venues, some reporting that they went out even more than when they had been married. Those who already belonged to organizations such as social clubs and church groups tended to continue their involvement, but were unlikely to invite the people they met at such organizations to their home. Some joined clubs after they had been widowed, often on the instigation of adult children. This supports the findings of Perren *et al.* (2003) that widowers were more likely to be members of sports clubs and social clubs than married men. Even though the widowers described the people they met in these social organizations as very friendly, they said they were unlikely to ask these new acquaintances back to their home.

> Archie (80, widowed): When my wife was alive, we used to have people here all the time, we had lots of friends. I still play bridge with a group of ladies around here.
> Interviewer: Do you ever ask them back here, a cup of tea or something or a drink?
> Archie: No, no I haven't. I have organized a 'bridge four' here with them across the road, with a couple who we both know, but that's only three of four times a year, if that.

The widowed men reported that they chatted to neighbours, especially if they had lived in the area for some time, and said they 'looked out for each other'. However, the widowers were unlikely to go into neighbours' houses, 'unlike their wife had', which contrasted with widows, who continued to visit their neighbours. Interestingly, some widowers said they were very cautious about being seen to talk with, and offer help to, neighbouring widows, since it might attract 'gossip', which was seen as unwelcome to both parties. Since men tend to pre-decease their wife, widowers can feel threatened by the presence of many widows. There may be a need to find creative new ways for widowers to interact 'safely' with the opposite sex in order to avoid misunderstandings about both their possible interest in remarriage and their desire or lack of desire to engage in intimate activity (van den Hoonaard 2002). This may be achieved by widowers reducing the amount of domestic interaction (hosting or visiting) of non-family members, and by meeting in public places, restaurants and clubs, for example, where they can enjoy congenial company without perceived pressure for (or assumptions about) an unwanted relationship.

> You see, I've been a member of the golf club for 40 years and my wife was a member as long as me, until she died. And of course, we had a great many husbands and wives up there that we played regular golf with. Well most of them did the right thing, the men died first as they're supposed to [laughs] . . . So quite often, I'll ask them out to dinner . . . there's safety

in numbers. I don't wish to be committed to any of them. We're all marvellous good friends.

(Barry, 77, widowed)

Men are much more likely than women to deposit all their 'emotional eggs in one basket' – that is, with their partner – and upon the death of the partner have a smaller network of friends upon whom to call (Arber and Ginn 1991: 169). This was echoed by many interviewees.

No, not many close friends. I know my neighbours well. They're not friends but we get on extremely well together. But I've not really got any close friends round about here . . . my daughter is in touch two or three times a week. The other sons certainly telephone me once a week and I visit them both about once a month for lunch or something.

(Kevin, 75, widowed)

But here, nobody will ring me up and say 'Look, Roy. Come out, we'll go out to so-and-so.' My daughter is the only one that would do that. I don't have any close friends. It could be my lack because with my wife, I was so close to her. We did everything together.

(Roy, 86, widowed)

Adult children of widowed men tend to 'rally round' their father on the death of their mother (Carr and Utz 2002), and to stay in close instrumental contact (in terms of helping with domestic chores and self care) with him for longer than with a widowed mother, primarily because he is less likely to have a large circle of supportive friends (Davidson 2001). Widowed men reported a smaller circle of friends than when they had been married, but closer relationships with their adult children. They were likely to say that their wife had primarily instigated and maintained the social network and that, as a couple, they hosted and visited friends in their home.

Older men and family relationships

Sociological discourse on the family has tended to concentrate on gender dynamics of equity and empowerment within relationships comprising young adults with children. In the past decade, there has been increased scholarly interest in the role of men in families, in large part because men are not seen as living up to the contemporary ideal of the 'new man' who does an equal share of the practical and emotional work associated with family life (Seidler 1998). Less attention has been paid to how older fathers interact with their adult children. Nydegger and Mitteness (1991) found that fathers report different responsibilities toward sons and daughters; for example, sons are guided and advised, and daughters are protected. Fathers share a male world with sons, providing a commonality not available to daughters.

However, relationships between fathers and sons are complex and multi-dimensional, change over time and involve tensions that often remain unresolved until the sons are in their thirties. The key to good relations between these men, Nydegger and Mitteness (1991) suggest, is the development of mutual respect. Relationships with daughters are more simple, relaxed and stable and are characterized by mutual affection. Mothers, on the other hand, tended to report more relaxed and stable relationships with both sons and daughters.

Many of the fathers in our sample, even those who reported a very good and close relationship with their children, viewed their wife as 'exemplar' for showing appropriate affection.

> I try to be a good father – I'm not. I'm not as good a father as my wife is a mother. She is far more relaxed and fonder of children than I am. I look on it as a duty to have a family. Ah – and I'll provide all the necessities and a bit more for them but my wife is a better mother than I am a father. I am totally aware of that.
>
> (Clive, 72, married)

> I wasn't the sort of father who talked a lot. Some fathers talk a lot to their sons or daughters. I may have done more perhaps if it had been a girl, I don't know, it might have been different. No, I didn't talk to him a lot. He talked to his mother much more than to me.
>
> (Gary, 80, widowed)

Interestingly, both these men were measuring their relationship with their children, with what Cancian (1987) describes as the 'feminine ruler'. There was a consensus between all the interviewees that women 'do relationships' better than men, and that children, whatever their age, would be more likely to turn to their mother when stressed. This is not to say that men do not also acknowledge the negative life stressors experienced by their adult children, just that they tend to react to them differently.

> For fathers, acting as a resource for adult children in need may be stressful – as it may be for mothers. However, the source of stress is different for men and women. Interviews with parents who were helping adult children cope with serious problems such as divorce . . . showed that mother typically noted the stress that their children's problems caused them personally. Fathers, however, were more likely to be distressed over the anxiety that their wives experienced and thus were indirectly affected by their children's life problems.
>
> (Thomas 1994: 207)

An important and potentially paradoxical new role for older men is that of grandfather. It is paradoxical because, on the one hand, men may be exhibiting a 'gentler', more nurturing relationship with a grandchild than they had with their own children but, on the other hand, may still be viewed, and view themselves, as having the traditional patriarchal role as 'sage' or 'wise man'. Thomas (1994) found that although women report enjoying grandparenthood more than men, grandfathers express higher levels of obligation to offer childrearing advice than grandmothers. She also found that grandfathers were more likely to provide instrumental types of help, such as financial assistance and career guidance. They tended to have an 'active' relationship (exchange of services and support of sporting activities), especially with a grandson, in contrast to the 'expressive' relationship (sympathy and guidance in personal issues) more commonly reported by women with both granddaughters and grandsons. However, grandfathers also reported enjoying the opportunity for indulging their grandchildren, with their time, as well as the provision of instrumental help and advice.

Throughout the interviews, many men spoke of their grandchildren with great affection. Some said they felt closer to their grandchildren than they had to their own children when they were young. This could reflect the difference in time available to spend with growing children. The imperative to work, coupled with the gendered expectations of childcare responsibilities for a cohort born during the first four decades of the twentieth century, meant that generally speaking, these men had less opportunity to engage with their own children as they grew up.

> I'm close with my sons now, but the rest of the family – we aren't a close-knit family as such, it was just how we were brought up. When the boys were younger, I didn't have so much to do with them . . . But Saturdays we go and watch the grandson play football. It's one of our great loves, is that . . . I think the break up of my son's marriage, that was sad. The thought of the grandchildren, they had to grow up far quicker than they would've.
>
> (Brian, 68, married)

Widowed men also reported a special relationship with grandchildren. It is possible that the death of a grandmother means widowers are encouraged to fulfil roles more commonly carried out by a grandmother, such as babysitting or taking grandchildren out on excursions. This contact often resulted in a closer relationship than they might have enjoyed with their grandchildren had their wife still been alive.

Divorced men and social networks

Divorced and separated men were the least likely group to chat to neighbours and were less likely than married/cohabiting or widowed men to entertain people in their home or to visit the homes of friends or family members. Divorced men also reported smaller social networks than when they had been married, but unlike widowed men, they were more likely to report strained relationships with adult children and infrequent contact with grandchildren.

There was also less acceptance of reduced social interaction and a greater desire than expressed by the widowed men to establish new intimate relationships. Divorced men, particularly those who had experienced an attenuated relationship with adult children, frequently articulated a desire for another close relationship as discussed by Borell and Ghazanfareeon Karlsson (in Chapter 4). 'Oh, I would love to have a partner . . . to share life; not just the sexual side am I speaking. I mean a *real* relationship' (Reg, 70, divorced).

Divorced men who did not have a particularly close relationship with their children, or felt that their former wife had 'turned' children against them, were less likely to have maintained or established a good relationship with children after divorce.

> I hadn't spoken to her for about six years. She bought this house and she said 'Oh dad can you come and have a look at it and do some work for me.' So of course dad went along and done all the work for her and after that I never heard anything. I mean over the last – about the last six months, I have had about three phone calls, which are just left on my answer machine, and I have got to the point where I think she is using me, so I am not responding to her calls now. She has got to come and tell me what sort of a relationship she wants. I just feel that all I am getting is a 'phone call' relationship. And I don't want that. I want something solid.
>
> (Dan, 72, divorced)

Dan, a builder, gave his daughter practical help, but still he wished to have a 'solid relationship' to underpin this exchange. On a more encouraging note, Mike (67) described how, after the death of his ex-wife seven years before, he and his daughters were reconciled, and how having contact with his grandchildren had transformed his life.

> When we split up they [daughters] were teenagers – you know what they can be like, didn't want anything to do with me. Since she [ex-wife] died, we sort of got together again and it's been great. The grandchildren are – I spend such a lot of time with them. I've actually got my granddaughter interested in bird watching, and she's only three and a half, it's amazing isn't it?
>
> (Mike, 67, divorced)

As a result of reduced contact with family, and the greater likelihood of having moved from the marital home environs, older divorced men reported smaller social networks than widowers. Perren *et al.* (2003) found that older divorced men were also less likely to belong to clubs, and would consequently lack the support and companionship offered within social organizations. We found that the divorced men in our sample were the least contented with their situation, and viewed a future of loneliness with some concern. For these divorced older men, there would have been an expectation when they married that they would continue to have caring, female companionship in their latter years. With the dislocation of their divorce, this expectation had disappeared and they were left with the possibility of a lonely old age. For some, the prospect was perceived as very bleak.

> It's something I long for, I'm not sufficient unto myself. I've never been a loner. I think one of the things I've always been terrified of all my life is not having a partner and finding myself like this. I'm sort of, kind of, gazing around saying, how did it happen? [laughs] I know perfectly well how it happened, but no, that is something which rather terrifies me. I don't like thinking of it [drops voice and sighs].
>
> (Jasper, 70, divorced twice)

For never married men there was not the same feeling of discontinuity. Given that they had never married, or indeed in some cases never wished to marry, they had placed less reliance on anyone, male or female, on whom they would depend for their sense of well-being and care.

Social independence among never married men

Despite a degree of residential stability, the older never married men reported the least interaction with friends and family within the domestic sphere. When we asked older never married men if they missed having company at home, they tended to say it was not very important to them: 'No. No. I am a bit of a loner in that respect . . . Yes. That is what I am, independent. Almost completely independent' (Karl, 80, never married). 'Yes from time to time. No – not too much because I'm used to my own company' (Guy, 79, never married).

When we asked if they had anyone they could confide in, they were more likely than any other group to say that they did not have a very close friend. 'I have suffered from a lack of true friends [laughs] all my life really, I haven't had firm friends. Maybe I did at school' (Guy, 79, never married).

Jeremy (71, never married): I'm a proud individualist, I mean I don't mind. You know, 'This man is an individualist.' So there you are . . . that was visible at 18.

Interviewer: The close friend you mentioned?

Jeremy: Yeah, but I don't go and stay with him, because, we bachelors, oh, we're very idle we don't want to be toiling after each other . . . I don't seek a lot of human company, I never say anything profound, I don't need someone sitting there particularly, I've never felt this great yearn for companionship, or, you know, 24 hours a day, so I don't know. There's a sad reflection on me.

It could be argued that Jeremy is viewing this 'sad reflection' by using a feminine mirror, as described by Cancian (1987). Even though he has never yearned for companionship, he views this behaviour as deviant from the cultural norm of sociability. However, the never married men generally reported being content with their level of social interaction. Despite the GHS data showing reduced social interaction among single men (in Figure 11.1), the men we asked did not view their situation as problematic. They talked proudly of their autonomy and independence and how they maintained mastery of their environment, organizing their routines around looking after themselves.

The homes of most of the older never married men were clean and tidy, and they did not report a dislike of housekeeping. Four of the never married men had spent several years in the army or navy and explained their orderliness as emanating from their military training. Jeremy (71), a pharmacist, had cared for his ailing mother for many years, and reported that he could not have held his job and cared for his mother without a strict routine of housework. Since an untidy home was more unusual among never married men, this was unlikely to pose a deterrent to asking people in, yet, as the analysis in this chapter has shown, these men were the least likely to invite friends to their home. A more likely explanation is the wish to maintain a distance from intimate relationships.

Conclusions

This chapter has examined to what extent marital status influenced the size and quality of an older man's social network. There was a widely held belief among the men interviewed that women (wives, mothers, daughters, nieces) played a pivotal role in the establishment and maintenance of wide social networks. Older men enjoy and maintain close relationships, although the scope and intensity vary according to current and former marital status. Within the four groups of older men we examined (married, widowed, divorced and never married), issues of continuity and discontinuities are important for understanding social involvement. Married men reported large, stable social networks, primarily (but not exclusively) couple-oriented. In widowhood, these networks contracted and the men tended to rely more heavily on their adult children for support. Divorced men, who reported more attenuated relationships with their adult children, tended to seek another close companionship (which did not necessarily involve sexual intimacy). Older never married men, who had established few close relationships in younger years, did not seek intimacy, and did not report feeling deprived, but they did see themselves as 'different'.

In the life course, men's friendships are principally forged and maintained within a workplace setting (Adams 1994). Friendships outside the workplace are frequently associated with social club, sports and leisure venues (Arber et al. 2002). These friendships are characterized by side-by-side sociability, focusing on activity and often on competitive pursuits, as outlined in Table 11.1. On retirement, the majority of men, regardless of marital status, report a reduction in their circle of friends. However, partnered men maintain couple-oriented social involvement as long as they have reasonable health and sufficient funds to enjoy social activity. Men who live alone are more likely to meet with friends in a public setting than in their home, but do entertain family within the home if they have continued to maintain contact. However, lone older men experience a much reduced social network if physical disabilities mean they are unable to get out, because unlike women, they have a restricted history of entertaining within the private sphere.

Current gerontological literature treats older men as genderless and frequently fails to recognize that men exhibit masculinities that have adapted to changing roles and relationships in later life. For men, increasing age does not necessarily herald a reduction in masculine identity. For the majority of previously married men, the need for close companionship does not diminish in later life, but the imperative of 'separateness' allied to masculine self-identity may hamper the establishment of new relationships in later life. Nevertheless, as Cancian (1987) points out, instead of continuing to measure the quantity and quality of social networks with a 'feminine ruler', we need to seek different ways of viewing intimacy and friendship patterns in the lives of older men. We need to consider the scenario that older men may wish to have a smaller, closer network of friends and acquaintances, like Jeremy and his close friend who do not wish to 'toil after each other'.

This chapter has revealed that much importance is attached to individual autonomy and independence and many men hold ambivalent attitudes towards central features of the 'female script', such as the need for intimacy and social engagement. Most prescriptions for well-being in later life derive from the experiences of the female majority, and as such may be ill-suited to the perspectives of older men.

Acknowledgements

We are grateful to National Statistics for permission to use General Household Survey data, and to the UK Data Archive and Manchester Computing Centre for access to the data. The material presented in this chapter is based on research supported by the Economic and Social Research Council under the Growing Older Programme, grant no. L480 25 4033.

References

Adams, R. (1994) Older men's friendship patterns. In E. Thompson (ed.) *Older Men's Lives*. Thousand Oaks, CA: Sage.
Arber, S. and Ginn, J. (1991) *Gender and Later Life: A Sociological Analysis of Resources and Constraints*. London: Sage.

Arber, S., Perren, K. and Davidson, K. (2002) Involvement in social organizations in later life: variations by gender and class. In L. Andersson (ed.) *Cultural Gerontology*. Westport, CT: Greenwood Publishing Group.

Burgoyne, J., Ormrod, R. and Richards, M. (1987) *Divorce Matters*. Harmondsworth: Penguin.

Cancian, F. (1987) *Love in America: Gender and Self Development*. New York: Cambridge University Press.

Carr, D. and Utz, R. (2002) Later-life widowhood in the United States: new directions in research and theory. *Ageing International*, 27(1): 65–88.

Chodorow, N. (1991) The reproduction of mothering: psychoanalysis and the sociology of gender. In M. Humm (ed.) *Feminisms*. London: Harvester Wheatsheaf.

Cliff, D. (1993) Under the wife's feet: renegotiating gender divisions in early retirement, *Sociological Review*, 41(1): 30–53.

Davidson, K. (2001) Reconstructing life after a death: psychological adaptation and social role transition in the medium and long term for older widowed men and women in the UK, *Indian Journal of Gerontology*, 15(1/2): 221–36.

Davidson, K., Daly, T. and Arber, S. (2003) Older men, social integration and organisational activites. *Social Policy and Society*, 2(2): 81–89.

Davies, M., Falkingham, J., Love, H., McCleod, T., McKay, A., Morton, O., Taylor, L. and Wallace, P. (1998) *Next Generation*. London: The Henley Centre.

de Jong Gierveld, J. (1998) A review of loneliness: concept and definitions, determinants and consequences, *Reviews in Clinical Gerontology*, 8: 73–80.

Duncombe, J. and Marsden, D. (1998) 'Stepford wives' and 'hollow men'? Doing emotion work, doing gender and 'authenticity' in intimate heterosexual relationships. In G. Bendelow and S. Williams (eds) *Emotions in Social Life: Critical Themes and Contemporary Issues*. London: Routledge.

Field, D. (1999) Continuity and change in friendships in advanced old age: findings from the Berkeley Older Generation Study, *International Journal of Aging and Human Development*, 48(4): 325–46.

Goldman, N., Korenman, S. and Weinstein, R. (1995) Marital status among the elderly, *Social Science and Medicine*, 40(12): 1717–30.

Hess, B. (1982) Aging, gender role and friendship, *Educational Horizons*, 60(4): 155–60.

Keith, P. (1994) A typology of orientations toward household and marital roles of older men and women. In E. Thompson (ed.) *Older Men's Lives*. Thousand Oaks, CA: Sage.

Kulik, L. (2002) Marital equality and the quality of long-term marriage in later life, *Ageing and Society*, 22(4): 459–81.

Miller, S. (1983) *Men and Friendship*. San Leandro, CA: Gateway Books.

Nydegger, C. and Mitteness, L. (1991) Fathers and their adult sons and daughters, *Marriage and Family Review*, 16(3/4): 249–66.

O'Connor, P. (1992) *Friendships Between Women: A Critical Review*. Hemel Hempstead: Harvester Wheatsheaf.

OPCS (1997) *General Household Survey: 1994–1995*. Computer file. Colchester: The Data Archive.

OPCS (1998) *General Household Survey: 1995–1996*. Computer file. Colchester: The Data Archive.

OPCS (2000) *General Household Survey: 1998–1999*. Computer file. Colchester: The Data Archive.

OPCS (2002) *Marriage, Divorce and Adoption Statistics*. London: HMSO.

Perren, K., Arber, S. and Davidson, K. (2003) Men's organisational affiliation in later life: the influence of social class and marital status on informal group membership, *Ageing and Society*, 23(1): 69–82.

Pleck, J. (1975) Man to man: is brotherhood possible? In N. Glazer-Malbin (ed.) *Old Family, New Family*. New York: Van Nostrand.

Scott, A. and Wenger, G. C. (1995) Gender and social support networks in later life. In S. Arber and J. Ginn (eds) *Connecting Gender and Ageing: A Sociological Approach*. Buckingham: Open University Press.

Seidler, V. (1989) *Rediscovering Masculinity*. London: Routledge.

Seidler, V. (1998) *Man Enough*. London: Sage.

Thomas, J. (1994) Older men and fathers and grandfathers. In E. Thompson (ed.) *Older Men's Lives*. Thousand Oaks, CA: Sage.

Thompson, E. (1994a) Older men as invisible men. In E. Thompson (ed.) *Older Men's Lives*. Thousand Oaks, CA: Sage.

Thompson, E. (ed.) (1994b) *Older Men's Lives*. Thousand Oaks, CA: Sage.

van den Hoonaard, D. K. (2002) Attitudes of older widows and widowers in New Brunswick, Canada towards new partnerships, *Ageing International*, 27(4): 79–92.

Webster, J. (1995) Age differences in reminiscence functions. In B. Haight and J. Webster (eds) *The Art and Science of Reminiscing*. Washington, DC: Taylor and Francis.

12

SLEEP AS A SOCIAL ACT: A WINDOW ON GENDER ROLES AND RELATIONSHIPS

Jenny Hislop and Sara Arber

The sociology of sleep is a new and hitherto under-explored area of everyday life. This chapter explores women's sleep against a vivid backdrop of their social world, reflecting the multiplicity of roles and relationships that characterize their lives. As such, for many women, a central theme is the relationship with their partner and the key role this plays in shaping and influencing their sleep patterns throughout the life course. As couples age, physiological factors may coincide with life events and transitions to change not only the structure of sleep but also the nature of the couple relationship. To study sleep in its social context is thus to open a window on to gender roles and relationships in later life.

Drawing on qualitative research, this chapter shows the link between women's sleep in later life and their sleeping relationship with their partner. Women's sleep may be affected by their partner's increased restlessness as they age, with snoring, prostate problems and the pain and discomfort of poor health creating an unfavourable sleeping environment. Changing identities, gender roles and relationships that accompany later life transitions may also contribute to a restructuring of women's sleep. Reflected in these changes may be an underlying ambivalence, as women seek to accommodate their own sleep needs while remaining committed to a relationship with their partner in which the balance of gender roles has shifted. Moreover, the salience of the sleeping relationship in structuring women's sleep is highlighted as women try to establish a viable sleeping pattern in the absence of their partner following divorce or widowhood. Alongside these transitions, the double bed may become a powerful symbol of the changing nature of the couple relationship in later life.

The changing nature of sleep with ageing

I said to my friend that I thought perhaps as I got older my sleep wasn't quite so deep as it used to be when I was a lot younger. Say up to the age of 55 or even 60 I slept very deeply, but maybe now I don't sleep so deeply – I sleep well, quite satisfactorily, but not like a log. My friend said he thought the same.

(SD023: Claire aged 71)

Claire's instincts about her sleep are right. The patterning of sleep in later life changes in response to physiological and psycho-social factors. From a physiological viewpoint, ageing is associated with major changes in sleep structure, quality and timing (Dijk *et al.* 2001). Sleep patterns become lighter and more fragmented and are characterized by more frequent and prolonged awakenings as the amount of slow wave or deep sleep declines (for example, Bixler *et al.* 1984; Bliwise 1998; Morgan 1998). According to Dement (2001: 122), many people over 60 have 'very little stage 4 [deep sleep] left at all', leaving them more vulnerable to sleep disruption from external factors such as noise, light and movement. Moreover, changes in the circadian regulation of the sleep–wake cycle with ageing create a tendency for people to become 'more larklike, falling asleep earlier and getting up earlier' (Dement 2001: 122). Shifts in the circadian clock may also lead to patterns of daytime napping and increased fatigue, further compromising the ability to sleep at night. The discontinuity in sleep patterns arising from these age-related changes may cause feelings of anxiety and dissatisfaction with sleep as the gap between sleep expectations, based on lifetime experiences, and new sleep realities becomes apparent.

The process of change in sleep patterns associated with ageing is unique and different not only between individuals but also between men and women. Studies of brain wave patterns in sleep indicate that, from a physiological perspective, it is men who experience the greater deterioration in sleep patterns with ageing (for example, Webb 1982; Reynolds *et al.* 1985; Hume *et al.* 1998; Schubert *et al.* 2002). Redieh *et al.*'s (1990) meta-analysis of 27 sleep studies addressing differences in sleep behaviour between men and women aged 58 and over found a number of significant differences. While older men had a higher percentage of lighter sleep stages, women enjoyed a greater percentage of deeper restorative sleep. Moreover, the incidence of respiratory disturbances such as obstructive sleep apnoea (OSA, a snoring-related disorder in which the airways collapse blocking breathing) and periodic limb movements (PLMS, a condition in which people experience periodic leg jerks throughout much of the night) was significantly higher in men than women.

Redieh's review is supported by more recent studies. Ancoli-Israel *et al.*'s (1991) study of 192 men and 228 women aged 65 and over in the USA found that PLMS becomes more severe with age. Although equally distributed among men and women across all ages 65 to 89, relatively severe PLMS is almost twice as prevalent in men aged 65 to 79 as in women. Enright *et al.*'s (1996) study of self-reported sleep disturbances in 5201 men and women aged 65 and older in the USA found that the prevalence of snoring increases with age until the age of 70, with men more likely than women to report that others had complained about their loud snoring (33 per cent versus 19 per cent). The implications of increased movement from partners and the sound of snoring and strained grunting and gasping as partners fight for breath (Hobson 1995) on maintaining sleep quality and harmony in the couple relationship are considerable.

Alongside these physiological changes in sleep patterns, the ageing process is characterized by an increase in health problems, which can cause discomfort and sleep disturbance for both the sufferer and, by association, their partner. Medical diseases and chronic illness play an important role in influencing sleep quality in old age (Bliwise 2000). Foley *et al.* (1995), studying sleep complaints among 9000 men and women aged 65 and older, concluded that a considerable proportion of sleep complaints may be associated with co-morbidity. Heart and respiratory problems, sleep apnoea, joint pain, arthritis, prostate problems, hypertension, cancer and dementia, as well as the medications used to treat these disorders, can increase the potential for sleep disturbance. A survey conducted by the Arthritis Research Campaign (2002) found that people aged 55 and over were almost three times more likely to suffer from arthritis or joint pain than those aged under 55 years (52 per cent versus 18 per cent). The study found that the incidence of arthritic conditions was more prevalent in women than men, with associated pain having a major impact on sleep quality for both the sufferer and their partner. A study in the USA, for example, found that 60 per cent of all night-time pain sufferers over the age of 50 experienced pain from arthritis that resulted in frequent sleep loss (NSF 1996). Non-cancerous enlargement of the prostate affects about half of all men by the age of 60, rising to 80 per cent in their eighties, while prostate cancer increases in men from the age of 50, with a lifetime risk of one in 12 (www.prostate-research.org.uk). The need to go to the toilet frequently during the night can be an impediment to sleep maintenance for both men and women. As one GP in our study says:

I think older people have more interrupted nights and so feel tireder because the old men are getting up to wee from their prostates and the old women are getting up because they also have uro-genital ageing and can't sleep through the night without weeing, or they have arthritis in their hips, back, neck that wakes them up.

(GP002)

From a physiological viewpoint, therefore, the potential for increased sleep disruption with ageing is high. However, if, as we assert, sleep is a social act, then to consider only the physiological aspects of sleep is to ignore the influence of psycho-social factors on sleep patterns in later life.

From a psycho-social perspective, ageing is accompanied by changes in status and identity as people make the transition from work to retirement, from good health to poor, from an active to more sedentary lifestyle, from caring for children to caring for elderly parents or a spouse and from spouse to widow(er). The psychological stress associated with these transitions inevitably impacts on sleep. As lives and lifestyles are restructured, so too are sleep patterns, with earlier expectations and patterning of sleep no longer viable as roles and relationships undergo change. Few of these life changes take place in isolation, however. They take place within and are structured by our relationships with others. Our sleep, therefore, is the outcome of the interaction of life events in association with the physiological ageing of both the mechanisms of sleep and the body. These factors, set within the context of our social roles and relationships, interact to produce a fertile environment for the emergence of compromised sleep patterns as individuals age. We suggest, therefore, that it is women's relationship with their partner and the roles and responsibilities embedded within this relationship that play a key role in structuring women's sleep in later life.

Couples, relationships and sleep

Sleeping as a couple, while considered by some to be symbolic of a loving relationship, is fraught with the potential for sleep disruption. In their study of 46 couples aged between 23 and 67, Pankhurst and Horne (1994) found evidence that men are more likely to affect their partner's sleep than women, with women reporting significantly more awakenings because of their partner than men. If this is the case, then the higher incidence of reported complaints of sleep disturbance in women found in other studies may be attributable at least in part to the impact of partner behaviour (Redieh et al. 1990; Morgan 1998; Schubert et al. 2002). Morgan's study of sleep in people aged 65 and over in Nottingham in the late 1980s showed a prevalence of insomnia (problems with sleep onset, sleep maintenance and early awakening) in almost twice as many women as men (28 per cent versus 15 per cent) (Morgan 1998). Similarly, Schubert et al. (2002) found that the problem of waking and having a hard time getting back to sleep, although experienced by both men and women, was more commonly reported by women than men up to the age of 80.

While focusing primarily on the sleep patterns of younger couples (only 5 per cent of the sample were aged 55 and over), research conducted in the UK (Sleep Council 2002) into the sleep patterns of 1000 couples provides insights into how sleep disruptions can impact on the couple relationship. The survey found that 49 per cent of respondents complained about being awakened by their partner during the night. Partners' snoring, tossing and turning, hogging the bed clothes, waking them up to chat, reading, watching TV or listening to the radio were cited as contributing to sleep disturbances. Partners' snoring was ranked as the major cause of complaint by women in the survey (63 per cent versus 32 per cent of men). There is little doubt that intrusions into sleep from sources such as these play a significant role in determining the quality of couples' sleep in later life.

From a sociological viewpoint, however, it is the nature of the couple relationship as revealed through sleep that is of more interest in this chapter. The period of sleep provides a valuable resource for understanding the changes in gender roles and relationships that accompany transitions in later life. To analyse these changes, however, we need first to examine the gendered roles and relationships that have structured the lives of older women and their partners.

For the majority of couples born prior to the Second World War, their relationship has been structured according to a traditional gendered division of labour, with men as providers and protectors balancing women's roles as servicers and carers within the home. In addition to the more visible domestic tasks, women's roles incorporate the often invisible 'sentient activities' through which they often unconsciously attend to, notice and respond to the needs, health and well-being of their partner and children (Mason 1996). Women carry out the multifaceted tasks associated with caring from a sense of commitment and responsibility, or 'active sensibility', which ensures the continuity of the caring role throughout the life course (Mason 1996).

Structured and reinforced by active sensibility and the marriage vow of 'in sickness and in health' (Davidson et al. 2000), the provision of caring services remains a constant commitment as women age. In the 'bridge between marriage and widowhood' (Davidson 1999: 141), caring responsibilities can grow in intensity as their partner's health declines, impacting significantly on women's sleep (for example, McCurry and Teri 1995; Wilcox and King 1999; Mahler and Green 2002). A recent study of carers in the UK, for example, showed that 34 per cent of carers reported tiredness and 31 per cent reported disrupted sleep arising as a consequence of their caring responsibilities (Mahler and Green 2002: 25). For many women the bedroom becomes an 'invisible workplace' where they carry out the sentient activities associated with their caring responsibilities, rather than a sanctuary providing respite from the day's activities (Hislop and Arber 2003).

The decline in the quantity and quality of women's sleep during later life, while on one level the result of changes in their partner's sleep behaviour, may also be associated with other changes in the nature of the couple relationship. The increased responsibilities for caring for a partner in later life and the consequent intrusions into women's sleep may take place in the context of a corresponding change in their partner's previous gendered role as provider and protector. To examine sleep disruption in later life, therefore, is to bear witness to changes in lifetime gendered roles and identities.

One of the strategies that women may consider when partners constrain their access to the sleep resource is to move from the double bed. The decision to sleep apart while remaining together is not straightforward, however. The double bed is central to the sleeping relationship of most couples. As the site of sleep as well as sex, it symbolizes the interactional nature of the partnership. For women whose sleep is compromised by their ageing partner's sleep behaviour, the double bed may become symbolic of a growing ambivalence in the couple relationship. According to Connidis (see Chapter 6), ambivalence 'captures the coexistence of harmony and conflict in family relationships', reflecting 'the contradictions and paradoxes of their ties to one another'. This ambivalence may be evident as women weigh up the pros and cons of moving from the double bed to a single bed or to another room to reclaim their right to sleep. According to the Sleep Council's (2002) research, although fewer than one couple in ten (7 per cent) currently have separate beds, almost 20 per cent would do so if their partner suggested it, while 5 per cent would like to suggest it but know their partner would refuse. Fear of causing offence, putting a strain on the relationship, habit and concern over the reaction of family and friends are cited as reasons for continuing to share a bed despite this being the cause of sleep disruption.

We suggest that the reasons for the reluctance of couples to sleep apart may be more subtle than this, however. We propose that the decision to move or to stay is inextricably linked to the gendered expectations of the couple relationship and to the cultural values of the society in which the partnership exists. This chapter explores to what extent among ageing women part of the 'doing of gender' as 'wife' or 'partner' involves the sharing of a double bed. If, as West and Zimmerman (1987: 147) maintain, doing gender 'furnishes the interactional scaffolding of social structure', then to sleep apart may represent a challenge to the couple relationship, bringing into question women's gendered identity as 'wife' or 'partner'. Moreover, in a culture in which the 'norms' of couple behaviour are defined as sleeping with one's partner, to sleep apart is to challenge the overriding ideology on which the couple relationship is based.

With increasing age, for many women divorce or the death of their spouse represents a disengagement from the couple relationship and its concomitant roles and responsibilities. After a period of grieving, women have the opportunity to restructure their sleeping patterns and arrangements as part of the building of a new identity. The sleeping experiences of these women, symbolized in the form of an empty double bed at night, thus provide insights into the role transition from couple to lone woman.

This chapter explores the interrelationship between sleep and gendered roles and relationships from the perspective of women aged 60 and over who participated in a study of women's sleep in the UK. Following discussion of methodology, the chapter draws on empirical data to uncover insights into the interrelationship between sleep patterns and gender roles and relationships. It examines the impact of partners' behaviour, increased caring for their partner and relationship loss on women's sleep and the management of sleep disruption. Central to the discussion is the contention that as the couple relationship structures sleep patterns, so too do women's experiences of sleep reflect the intricate and changing nature of the couple relationship in later life.

Method

Qualitative research was conducted on the sleep of women aged 60 and over in a medium-sized city in southern England in 2001–2. Using a multi-method approach, data were drawn from three main sources: focus groups (coded FG), in-depth interviews (coded IV) and audio sleep diaries (coded SD). Participants were recruited in response to poster advertisements throughout the community and through coordinators of social and educational groups approached by the researcher. Snowballing from initial recruits also proved a successful recruitment strategy, with respondents asked to publicize the project through their own professional and social networks.

Four focus groups ($n = 34$), each 1.5 hours in length, were held comprising two groups each for ages 60 to 69 and 70 and over, to gain an overview of the experiences of sleep among older women. Discussion and interaction among participants ranged around broad topic areas, including attitudes to sleep, patterns of sleep, sleeping as a shared experience, ageing and sleep, the effects of poor sleep and strategies for overcoming sleep problems.

In-depth interviews with a further 28 women were conducted, providing opportunities for these women to discuss changes in their sleep patterns in relation to major life events and transitions. Following the interview, these women were asked to complete an audio sleep diary in which they tape recorded an assessment of their sleep each morning for a seven-day period. Data from these diaries highlighted the inter-relationship between women's gendered roles and responsibilities and their sleep patterns.

At the beginning of each focus group session or interview, participants were asked to complete a short questionnaire. In terms of socio-demographic characteristics, the 62 women participating in the study ranged in age from 61 to 86. Of these, 27 were married, 15 were separated or divorced, 18 were widowed and two had never married. The majority of women had children ($n = 55$). Although 42 per cent of participants had qualifications at or below O level, just over one-quarter had degrees, perhaps a reflection of the population of the university city in which the research was conducted. All participants considered themselves retired, although eight were working part-time. In terms of household composition, half the women lived alone ($n = 31$), 25 were living with a partner only, two with a partner and adult children, three alone with adult children and one with a tenant.

All data were recorded, transcribed and imported into the qualitative data analysis package *QSR NVivo*. Data were then analysed for emergent themes reflecting the influence of life events and transitions, and roles and relationships, on sleep. Almost all women in the study were, or had been, part of a couple, with just under half currently partnered and the balance widowed or divorced. As such the sample is ideal for analysing the impact of being part of a couple, now or in the past, on women's sleep.

The impact of partners on women's sleep in later life

Laugh and the world laughs with you, snore and you sleep alone.

(Anthony Burgess)

Sharing the same sleeping space as a partner, while important for warmth, love and companionship, can also be detrimental to the maintenance of good sleeping patterns in later life. Women in our study reported a strong association between deterioration in their sleep quality arising from their partner's snoring, prostate problems and ill-health. We examine each of these factors in turn, revealing that for some women the reality of sleep in later life can be more a 'bed of thorns' than a 'bed of roses'.

Partner's snoring is an intrusion into sleep experienced by many women in our study. Its chronic nature leads to impaired sleep accompanied by increasing frustration and irritation. Although often portrayed in a humorous vein, accounts of snoring can also reveal the emotional labour expended in concern for a partner's well-being throughout the night:

He used to make a lot of noises, like a farmyard he was.

(FG2: 70+)

My husband used to be asleep then all of a sudden he would stop breathing. I used to lie there and think, 'for god's sake breathe'. I would give him a kick and he would say, 'what the hell are you kicking me for?'

(FG1: 70+)

The need to go to the toilet during the night increases with ageing for both men and women. While for most women this is a source of inconvenience, the increasing incidence of diseases of the prostate in ageing men is a major source of sleep disruption for both the man and his bed partner. For most men, frequent getting up to go to the toilet during the night will be a feature of their sleep patterns as they age. As these excerpts show, among couples the consequences of these disturbances are considerable, with women at times assuming the added responsibility for ensuring their partner seeks medical advice for his condition:

My husband is in and out of bed a few times a night and disturbs me as well because he is larger than me so the weight of him getting out of bed, that disturbs me, and I'm a very light sleeper anyway.

(FG2: 60–69)

My husband needs to pee so that sometimes does wake me up. He's getting something done about it *by my instigation*. He gets up about three times a night so that sometimes disturbs me.

(FG2: 60–69, emphasis added)

The deprioritizing of individual sleep needs in response to women's commitment to care for the well-being of their partner is also evident when partners experience poor health in later life. In the following excerpts from her sleep diary, Mary describes the causal relationship between her husband's illness and the quality of her sleep. She speaks of her concerns about her husband's illness as well as the intrusive nature of his symptoms on her sleep:

Tuesday

Quite a good night – my husband wasn't having any problem with his breathing and so he didn't disturb me at all.

Wednesday

I didn't sleep very well last night, very poor sleep. I went to bed at the usual time about ten o'clock and read for half an hour which is what I usually do. I was quite happy and lay down at half past ten but I just could not sleep. I was still awake at one o'clock, a bit restless, not too bad and I really put it down to being a bit *apprehensive* about today because my husband has to go to hospital and get some results of tests. So I suppose it is a bit of *stress* . . . My husband *coughed* quite a lot during the night which I was *concerned* about, and that of course didn't help me to sleep either.

(SD001: Mary, aged 64, emphasis added)

As women age, their own health problems may interact with those of their husband to increase the potential for sleep disturbance and poor quality sleep. While, for Mary, the pain from arthritis exacerbates the disruption caused by her husband's ill-health, Alice's sleep is affected by her husband's snoring and her own pain:

Very poor sleep last night . . . My husband didn't come to bed straight away and I suppose I was aware that he was downstairs. He was coughing a bit and I got up and just checked to make sure he was alright . . . My knees were aching, I suppose it's a bit of old age or arthritis or something . . . I feel very tired this morning and I obviously didn't rest easily during the night. (Sunday)

(SD001: Mary, aged 64)

[My husband] snores a lot and keeps me awake half the night. I don't sleep very well. I also get a lot of earache if I lay on this side. It's bad and I'm up all night.

(FG2: 60–69)

With ageing, sleep disruption can become a feature of the couple relationship. Yet, while physiological changes such as increased snoring, prostate problems and ill-health of their partner can interact with women's own health problems to compromise their sleep, they are not the only factors that impact on women's sleep quality in later life. The women above, for example, reveal the emotional labour that underpins their gendered roles within the couple relationship. We contend that it is this overlay of 'worry' work, or sentient activity, that plays a significant role in compromising women's sleep within the couple relationship.

Sleep problems in ageing, therefore, must be seen within a social context, responsive not only to physiological changes but also to gendered divisions of labour and life events and transitions that may alter the balance of the relationship between men and women. To exemplify this, we next examine the impact on older women's sleep of increased caring responsibilities as their partner's health declines.

The caring role and the sleeping relationship

> Care keeps his watch in every old *(wo)*man's eye,
> And where care lodges, sleep will never lie.
> (Shakespeare, *Romeo and Juliet*, Act 2 Scene 3, adapted)

Many women in our study, who care for husbands in later life, would attest to the validity of Shakespeare's words describing the impact of care on sleep. In describing their sleep in relation to these caring experiences, the women allude not only to the physical and emotional labour associated with caring but also to the changing nature of the couple relationship.

Caring for a partner with dementia, for example, can be a long-term commitment resulting in chronic sleep disruption and adverse consequences on the quality of the carer's daily life. Florence, a widow, describes her experience of caring for her husband:

> For ten years I looked after my husband with dementia and I mean I never stopped, I never slept really and that was my worse time for sleep. I kept a diary all the time he was ill and 25 times a night I got up once and in the morning I was just absolutely shattered.
>
> (FG1: 70+)

Rita, currently caring for her husband after a major heart attack, speaks not only of the impact on her sleep, but of the change in identity within their relationship from 'husband–wife' to 'mother–child', describing her husband's behaviour in terms of that of a recalcitrant child over whom she needs to watch constantly:

When he had the actual heart attack I was so tired, but when he came home it was bad. That would be the only time I'd say my sleep has been bad . . . It affected me from the point of view, it is like having a *baby*. I have always got *one ear listening for him*. But he is very *naughty* actually because he wakes up and has pains and he uses his spray and sits up in bed and I give him an aspirin and then after about half an hour he says, 'Oh, I think I will try and sleep now', and he goes to sleep. But of course I don't. *I lay awake listening to him breathe*.

(IV007: Rita, aged 63, emphasis added)

In the following extract, Bea describes the consequences on her sleep at present as she cares for her 89-year-old husband, who suffers from Parkinson's disease, multiple strokes and arthritis:

I get into bed and then I can't lie down and go straight to sleep. And for the past three years I haven't been able to concentrate on reading a book. I lay down to go to sleep at 12.10, I woke at 2.30 and from 2.30 until 4.25 I couldn't get back to sleep. I take Tamoxifen [for breast cancer], and that can give you hot flushes and this was continuous. I couldn't go back to sleep. [My husband] was moaning, I didn't know what was wrong. I went off into the other bed and took the radio. I had a little doze then, up at 5.30 [to attend to husband], that took half an hour, no point going back to bed. So I got a couple of hours sleep . . . It is a battle and *I haven't got a husband*. That is the awful part about it. So *the man I love is not there* . . . I often wonder what is going to happen . . . I know if he went into a home, then he would never come out again, and *I couldn't live with myself*.

(IV005: Bea, aged 68, emphasis added)

Bea paints a vivid description of nights of continual sleep disruption and the sheer awfulness of her predicament. Yet her account reveals many insights into the evolving nature of the couple relationship in later life. In the final months of her husband's life, Bea continues to fulfil the physical and emotional labour intrinsic to her role as wife in a situation where, through his illness, her husband's identity has changed from active partner to passive dependant. For her the partnership has changed beyond recognition. In the transition to widowhood, what remains is an expectation that she continue to care without the recompense of the loving relationship she once enjoyed. Moreover, Bea is burdened with guilt at the prospect of being unable to continue to fulfil her commitment to care for her husband 'till death us do part'.

As the above excerpts show, caring responsibilities can be a major predictor of sleep disruption in later life. Moreover, these responsibilities may reflect a gradual loosening of the couple relationship as gender roles become unbalanced and identities change in the transition to widowhood. The influence of the couple relationship, however, forged over a long lifetime, can continue to affect women's sleep long after it has ended through divorce or widowhood.

Relationship loss and its impact on women's sleep

For over half the women in our study, the loss of a husband through either divorce or, more commonly, bereavement has a significant impact on their sleep. In talking about their current experiences of sleep, widows and divorcees may shed light retrospectively on dimensions of the couple relationship not previously apparent.

Divorce in later life can bring a sense of freedom to some women and, after an initial period of mourning the relationship, often an improvement in sleep patterns. Lana, who divorced in her late fifties, describes how, in retrospect, her ex-husband's behaviour in bed reflected the nature of their relationship.

> When I was sleeping with my ex-husband in bed I felt I was being strangled. And he wouldn't sleep without his arm around me. Sometimes it was round my neck. Possession . . . Now I am myself . . . my sleep is much improved. I have just gone back to the pattern I had when I was young basically.
>
> (IV015: Lana, aged 62)

Amy, whose husband left her for another woman when she was 57, describes the impact of separation and divorce on her sleep. Her description parallels that of the mourning period experienced following the death of a husband, and illustrates the strength of the marital bond on sleep, even after the relationship ends and significant time elapses:

Amy: My sleep went to pot. I found sleep very difficult, not initially. Initially I just slept but after a few weeks or so I began to be unable to sleep for very long. I took a long while to get to sleep and I woke up a lot in the night. Very poor sleep . . . My sleep did improve gradually and I just can't remember at what point, but within a couple of years it had improved.
Interviewer: So since then, how has your sleep been?
Amy: At the moment it is mostly OK. There are always times, I think with all of us particularly, when memories come into this, when perhaps you have a wakeful spell, particularly the break-up of the marriage.   (IV009: Amy, aged 71)

As discussed in the previous section, the transition to widowhood for many women is characterized by a period of intensive caring responsibilities, which play havoc with their sleep. Patterns of sleep established during this period, coupled with grieving, can create a predisposition to poor sleep quality, particularly during the initial stages of widowhood. June, whose husband

died three years ago, six months after her retirement, links the deterioration
in her sleep to the period of caring and mourning:

> *Interviewer:* How was your sleep when your husband died?
>
> *June:* Oh, that was terrible. That was probably when the rot set in
> actually. I just didn't sleep well or for very long ... It was
> probably creeping on before then. Obviously if someone beside
> you is not very well, you are very keen to see what is going on,
> even half asleep really ... I think I just carried on [after he
> died] in the same waking up sort of pattern.
>
> *Interviewer:* How long did this pattern continue?
>
> *June:* Well, I'm obviously sleeping better than that now, but I'm still
> not sleeping well.   (IV008: June, aged 63)

After a lifetime of sharing a bed with a partner and the sense of companionship this implies, widows experience a sense of loss symbolized by the empty
double bed at night. For many widows, the empty bed is a constant reminder
of the couple relationship that was, and an expression of their new identity as
widow. The long hours of night are often permeated by reminiscences about
the past:

> I go to bed and don't go to sleep until four or five in the morning, but
> another night I could go in and drop off straight away you know. But I
> think, myself, it is missing somebody in bed, because I have been a widow
> two and a half years, and I think you miss the company.
>
> (FG2: 70+)

> When my husband was alive, I used to find sex was the best sleeping pill.
>
> (FG1: 70+)

> You still remember things you done years ago. And I think that is one of
> the reasons I wake at night, or when you can't sleep you are thinking of
> all those times that you had.
>
> (FG2: 70+)

Alongside this sense of loss, the reality of sleeping alone without the security
or companionship of a partner can create a sense of fear that impacts on
women's sleep in widowhood and/or divorce. In the following excerpt, Anna
and June speak of the consequences of living alone in the absence of the
protective role of their partner, and suggest a link between companionship
and improved sleep.

> *Anna:* Living on your own, you're just aware of sounds ... I'm too
> much of a coward ... if I get up in the night it is because I think
> I heard something and this is living on your own.
>
> *June:* It sounds funny because I wedge my bedroom door open
> because I want to know if there is something going on in the
> house.   (FG2: 60–69)

Women's accounts of sleep after divorce or widowhood can heighten understanding of the impact of loss of a partner on sleep patterns. For many widows, this period of adjustment is often accompanied by a continuation, at least in the short term, of the disrupted sleep patterns that marked the intense period of caring during the final stages of their partner's life. This may be followed by greater freedom to create a sleeping environment free from the constraints imposed by their late partner. As women restructure their sleep in accordance with their new identity as widows or divorcees, talking about their past can provide valuable insights into the gendered roles and relationships that once characterized their lives. As we discuss in the next section, these reflections can also reveal the influence of the couple relationship on women's management of sleep disruption.

Relationships and the management of sleep disruption in later life

> All this fuss about sleeping together. For physical pleasure I'd sooner go to my dentist any day.
>
> (Evelyn Waugh)

Not all women would agree with Waugh's statement, but the issue of how women manage sleep disturbance emerges as a major theme in the study of women's sleep in later life. The strategies women use to manage sleep disturbances are diverse, ranging from simple pre-bed rituals such as having a hot bath or a warm drink, to taking sleeping pills or relocating either to a single bed within the same room or to a different room. These strategies have been discussed in more detail elsewhere (Hislop and Arber 2002, forthcoming) and are not the focus of this discussion. Instead, we now examine two issues associated with sleep management: first, how partners impact on women's strategy choice; second, the issue of relocation and its repercussions in terms of the couple relationship.

How partners impact on strategy choice

While women have access to a range of strategies designed to improve their sleep, not all are readily accessible. With sleep taking place within a social context, women are aware of the need to protect the sleep of others in the household as part of their practice of sentient activity. In the following audio sleep diary excerpt, Rita highlights how her respect for her partner's sleep and well-being can impose constraints on her choice of strategies to help her sleep:

> I would have liked to have got up and made a drink and read for a while but [husband] was fast asleep and if I had got out of bed I would have disturbed him.
>
> (SD007: Rita, aged 63)

Ironically, widowhood provides the best insights into former constraints imposed on strategy choice by the couple relationship. Released from concerns about disturbing their partner's sleep by moving around the house at night, or reading or listening to the radio in bed, widows are able to choose from a wider range of strategies to help to overcome sleep disruption:

> I always read a book when I go up to bed until about 12 o'clock. I never used to when my husband was alive, I never read a book then.
>
> (FG2: 70+)

> When you have a partner you disturb him [if you get up]. There is this thing [with a partner] about I will lie, I will wait and then I will fall asleep. But now [as a widow] I will get up and go downstairs and make a drink. I think doing something is better than lying there.
>
> (FG1: 60–69)

Widows' reflections on the past and their descriptions of sleep arrangements since the death of their husband highlight how partners' behaviour during the relationship may act as a barrier to better sleep. For Connie, whose relationship had dictated her sleeping arrangements, her husband's death provided an opportunity to move to what she considered a preferable environment. Her comments highlight the dynamics of a relationship in which her sleeping comfort was compromised by her acquiescence to the wishes of her husband:

> *Interviewer:* Was it strange sleeping alone after [your husband] died?
> *Connie:*   Oh, yes.
> *Interviewer:* But you stayed in the same bed?
> *Connie:*   Yes, but then I got fed up with it, so I moved into one of the other rooms and moved a single bed in there.
> *Interviewer:* You missed your husband?
> *Connie:*   No, it wasn't that. I never did like the bed. He did. I didn't like it.
>
> (IV014: Connie, aged 83)

For May, widowhood has meant a restructuring of the patterning of her sleep. Away from the fear of her domineering husband who died four years ago, she describes the freedom she now enjoys:

> *May:*   I wake up at 7 a.m. and just lay there thinking you know.
> *Interviewer:* Is that a nice time for you?
> *May:*   Yes.
> *Interviewer:* So how has your sleep changed since your husband died?
> *May:*   Well he didn't like laying in bed and if he got up he expected everybody else to get up so you were always up between seven and eight. And bed time was usually half ten. He expected everybody to go to bed before him . . . Now I'm often still down here at 11.30.   (IV016: May, aged 74)

To examine sleep management is thus to reveal the complex interplay between women's own sleep needs and those of their partners. In protecting the sleep needs of their partners as part of their commitment to the couple relationship, women may relinquish their access to the full range of strategies available to improve their sleep outcomes. Moreover, the strategies that women choose, or fail to choose, may be illustrative of the constraints inherent in the couple relationship. One such strategy, which we now consider in more detail, is relocation.

The double bed and relocation

With partners increasingly affecting each other's sleep because of the physiological changes associated with ageing outlined earlier, it would appear that to sleep apart while remaining together, either in separate beds or in separate rooms, may be a pragmatic solution to the dilemma of disturbed sleep. For twice-widowed Claire, single beds and earplugs proved an antidote to a first husband who 'snored like crazy', and a second husband who snored, suffered from cancer of the prostate and had 'a type of shake' (IV023: Claire, aged 71). For Vi, the decision to get single beds arose from the guilt she felt at disturbing her husband's sleep by fidgeting at night:

> It's me that is the fidgety one and we've now got single beds and I tell you I wouldn't want to go back to a double one . . . because I fidget and then of course he says, 'can't you sleep?' and all that and it makes me feel worse . . . Even though I still fidget in my own bed, at least he is getting a good night's sleep.
>
> (FG1: 70+)

Yet the decision to shift from the double bed is not without its costs in terms of a couple relationship founded on the concept of togetherness. The double bed, as the site of the sleeping relationship, is a powerful symbol of the couple partnership. To move beds can thus be interpreted as symbolic of a weakening of this partnership. The following extracts from our research highlight the feelings of ambivalence facing this cohort of women, for whom the prospect of changing sleeping arrangements after long marriages, although in some cases desirable, is not acceptable within the terms of their relationship:

> He snores and I'm sure that he's disturbing me. I was trying to get him to think perhaps it would be better in twin beds, but he won't cave into that.
>
> (FG1: 70+)

> *Interviewer:* Have you ever thought of sleeping in separate beds?
> *Jane:* He says we may as well get a divorce then. (FG2: 70+)

> *Interviewer:* When he came back from hospital did you stay in the same bed?
> *Rita:* Oh yes, he's not allowed out of my sight at night. I don't like sleeping on my own actually.

Interviewer: Why is that?

Rita: I don't know. We've been married 44 years and when he's not there, when he's in hospital, I don't like it. There's nobody there except the cat.   (IV007: Rita aged 63)

Culturally, there is a strong expectation for the couple to sleep together throughout their relationship. Reactions from family and friends are indicative of the stigma attached to separate rooms:

Donna: We started to sleep in separate beds because he didn't sleep well – except when we wanted, you know, a bit of hanky panky, but even then he would move out so that I could go to sleep. We now have two separate rooms because his sleep pattern is so irregular.

Interviewer: What was the reaction to this?

Donna: The kids [when they came home from university] said, 'Oh, you two aren't splitting up?' I explained and they knew anyway that dad used to wander around the house at night.
                                         (IV002: Donna, aged 61)

Yet while, as in Donna's situation, the couple continues to relate as man and wife despite sleeping separately, in some cases the night-time separation of couples after a lifetime of sharing a double bed can symbolize the effective ending of the partnership. Sarah, caring for a husband with dementia, describes the circumstances of her move to a separate room. In this case, sex, once a key reason for sharing a bed, seriously jeopardizes the marriage, with changing rooms the only viable alternative:

I had to get out of the bed because [husband] had a problem. [His illness] affected his sexual drive and he just wouldn't leave me alone so I had to say to him, 'Look I'm going to have to sleep in a different bed' . . . I just couldn't cope with that . . . *I nearly left him.* I was married 51 years and after about 41 years I was thinking of leaving because I thought *he wasn't the man I married.*

                                         (FG1: 70+, emphasis added)

As our data show, making the decision to move or not from the marital bed in later life involves a complex process of negotiation with self and/or partner. Reflected in this process is a growing sense of ambivalence as women weigh up the promise of improved sleep against the consequences of sleeping apart for the couple relationship. Implicit in the move may be a loss of identity as 'wife', symbolized by the double bed; a loss that few women, or men, are prepared to countenance. Our data suggest that it is only when relationship identity and roles are lost either through extreme ill-health and dementia, or through divorce or widowhood, that women are able to restructure their sleeping arrangements to help to overcome sleep disruption arising from sleeping with their partner in the marital bed.

Conclusion

This chapter has shown how the interactional nature of the sleep relationship for couples can provide valuable insights into sleep disruption in later life. It also shows how the study of sleep can provide insights into the changing nature of the couple relationship across the life course. With ageing, women's sleep is affected by disturbances from partners who snore, experience prostate problems or suffer from increasing physical and/or mental disabilities. Intrusions into women's sleep from partners are often compounded by women's own health problems with ageing and by the emotional labour expended in concern for their partner's health and well-being. Following divorce or widowhood, the emptiness of the double bed serves as a constant reminder of the loss of a partnership and the identity attached to the role of wife. Retrospective accounts of the couple relationship during this period of adjustment can contribute to our understanding of the way in which couples interact to structure the sleep experience.

In the transition period before widowhood, women's sleep may be affected by an intensification of their gendered roles as service provider and carer, at a time when men's role as provider and protector is in decline. In some cases, the couple relationship as it has existed throughout the marriage is lost through dementia, serious illness or disability. This gradual undermining of the basis of the couple relationship forged over long years in the togetherness and companionship culture of the double bed is highlighted in the ambivalence that often accompanies women's response to sleep disruption. In choosing whether or not to vacate the double bed and remove themselves from the source of sleep disruption, women are caught in a bind. To prioritize their own sleeping needs and move from the double bed, they not only risk losing access to their own sleeping space but also challenge the foundations on which the couple relationship has been built over time. Similarly, when women are forced to move to another room because of their husband's illness, they may also lose the companionship of the relationship and the benefits of sleeping in the room symbolic of their couple relationship. In these circumstances, the management of sleep disruption reflects the complexity of meanings associated with the structuring of the couple relationship in later life.

For the sociologist, the study of sleep provides a rich and relatively untapped resource. Sleep, like breathing, is a central part of our lives, essential to our well-being and ability to function. Yet while ageing may precipitate changes in the physiology of sleep, we contend that it is only by examining sleep within its social context that a better understanding of the underlying meanings of sleep disruption can be gained. As a social act, sleep takes place within a social context, influencing, and being influenced by, the gendered roles, relationships and life course transitions that characterize our social world. For couples, sleep is, in essence, a barometer, sensitive to shifts in the nature of the relationship arising from fluctuations and changes in the health of partners and the impact of life course transitions. Through studying sleep we open a window on to the gendered roles and relationships that form the fabric of our lives.

Acknowledgement

This chapter is part of a larger study of sleep in women aged 40 and over. It is funded by the Commission of the European Communities, contract number QLK6-CT-2000-00499.

References

Ancoli-Israel, S., Kripke, D., Klauber, M., Mason, W., Fell, R. and Kaplan, O. (1991) Periodic limb movements in sleep in community-dwelling elderly, *Sleep*, 14(6): 496–500.

Arthritis Research Campaign. (2002) *Arthritis: The Big Picture*. ARC Epidemiological Unit and ARC/MORI poll (http://www.arc.org.uk).

Bixler, E., Kales, A., Jacoby, J., Soldatos, C. and Vela-Bueno, A. (1984) Nocturnal sleep and wakefulness: effects of age and sex in normal sleepers, *International Journal of Neuroscience*, 23(1): 33–42.

Bliwise, D. (2000) Normal ageing. In M. Kryger, T. Roth and W. Dement (eds) *Principles and Practice of Sleep Medicine*. Philadelphia: Saunders.

Davidson, K. (1999) Marital perceptions in retrospect. A study of older widows and widowers. In R. Miller and S. Browning (eds) *With this Ring: Divorce, Intimacy and Cohabitation from a Multicultural Perspective*. Stamford, CT: JAI Press.

Davidson, K., Arber, S. and Ginn, J. (2000) Gendered meanings of care work within late life marital relationships, *Canadian Journal on Aging/La Revue canadienne du vieillissement*, 19(4): 536–53.

Dement, W. (2001) *The Promise of Sleep*. New York: Pan.

Dijk, D.-J., Duffy, J. and Czeisler, C. (2001) Age-related increase in awakenings: impaired consolidation of nonREM sleep at all circadian phases, *Sleep*, 24(5): 565–77.

Enright, P., Newman, A., Wahl, P., Manolio, T., Haponik, E. and Boyle, P. (1996) Prevalence and correlates of snoring and observed apneas in 5201 older adults, *Sleep*, 19(7): 531–8.

Foley, D., Monhan, A., Brown, S. Lori, S., Simonsick, E., Wallace, R. and Blazer, D. (1995) Sleep complaints among elderly persons: an epidemiologic study of three communities, *Sleep*, 18(6): 425–32.

Hislop, J. and Arber, S. (2003) Understanding women's sleep management: beyond medicalisation–healthisation? *Sociology of Health and Illness*, 26(6): 815–37.

Hislop, J. and Arber, S. (2003) Sleepers wake! The gendered nature of sleep disruption among mid-life women, *Sociology*, 37(4): in press.

Hobson, J. A. (1995) *Sleep*. New York: Scientific American Library.

Hume, K., Van, F. and Watson, A. (1998) A field study of age and gender differences in habitual adult sleep, *Journal of Sleep Research*, 7(2): 85–94.

McCurry, S. and Teri, L. (1995) Sleep disturbance in elderly caregivers of dementia patients, *Clinical Gerontologist*, 16: 51–66.

Maher, J. and Green, H. (2002) *Carers 2000*. ONS. London: The Stationery Office.

Mason, J. (1996) Gender, care and sensibility in family and kin relationships. In J. Holland and L. Adkins (eds) *Sex, Sensibility and the Gendered Body*. Basingstoke: Macmillan.

Morgan, K. (1998) Sleep and insomnia in later life. In R. Tallis, H. Fillit and J. Brocklehurst (eds) *Brocklehurst's Textbook of Geriatric Medicine and Gerontology*. Edinburgh: Churchill Livingstone.

National Sleep Foundation (2001) *Sleep and Aging* (http://www.sleepfoundation.org/publications/sleepage.html).

Pankhurst, F. and Horne, J. (1994) The influence of bed partners on movement during sleep, *Sleep*, 17(4): 308–15.

Prostate Research UK. (2003) *About the Prostate* (http://www.prostateresearch.org.uk/aboutprostate.htm).

Redieh, M., Reis, J. and Creason, M. (1990) Sleep in old age: focus on gender differences, *Sleep*, 13(5): 410–24.

Reynolds, C., Kupfer, D., Taska, L., Hoch, C., Sewitch, D. and Spiker, D. (1985) Sleep of healthy seniors: a revisit, *Sleep*, 8(1): 20–9.

Schubert, C., Cruikshanks, K., Dalton, D., Klein, B., Klein, R. and Nondahl, D. (2002) Prevalence of sleep problems and quality of life in an older population, *Sleep*, 25(8): 48–52.

Sleep Council (2002) *Separate Beds – The Secret of Wedded Bliss?* (http://www.sleepcouncil.com).

Webb, W. (1982) Sleep in older persons: sleep structures of 50- to 60-year-old men and women, *Journal of Gerontology*, 37(5): 581–6.

West, C. and Zimmerman, D. (1987) Doing gender, *Gender and Society*, 1(2): 125–51.

Wilcox, S. and King, A. (1999) Sleep complaints in older women who are family caregivers, *Journal of Gerontology: Psychological Sciences*, 54B(3): 189–98.

INDEX

RESEARCHING AGEING AND LATER LIFE
THE PRACTICE OF SOCIAL GERONTOLOGY

Anne Jamieson and Christina Victor (eds)

The changing demographic profiles of modern societies have led to a growing interest in understanding ageing and later life among those working within the social sciences and humanities. This edited volume addresses the methodological challenges entailed in studying the process of ageing and life course changes, as well as the experience of being old. The book focuses on the theory and practice of doing research, using a wide range of examples and case studies. The contributors, who are prominent researchers in the field, review the range of practices in the use of different methodologies and give in-depth examples, based on their own research experience. The book covers a variety of disciplines and methodologies, both quantitative and qualitative, and a diversity of sources, including fiction, photographs, as well as the traditional social science sources. *Researching Ageing and Later Life* will be essential reading for those wishing for an insight into the realities of doing research in this area.

Contents
Introduction – Part 1: The who, what and how of social gerontology – Theory and practice in social gerontology – Strategies and methods in the study of ageing and later life – Part 2: Using existing sources – Using documentary material : Researching the past – Using existing research and statistical data: Secondary data analysis – Using the Mass Observation Archive – Using 'cultural products' in researching images of ageing – Part 3: Creating new data – Doing longitudinal research – Doing life history research – Doing case study research in psychology – Doing diary based research – Doing evaluation of health and social care interventions – Part 4: The roles and responsibilities of the researcher – Researching ageing in different cultures – Ethical issues in researching later life – The role of older people in research – The use of gerontological research in policy and practice – References – Appendix: Web resources – Index.

288pp   0 335 20820 7 (Paperback)   0 335 20821 5 (Hardback)

SOCIAL THEORY, SOCIAL POLICY AND AGEING
A CRITICAL INTRODUCTION

Carroll Estes, Simon Biggs and Chris Phillipson

In this important new book, three leading social theorists of old age present a critical review of key theoretical developments and issues influencing the study of adult ageing. The authors explore contemporary trends in social policy drawing on the experience of ageing in the USA, Europe and an increasingly global environment.

Particular attention is given to feminist perspectives on ageing, ethics and bio-medicine, successful and productive ageing, globalization and migration and the politics of ageing. Consideration is given in each case to the interaction between structural influences on social ageing and the experience of age and identity. The work ends with a manifesto for social theory, social policy and social change.

Social Theory, Social Policy and Ageing will be valuable reading for advanced students and practitioners taking courses in social theory, the sociology of old age and social gerontology.

Contents
Introduction – Social theory and ageing: From functionalism to critical gerontology – Social theory and ageing: From identity to critical identities – Ageing, migration and globalization – Feminist perspectives and old age policy – Productive ageing, self-surveillance and social policy – The bio-medicalization of ageing – The politics of ageing in Europe and the USA – A manifesto for social theory and social change – References – Index.

200pp   0 335 20906 8 (Paperback)   0 335 20907 6 (Hardback)